Financial Management Techniques

FOR SMALL BUSINESS

By Arthur R. DeThomas, Ph.D.

Edited by Scott Crawford

The Oasis Press® / PSI Research
Grants Pass, Oregon

Published by The Oasis Press

Financial Management Techniques for Small Business

This publication is designed to provide accurate and authoritative information with regard to
the subject matter covered. It is sold with the understanding that the publisher is not engaged in
rendering legal, accounting, or other professional service. If legal advice or other expert assistance
is required, the services of a competent professional person should be sought.
*—from a declaration of principles jointly adopted by a committee of the American Bar Association
and a committee of publishers*

Edited, page design and typography by Scott Crawford
Editorial Assistance: Vickie Reierson
Typographic Assistance: Melody Joachims

Please direct any comments, questions, or suggestions regarding this book to The Oasis Press,
Editorial Department, at the address below.

The Oasis Press offers PSI Successful Business Software for sale. For information, contact:

PSI Research/The Oasis Press
300 North Valley Drive
Grants Pass, OR 97526
(503) 479-9464

The Oasis Press is a Registered Trademark of Publishing Services, Inc., a Texas corporation
doing business in Oregon as PSI Research.

ISBN 1-55571-116-2 (binder) 1-55571-124-3 (paperback)

Printed in the United States of America

First edition 10 9 8 7 6 5 4 3 2 1 Revision Code: AAA

Table of Contents

PART TWO — FINANCIAL PLANNING

PART THREE — WORKING CAPITAL MANAGEMENT

List of Illustrations

Preface

One of the many advantages of small business ownership is complete control over the operation of the business. Free from the multiple levels of management authority associated with large firms, decisions can be made and implemented quickly. What's more, the entrepreneur is his or her own boss and, as the song goes, has the satisfaction of saying, "I did it my way."

Unfortunately, as any experienced small firm manager will readily admit, it is often lonely at the top. Along with the luxury of complete control goes the demanding responsibility for wearing many different administrative hats. The entrepreneur is usually forced by circumstances to be knowledgeable about each facet of the business, and must often make decisions in isolation without the benefit of expert advice or capable staff assistance.

For the harried manager, this means that some important administrative activities frequently receive only minimal attention, or worse, are totally ignored until a crisis develops. As revealed by the dismal statistics on business failures, financial management is the area of small firm administration that is usually neglected. All too often, financial decisions are made without the benefit of formal analysis and planning, or are made by default after the firm's financial position has been damaged beyond repair.

While all management activities are important to the efficient operation of the firm, prudent management of the firm's finances is critical. The typical small firm operates in a fiercely competitive environment with limited resources, and no resource is more scarce than its financial wealth. Sound financial management of this vital asset, therefore, is the difference between successful financial performance of the business and its failure.

The Concept of Financial Management

Simply stated, the subject of finance deals with the often scarce commodity of money or more accurately, financial resources, which includes both cash and the ability to obtain credit. Finance, then, is a subject that is near and dear to all small business managers. Without adequate financial resources, activities normal to the firm's operation, such as meeting payroll, buying inventory or equipment, carrying receivables, and implementing plans, cannot be conducted effectively. On the other hand, merely having cash and credit capability does not automatically ensure a financially successful business. Achieving financial success for the firm requires the combination of adequate financial resources and sound financial management.

All too often, financial management of the firm is mistakenly thought of as consisting of nothing more than raising needed financing. Certainly, obtaining funds is an important part of good financial management, but this critical administrative function involves much more. To get a feel for how much more, consider that most business decisions made by management involve money or credit, or both. Decisions as diverse as what product mix to offer, what pricing strategy to employ, what inventory level to maintain, whether to carry receivables, and the number of employees to hire, all cause cash and credit to flow into and out of the business. To increase the likelihood that such decisions will not endanger the firm's financial health, they must be made with a clear understanding of their financial impact. This understanding is the first and most important step toward sound financial management of the firm.

So, while financial management is about managing money and credit, it is also about the analysis of and planning for the financial effects of all management decisions. In short, financial management involves:

- Systematically evaluating the firm's financial performance and financial position to determine when operations are going according to plan and when corrective measures must be taken.

- Developing sound plans for the firm's financial future.

- Developing reliable financial controls.

- Planning for the financing necessary to implement plans and to ensure continued operations.

- Managing and controlling the assets and liabilities that are critical to the firm's operations.

In order to conduct these fundamental finance functions effectively, you, as the small business manager, must:

- Understand financial principles.

- Have facility with the basic tools and techniques of finance.

- Stay financially tuned to each phase of your business.

Financial Management Techniques for Small Business

As the title suggests, this book deals with financial management for the practicing small business manager. It focuses on those areas of finance that have been shown to be of greatest importance to the financial success of the business: financial analysis, financial planning, and what is known as working capital management, which consists of the management of accounts receivable, inventory, and accounts payable. This book is designed and written as an easy-to-read, how-to primer that will quickly improve the financial understanding, skills, and practices of the entrepreneur. Prior financial knowledge is not required to master the principles discussed and illustrated throughout its pages. What is required is an small investment of the reader's time.

This suggestion is not made lightly. The author is fully aware that the small firm manager's time is limited. The decision to read this book and develop facility with the financial principles discussed in its pages, however, is a decision that will return countless, long-term benefits for the time invested.

Years of experience as a small business consultant have convinced the author that the typical entrepreneur wants to improve the financial management of his or her business. Unfortunately, the knowledge and means to do so are often lacking. This is no longer the case. *Financial Management Techniques for Small Business* provides both the knowledge and the means. Applying the principles and tools that are discussed and illustrated in the following pages will produce benefits that translate into bottom-line dollars and cents for the firm.

Reading and learning the text material should be exciting as well as rewarding. You will unmask details about business finance that in the past may have seemed mysterious and inscrutable. What's more, as you apply these financial principles to the analysis, planning, and management of your firm, you will discover a wealth of new information about something you thought you knew very well: the detailed operations of your firm.

A Final Thought

Introduction to Financial Analysis

Making the many financial decisions required to effectively manage the day-to-day operations of a business and to develop sound plans for its future requires reliable and pertinent information on the financial performance and financial position of the firm. This means having answers to such questions as:

The First Ingredient of Sound Financial Management

- Is the business generating cash flows sufficient to maintain a profitable level of operations?

- Are operating costs adequately controlled?

- Is the rate of inventory turnover sufficient to maintain satisfactory profit margins and avoid the unnecessary use of scarce cash?

- Is the collection rate on accounts receivables sufficient to maintain satisfactory cash flow and avoid the unnecessary use of cash?

- Are accounts payable effectively controlled?

- Is the firm generating a satisfactory return on its assets and on the owner's invested capital?

The more detailed information you have on how the business operates, the easier it is to provide reliable answers to critical questions such as these. As you will learn from the ensuing chapters, some of the needed information is provided by the basic financial statements (balance sheet and income statement) that are produced by a firm's accountant or bookkeeper, and some will come from other sources; the key is knowing what information is needed for a particular purpose, where it can be found, and how to use it. In the following section, you will discover that this task is not as difficult as you might imagine.

Much of the nuts and bolts activity of financial management involves financial analysis. Simply stated, financial analysis is a problem-solving process similar to that used in working a crossword puzzle. Solving a crossword puzzle is accomplished through a combination of using the information given by printed clues; using the clues provided by adjoining words and letters; and, using the skills and judgment of the analyst. Similarly, financial analysis combines clues from various sources of financial information with the skills and knowledge of the analyst to solve the firm's financial puzzle.

The Role of Financial Analysis

Part One

What you will learn about financial analysis from the first six chapters of this book is outlined in the table below.

TOPIC	CONCEPTS DISCUSSED
Financial Statements	The accounting concept of the income statement and balance sheet.
	How to interpret and use the information from these statements for financial analysis.
Cash Flow from Operations	How cash flow from operations is determined, and how operations can drain cash from the business.
	Why cash flow from operations is not profit from operations.
Sources and Uses of Cash	How non-operating and financial sources and uses of cash are determined.
	How to use the information provided by the sources and uses of cash statement.
Ratio Analysis	How to use financial ratios to evaluate the financial position of the firm.
	Which financial indicators should be monitored for effective financial control of the firm.
Contribution Format Statements	How to identify the firm's cost structure, and how these costs react to changes in operations.
	How to prepare a contribution format income statement, and how to interpret and use the information it provides.
Breakeven Analysis	The meaning of breakeven analysis.
	How breakeven is calculated and how the information is used.
Sales Analysis	The meaning of sales analysis and how it is performed.

There is no question that financial analysis, if done properly, will require some of your valuable time. If you are like most small business managers you are probably thinking that the last thing you need is more demands on your time. But the bottom-line benefits gained by financial analysis far exceed the cost of the time invested. The information produced by financial analysis allows you to:

The Benefits from Sound Financial Analysis

- Uncover potential problems before they reach crisis proportion. This gives you time to develop solutions and map alternative courses of action before emergency conditions force unpleasant choices.

- Establish standards for measuring your firm's performance.

- Identify and become familiar with the key factors that determine the success and well-being of your business. Small firm managers often become so immersed in day-to-day operations that they lose an overall perspective of the business, its customers, markets, and competitors. By doing financial analysis, you are forced to maintain this critical perspective.

- Present the business in a professional manner to those outside parties interested its financial health. For example, your firm's banker or other prospective creditors use the tools of financial analysis to provide answers to questions about the credit risk your firm represents. By using the same tools, you gain insight into your creditor's thinking. Being forewarned and forearmed when approaching a bank for a loan is no small blessing. What's more, approaching a bank with a well-developed set of plans goes a long way toward convincing the banker that the business is in the hands of capable management and is, therefore, a desirable candidate for a loan.

Financial analysis consists of two basic steps: generating the information, and evaluating the results. Manufacturing the information is a straightforward procedure that involves nothing more than directed number crunching. This can be done manually, or the effort can be simplified by using computerized financial models. For information regarding financial models software, see the card enclosed at the back of this book.

A Final Thought

Evaluating the information is the critical step in the analysis process. Effective analysis requires an understanding of the underlying financial principles, a knowledge of the business, and sound management judgment. There is no substitute for these ingredients. The necessary expertise is easily developed, however, by simply practicing what this book teaches.

Chapter 1
Basic Financial Statements

How often have you thought, or heard a fellow business person say, "Other than the bottom-line profit or loss figure, the firm's financial statements provide very little information about the business." If you are anything like the typical small business owner, you have probably expressed or heard this sentiment expressed many times. Financial statements are the items most often received from your accountant (except perhaps for his or her bill), but are probably the most rarely used. This is unfortunate, since the data shown on these statements, when properly interpreted, can provide a wealth of information about the financial status of your business. Conversely, ignoring this information can be extremely hazardous to your firm's financial health.

Financial statements, in the form of the traditional balance sheet and income statement, reflect the continual changes in revenues, expenses, assets, liabilities, and owner's net worth that result from the operation of the business. Understanding these summary statements is the subject of this chapter, and the concepts that will be discussed are outlined in the table below.

TOPIC	CONCEPTS DISCUSSED
The Income Statement	How to interpret the format and terminology used by the accountant in preparing this statement.
	How profit or loss for the period is determined and how the figure is interpreted.
	Why profit or loss from operations is not the same as cash flow from operations.
	What information from the statement is useful for evaluating the performance of your business.

TOPIC	CONCEPTS DISCUSSED
The Balance Sheet	**How to interpret the format and terminology used by the accountant in preparing this statement.**
	How the accountant's approach to valuing assets and owner's net worth on the balance sheet differs from the concept of market value or liquidation value.
	What information from the statement is useful for evaluating the financial position of your business.

The Income Statement

The *income statement* or, as it is often called, the *statement of profit and loss*, is designed to reflect the financial results of the firm's operations over a specific time period (month, quarter, or year). It is designed in accordance with accounting convention, as a summary statement of the business transactions that produced sales revenue for the period, and the operating expenses and taxes the firm incurred in generating this revenue. For the manager with a grasp of elementary accounting conventions, the income statement can provide a great deal of information about the nature of the firm's operations and how effectively the cost of these operations have been controlled.

Accountants have adopted a number of conventions or guidelines for recording business transactions and preparing financial statements. These conventions are designed to provide reported financial statement information that is reasonably objective, consistent, and comparable for all types of business firms. Unfortunately, there is a trade-off. The statements produce information in a form suitable for reporting, but often not suitable for analysis, planning, and decision making. The reasons for this are discussed below.

The Income Statement Format

Sample income statements for The Avanti Company covering the latest two years of the firm's operations appear on the following page. Avanti is a hypothetical small firm that builds and sells customized bicycles and offers bicycle repair service. Note first that Avanti's income statements have two major sections: revenue as shown by the net sales figure, and operating and income tax expenses as shown by cost of sales, operating expenses, and income tax. The net income (profit figure) shown on the bottom line of the statement is determined as follows:

Net Income = Sales Revenue - Cost of Sales - Operating Expenses & Taxes

Understanding this statement and the information it does and does not convey requires an understanding of the accounting concept of revenue

Table 1.1

THE AVANTI COMPANY
Annual Income Statements
For the Periods 19X1 and 19X2

	19X1	**19X2**
Net Sales	$290,000	$340,000
Cost of Sales	148,000	194,500
Gross Profit	$142,000	$145,500
Operating Expenses:		
Wages & Salaries	$ 32,500	$ 34,700
Rent & Lease Payments	5,400	3,600
Utilities	5,100	5,093
Insurance	12,700	12,700
Advertising	6,000	5,100
Vehicle Operation & Maintenance	20,378	19,916
Accounting & Legal	2,400	2,400
Payroll Taxes	4,550	8,858
Depreciation	1,800	2,000
Total Operating Expenses	$ 90,828	$ 90,367
Net Operating Income	$ 51,172	$ 55,133
Less: Interest Expense	2,800	3,300
Net Taxable Income	$ 48,372	$ 51,833
Less: Income Taxes	19,349	20,733
Net Income	$ 29,023	$ 31,100

The income statement is the accountant's summary of the sales revenue produced and expenses incurred by the firm's operations for a given accounting period. When interpreting this statement or using its information for decision making, it is important to remember that (1) the sales revenue for a given accounting period is not necessarily the same as cash inflow from sales for that period, and (2) the expenses shown on the income statement are not necessarily cash outflows in that accounting period.

and expense. It may surprise you to learn that in accounting parlance these terms are not defined as, nor necessarily represent, cash inflows and outflows.

The Concept of Revenue and Expense

Revenue is defined in accounting as the inflow of value resulting from the sale of products or the services a firm renders in the normal course of business. The process of generating sales and incurring expenses that are associated with those sales is referred to as *normal operations*. For Avanti, normal operations produce the dollar amount of sales from its product line and the revenue its service department generates.

It is important to note the following two points about the concept of sales revenue:

- While you may think of the value produced by sales as cash received, an accountant measures the inflow of value by either a cash sale or a credit sale. To an accountant, a credit sale means the business receives something of value: a claim on the customer for the amount of the sale. This valuable claim appears as an asset known as accounts receivable. Accounts receivable are certainly valuable to the business, but they are not cash and, in the worst case, may never become cash.

- When preparing the income statement, an accountant recognizes a credit sale as revenue in the accounting period in which the credit sale is made. This means that the sales figure on the income statement for a given accounting period includes all credit sales made during that period, even though cash from the collection of those receivables may not flow into the business until a future accounting period. This means that there may be a significant difference between the sales revenue shown on the income statement and the amount of cash inflow a firm experiences in any given accounting period.

A clear understanding of its implications is essential to interpreting the income statement and to learning about the concept of cash flow from operations.

Expenses, which reflect the cost of operations for a given period, are defined as the amount of value used up in generating revenues for that period. This value may represent cash that has flowed out of the firm in some past accounting period, or may flow out in some future period. The expenses recognized in a given period are matched with the revenues realized in that period to determine the amount of accounting profit or loss (net income or net loss) for the firm. It is important to note the following point about expenses:

Similar to revenue, value is measured by the accountant at the time the expense is recognized and not when the cash flowed out of the business. As discussed on the following pages, the expenses that appear on the income statement for a given accounting period may represent cash that has flowed out of the business in a past period, in the current period, in a future period, or in the case of items such as depreciation expense, do not involve a cash flow.

As shown on Avanti's income statements, the first major expense item deducted from sales revenue is *cost of sales*. For Avanti, this figure represents the cost of the inventory purchased and sold, and the cost of rendering the services that were normal to the firm's operations. In a manufacturing firm, cost of sales would represent the cost of the inventory produced and sold, including the cost of raw materials, labor, and factory overhead.

Cost of Sales as an Expense of Doing Business

The accountant recognizes cost of sales as an expense on the income statement for the period in which the goods are sold or the service rendered. In some cases, this may be the same period in which the cash costs associated with producing or purchasing the goods or rendering the service are actually experienced. In others, there may be a significant difference between when the cash flows out of the business, and when the expense is recognized on the income statement. For example, if Avanti's trade supplier extends credit on purchases, the items could be purchased and sold in one accounting period but not paid for until a later period.

The difference between sales and cost of sales on the income statement is referred to as *gross profit* or *gross profit margin.* For Avanti, gross profit was $142,000 in 19X1 and $145,500 in 19X2. Gross profit is an important financial indicator for virtually any type of business. It indicates the amount available after cost of sales is deducted from revenue to cover overhead, other operating expenses, taxes, and to provide a profit. For a retailer like Avanti, maintaining an adequate gross profit margin means the difference between success and failure for the firm.

A useful way to depict gross profit is as a percentage of sales. This is accomplished by dividing the dollar amount of gross profit by the net sales figure.

Gross Profit as a Percentage of Sales = Gross Profit ÷ Net Sales

For Avanti in 19X2 this would be $145,000 divided by $340,000, or 42.8%. This percentage is an indicator of the average markup on sales that Avanti is able to maintain.

Operating Expenses as an Expense of Doing Business

The next major expense category deducted from sales revenue on the income statement consists of sales and administrative expenses normal to the firm's operations. As a group, these recurring expense items are referred to as *operating expenses*. On Avanti's 19X2 income statement, operating expenses totaled $90,367, and the difference between gross profit and operating expenses resulted in net operating income of $55,133. Thus,

Net Operating Income = Gross Profit – Operating Expenses

Net operating income (or possibly loss) is an important financial indicator. It represents the amount of profit generated by normal operations. Again, a useful way of depicting net operating income is as a percentage of sales. This figure is often referred to as *operating profit margin*, and is calculated as:

Operating Profit Margin = Net Operating Income ÷ Net Sales

Operating profit margin represents the average amount of each sales dollar that remains after normal operating expenses are deducted to cover interest and taxes.

Interest, Taxes, and Net Income

The remaining expense items that are deducted from sales revenue usually consist of interest expense and, if the firm is incorporated as is Avanti, an income tax based on the amount of taxable income generated by the business. The result of these deductions is the *net profit* or *net loss* figure. Net profit or net loss is defined in accounting terms as the difference between revenues and expenses for the period. For Avanti, net income was $29,023 in 19X1 and $31,000 in 19X2. It was calculated as follows:

Net Income = Net Operating Income - Interest Expense and Income Taxes

It is also revealing to depict net income as a percentage of net sales. This figure is referred to as the *net profit margin* and is calculated as:

Net Profit Margin = Net Income ÷ Net Sales

This percentage reflects the average amount remaining from each sales dollar after all expenses and taxes have been deducted. It is the average portion of the sales dollar available to the owners of the firm.

If you are like most small business owners, you have some feel for the term net income or profit. But since it is so important to financial analysis and, unfortunately, so often misunderstood, it would be useful to spend time investigating the concept before going further. What you discover about the profit generated by operations as shown on the income statement may surprise you.

An accountant's concept of revenue and expense focuses on the inflow and outflow of value and not the inflow and outflow of cash. In fact, you may have reasoned that if revenue does not necessarily involve cash inflows and expenses do not necessarily involve cash outflows, then net income, which is the difference between revenue and expense, may have very little to do with cash flow in a given accounting period. This is correct. While the amount of net income and cash flow generated by operations will be closely correlated over the long run, there may be no relationship between the two in the short run. It can be dangerously misleading, therefore, to confuse net income and cash flow.

The Truth About Profit from Operations

Understanding the subtle difference between profit and cash is the key to knowing what income statement information is and is not useful for financial analysis, planning, and decision making, and to understanding the crucial concept of cash flow from operations. This latter topic is the subject of the next chapter, but for now the income statement will be the focus.

A simple example will help clarify the distinction between revenue, expense, profit, and cash flow. Assume you own a rather peculiar retail store that only sells one item each year and the sale occurs during the month of December. Your one and only customer, Mr. Faithful, makes his purchase and, because he is a good credit risk, you extend 90-day credit terms. If your accountant closes your firm's books at the end of December, the income statement would show revenue in the amount of the sale. Value has been received even though no cash has been collected. Remember, accounts receivable (the customer's IOU) represents valuable consideration received in return for the item sold. An accountant recognizes this value as revenue on the income statement for this period.

Distinction Between Revenue, Expense, Profit, and Cash Flow

If you assume further that the amount of the sale to Mr. Faithful is greater than the amount of the expenses and taxes for the period, the income statement would show a profit. But having net income for the period is little consolation when you consider the important question: How much cash has flowed into the business this period? The answer is none. While net income is a reliable long-term measure of financial performance, it is not a short-term measure of the liquidity provided by operations.

To extend the example, assume that Mr. Faithful pays his bill at the end of 90 days. At this time, his accounts receivable balance is cleared and, more importantly, your firm's cash account is increased by the amount of the payment. If the books are closed at the end of this quarter, the income statement will not show any sales revenue. Operations have not produced revenue because there has been no increase in value through the sale of a product or rendering of a service in the normal course of business. Collection of a receivable causes cash, not revenue, to increase.

Since your firm has no revenue for the period, and will no doubt incur normal operating expenses, expenses will exceed revenue and the income statement will show a net loss. But again, ask yourself how much cash has flowed into the business. Even though there has been no sales revenue this period, and the income statement shows a net loss, your firm's cash account has increased by the amount of Mr. Faithful's payment.

The Effect on Profit and Cash Flow

The recognition of expenses on the income statement and the timing of cash outflows may also differ. Consider the effect on profit and cash flow of the examples listed below.

- **Cost of Goods Sold.** Assume the item sold to Mr. Faithful was purchased in December on credit terms of net 90 days. Although the income statement reflected the cost of the item as a deduction from sales revenue, no cash for the cost of the item flowed out of the business in this period. The cost of the item will not be paid for 90 days. Recall that an accountant recognizes cost of sales as an expense of the period in which the goods are sold, and not when payment for the goods is made.

- **Operating Expenses.** Other expense items on the income statement reflect differences between recognition and the timing of cash flow. For example, if the books are closed on dates different from the dates on which employees are paid or on which tax payments are made, a portion of the wage expense and tax expense that appear on the income statement for a given accounting period will not involve a cash outflow until a later accounting period.

- **Depreciation.** Depreciation expense does not involve a cash outflow in any accounting period. As discussed in the next section of this chapter, depreciation expense is an accountant's method of recognizing, as an expense of doing business, the portion of an asset's original cost assumed to be used up in a given accounting period. Although this expense item is deducted from revenue in calculating net income for the period, it does not involve a cash outflow. The cash flowed out of the business at the time the asset was purchased, not when depreciation expense appears on the income statement.

The message from this glimpse into the mechanics of the income statement is clear:

- The accounting conventions used to prepare the income statement may result in significant differences between the recognition of revenue and expense items on the income statement and the cash inflows and outflows experienced by the firm. Revenue and expense reflect the inflow and outflow of the accounting concept of the value associated with operations, and not the cash flow associated with operations.

- Net profit or net loss is not a measure of cash for the period. To obtain a measure of cash flow from operations you must look to another statement — the income statement can convey a great deal of information about the overall financial performance of a firm, if the data is properly manipulated.

As for Avanti, the company should have mixed emotions about the information shown on its income statements for 19X1 and 19X2. There is enthusiasm for the profit earned in each period, and for the increase in net income between the two periods; but questions should also be asked about what lies behind these figures and the information they convey.

As a business person, you know that things are not always what they seem. This is sometimes the case with net income. Unfortunately, there is more truth than humor in the old adage "many a business has gone broke earning a profit." The topic of revenue, expense, net income, and cash flow from operations is covered in Chapter 2. But for now, let's take a look at some of the subtleties associated with the balance sheet.

The Balance Sheet

While a firm's income statement summarizes operations for the entire accounting period, the *balance sheet* reflects an accountant's measure of the value of the business as of one moment in time: the end of the period. In the case of the Avanti Company, the balance sheet values shown on Table 1.2 reflect the close of business on December 31, 19X1 and 19X2. In the discussion that follows, you will discover that value is defined and measured on the balance sheet in a manner different from common usage of the term.

Avanti's balance sheet depicts two major divisions: *assets* and *equities*. Assets are the physical and monetary resources owned by the business and used in its operation. They consist of such things as cash, inventory, land, buildings, and equipment. The dollar value of Avanti's assets, $273,945 in 19X1 and $333,725 in 19X2, reflects an accounting concept known as *book value*. Familiarity with this concept is crucial to understanding what information the statement provides, or does not

Table 1.2

THE AVANTI COMPANY
Annual Balance Sheets
For the Periods Ending December 31, 19X1 and 19X2

	19X1	19X2
Assets		
Current Assets:		
Cash	$ 13,000	$ 3,000
Accounts Receivable	25,778	54,600
Inventory	24,167	56,125
Prepaid Expenses	0	5,000
Total Current Assets	$ 62,945	$118,725
Fixed Assets:		
Land	$ 30,000	$ 30,000
Building	150,000	150,000
Vehicles	32,000	35,000
Equipment	20,000	23,000
Less: Accumulated Depreciation	(21,000	(23,000)
Total Net Fixed Assets	$211,000	$215,000
Total Assets	$273,945	$333,725
Liabilities & Owner's Equity		
Current Liabilities:		
Notes Payable	$ 21,110	$ 38,000
Accounts Payable	12,200	16,912
Accruals Payable	2,280	3,690
Total Current Liabilities	$ 35,590	$ 58,602
Long-Term Liabilities:		
Installment Loan Payable	$ -0-	$ 25,668
Mortgage Payable	110,000	106,000
Total Long-Term Liabilities	$110,000	$131,668
Total Liabilities	$145,590	$190,270
Owner's Equity:		
Capital Stock	$ 30,000	$ 30,000
Retained Earnings	98,355	113,455
Total Owner's Equity	$128,355	$143,455
Total Liabilities & Owner's Equity	$273,945	$333,725

The balance sheet is the accountant's summary of the value of the firm's assets, liabilities, and owner's equity at the end of a given accounting period. When interpreting this statement or using its information for decision making, remember that (1) asset amounts represent values based on original cost, not liquidation, replacement, or earning power, and (2) the balance sheet is best viewed as a historical indicator of the sources of financing that have been made available to the firm, and how this financing has been invested in various assets.

to understanding what information the statement provides, or does not provide, for planning and decision making.

The other major division of the balance sheet is known as the equity section. In accounting parlance, equity means the claim on assets held by those groups that have provided funds for its operation. From Avanti's balance sheet, you can see that the equity claims are divided into two categories: liabilities, which represent the legal claims of creditors who have loaned money or goods to the business; and owner's equity, or net worth, which represents a claim resulting from the capital invested by the owners, and past profits retained in the business (not withdrawn or paid out as dividends).

The balance sheet value of the owner's interest in the business is calculated as the value of the firm's assets (what it owns) minus the value of its liabilities (what it owes).

Owner's Equity (Net Worth)= Assets – Liabilities

For Avanti, owner's equity was $128,355 in 19X1 (total asset value of $273,945 minus total liabilities outstanding of $145,590), and $143,455 in 19X2 (total asset value of $333,725 minus total liabilities outstanding of $190,270).

Notice that for each year, the value of total assets equals the combined value of total liabilities and owner's equity ($273,945 in 19X1 and $333,725 in 19X2). In other words, the balance sheet balances. This is as it should be. The total amount of funds provided by creditors and owners for Avanti management to invest in assets, must equal the total value of the assets owned by the firm. In financial terms, this simple identity is stated as: The total uses of funds in a given period equals the total sources of funds. These balance sheet sources and uses should be more closely examined.

Assets

From Avanti's balance sheet we see that assets are divided into two main categories: *current assets* and *fixed assets*. These items represent the manner in which management decided to use or invest the funds available to the firm over past periods. Current assets, which consist primarily of cash, accounts receivable, and inventory, are assumed by the accountant to be either cash or items that should be converted into cash or used up within a one-year period. These items are defined as follows:

- **Cash** is the amount of cash on hand or in the checking account plus any highly liquid, near-cash items such as a savings certificate or money market investment.

- **Accounts receivable** represents the dollar amount of outstanding credit sales on the books at the end of the accounting period.

- **Inventory** is the amount of raw materials, work-in-process, or finished goods (items ready for sale) that are available at the end of the period to meet the production or sales needs of the business. A merchandising firm such as a retailer or wholesaler would have only finished goods inventory; a manufacturer would have raw materials which are converted through work-in-process into finished goods; whereas a service firm may not have inventory.

- **Prepaid expenses** represent advance payment for services that will benefit the business in future accounting periods. A common example is payment of an insurance premium that will provide coverage over several accounting periods.

Both the amount of receivables and inventory carried by the firm represent the investment of sometimes scarce dollars. Since the money tied up in these assets cannot be used for other purposes, such as to meet ongoing expenses, pay liabilities, purchase new assets, etc., it is important that the level of investment in these assets be carefully controlled. Failure to do so has sounded the death knell for many small firms. Chapters 2 and 4 also discuss this point.

Fixed assets are the more long-lived resources owned by the firm. As shown on Avanti's balance sheets, they consist of such things as land, buildings, vehicles, and equipment. With the exception of land, these assets are valued by an accountant at what was previously indicated as book value. This concept is important to understanding the balance sheet, and the following example should make it clearer.

Cash Flow and Depreciation Example

Assume that you buy a new vehicle for your business at a cost of $18,000, and your accountant determines it will provide value to the business for three years. Because the assumed life of the asset extends beyond one year, your accountant does not write off the $18,000 cost as an expense of doing business on the income statement for this period. Rather, the cost of the vehicle is recorded as a fixed asset at the time of purchase. During each year of the vehicle's three-year life, that portion of the original cost or value that is lost is recognized as an expense of doing business. The expense write-off appears on the annual income statements as depreciation expense, and the difference between original cost and total depreciation taken on the asset appears on the balance sheet as book value of the asset for that year.

To illustrate, assume your accountant chooses to spread the cost of the asset equally over the three-year period. In this case, the annual depreciation expense would be $6,000 ($18,000 divided by 3). At the end of each year the value of the vehicle would appear on the balance sheet as $18,000 less all depreciation charged to date. This latter amount is referred to as accumulated depreciation. The accounting procedure and balance sheet and income statement effects would be as follows:

At the end of the first year, the accountant would charge $6,000 to the income statement as depreciation expense. This entry represents the assumed portion of the original cost or value of the asset that has been used up in that accounting period. The balance sheet account, accumulated depreciation, would also be charged for $6,000 to represent the expired portion of the asset's value, and the book value of the vehicle would be $12,000 ($18,000 minus $6,000). The process would be repeated in the second and third year. At the end of the second year $6,000 would be charged to the income statement as depreciation expense, and $6,000 would be charged to accumulated depreciation. The book value of the asset would then appear on the balance sheet as $6,000 ($18,000 minus $12,000 of accumulated depreciation). At the end of three years the asset would be fully depreciated and have a book value of $0.

From this discussion you should note two important facts about book value and the depreciation process:

- The balance sheet values for depreciated assets and, as a result, owner's net worth which reflects asset values, must be interpreted very carefully. The dollar amounts shown for fixed assets represent the accounting concept of book value. Since owner's equity is equal to asset value less liabilities outstanding, it also reflects book value. Remember, this concept of value is not related to the replacement cost of fixed assets, to the price at which they could be sold, or most important, to their value as measured by expected earnings and cash flows. In the case of land, which is not depreciated by the accountant or allowed by the IRS, the dollar value appearing on the balance sheet represents original cost. Obviously, any relationship between original cost of land and its current market value, replacement value, or resale value would be a rare coincidence. So the point about book value is clear: What your entire business or its individual assets are worth to you or to a prospective buyer is not measured on the balance sheet. In reality, value is measured by the ability of an asset or group of assets to generate cash flows.

- The depreciation expense figure that appears on each period's income statement as a deduction from sales revenue is a non-cash expense item. It is one expense item for which you will never be required to write a check. Note that the cash outflow occurred at the time the asset was purchased, and not when the subsequent depreciation entries are made. There will be more on this subject in the next chapter.

Liabilities

Liabilities are amounts owed to creditors. Like assets, the accountant divides liabilities into two categories: *current liabilities* and *long-term liabilities*. These categories represent the assumed time period within which the obligations will be paid.

Current liabilities, which consist of notes payable, accounts payable, and accruals, such as wages or taxes payable, are obligations that are assumed to come due within one year. These items are defined as:

- **Notes payable** are obligations owed to creditors, such as a bank or finance company, that have loaned money to the firm.

- **Accounts payable** are obligations owed to trade creditors for inventory or services purchased on credit.

- **Accruals payable** are obligations that have been incurred but not as yet paid. The primary items in this category are wages payable, taxes payable, and interest payable. Accruals are short-term items that arise because of differences between the date on which a firm's books are closed for a given accounting period, and the date on which cash payments will be made. For example, assume that Avanti's employees are paid every two weeks, and the end of the current accounting period falls in the middle of the two-week pay period. In theory, wages for one week have been earned by the employees but, since the pay period does not end until the following week, these wages have not as yet been paid. Since the firm has received the benefit of the employees' effort for the week, the accountant treats the wages for that period as a current obligation.

- **Current portion of long-term debt** is that portion of a long-term obligation assumed to be paid during the next accounting period; for example, that portion of an installment bank loan that will come due by the end of the next fiscal period would be treated as a current obligation.

Long-term liabilities are obligations assumed to mature and be paid sometime beyond a one-year period. Common examples are mortgage debt payable, installment debt payable, and bonds payable.

Owner's Equity

Owner's equity, or *net worth,* represents the owner's claim on the assets of the business. This is a residual claim since owners only receive what remains after all other claims, including taxes, have been satisfied. The value of the owner's claim results from the paid-in capital invested in the business (this is shown as capital stock for an incorporated firm such as Avanti) and retained earnings. As was true with assets, you must be extremely careful about interpreting the value implied by the net worth figure on the balance sheet.

The amount of owner's equity is not, nor is it intended by the accountant to be, a measure of the market value of the business. As is the case with any investment, what the business is worth on the open market (the amount a buyer is willing to pay for the business) is determined by valuing the amount of future cash flows it is expected to produce as a going concern. Owner's equity as shown on the balance sheet reflects the concept of book value, not market value.

Although you may now accept the fact that owner's net worth does not represent market value of the business, you may still wonder: Isn't there any real value in the amount of capital invested by the owner, and in the earnings that were retained and plowed back into the business? The answer is maybe. Realize that the cash represented by the amount of owner's investment and the amount of retained earnings has long since been used to meet operating expenses and purchase the assets needed to keep the firm going. Whether the investment of these funds has produced any value for the owner depends on whether operations and the firm's assets produced a satisfactory return in the form of earnings and cash flows. It is the process of generating a compensatory return on invested capital that produces value for the owner, and this measure of value is not reflected in the book values that appear on the balance sheet.

What Information Does the Balance Sheet Provide?

Now that you have become familiar with the accounting conventions that are used to prepare a balance sheet, you may question whether it provides any usable information for the practicing manager. The answer is yes. As shown in Chapter 4, the balance sheet for a single accounting period can provide useful information about the status of a particular asset, liability, or owner's equity account. Even more important, chapters 2 and 3 will show how changes in balance sheet accounts between two statement dates provide important information about a firm's financial health. Understanding the nature and implication of changes in financial statement accounts can help provide answers to questions such as:

- By how much did the amount of funds tied up in accounts receivable and inventory increase or decrease, relative to the change in sales for the period?

- Has the amount of debt financing increased to unsatisfactory levels since the last statement date?

- Are accounts payable rising to dangerous levels?

- Has net sales risen sufficiently to warrant the increased investment in fixed assets?

■ Has the firm maintained a satisfactory level of cash flow from operations?

A Final Thought

Remember: The income statement and balance sheet are prepared by an accountant using a very specific set of conventions. These conventions are designed to meet the accountant's needs for reporting and not for decision making. To use the information from financial statements effectively, you must understand the limitations created by these conventions.

Where to Now?

Probably the single most important indicator of the financial health of your business is the cash flow generated by normal operations. Without sufficient cash flow from operations, the business cannot run efficiently or provide a fair return on invested capital. Cash flow is the subject of the next chapter.

Chapter 2
Cash Flow & Cash Flow from Operations

Now that we have eliminated the mystery surrounding the balance sheet and income statement, let's investigate another perplexing phenomenon experienced by small business managers: the seeming absence of correlation between the profit figure shown on the firm's income statement and the amount of available cash. How many times have you thought to yourself, or heard a fellow business person say, "The business appears to be doing well, sales are up, profits are up, but there is never enough cash to pay the bills. If the business is doing so well, where is all the money?" Your study of the last chapter on financial statements provides part of the answer. Net income from operations is not a measure of cash flow from operations.

Profit is an accounting concept measured as the difference between two other accounting concepts: revenue and expense. Unquestionably, profit is a good long-term indicator of s firm's financial performance. It is also true that over the long run a firm's level of profit and cash flow will be closely correlated. The problem is, as a noted economist once observed, "in the long run, we are all dead." In the very important short run, you must be acutely aware of the difference that may exist between the amount of profit or loss from operations shown on your income statement and the level of cash available for use. This difference is the subject of the next two chapters. The following outlines what you will be learning about the subject.

TOPIC	CONCEPTS DISCUSSED
Cash Flow	The meaning of the term cash flow.
	What constitutes cash flow and how it differs from cash flow from operations.
Cash Flow from Operations	The meaning of the term cash flow from operations.
	What constitutes cash flow from operations and how it differs from profit from operations.

Understanding and controlling the forces that affect cash flow in the short run is a critical financial management responsibility. Cash is required to keep the business operating smoothly. In the short run, profit cannot be used to meet payroll, to repay maturing creditor obligations, to implement plans for the business, or to withdraw dividends. All such activities require cash. Considering the poor survival rate for small firms in general, cash flow management may be the single most important topic of this book.

The Concept of Cash Flow

The term *cash flow* is deceptive. It seems straightforward but, at the same time, it is difficult to explain. Even business people who use the term as part of their daily vocabulary are not always clear about its meaning. The reason for the confusion is simple: While the concept of cash flow is straightforward, identifying and tracking cash flow within the firm is complex. In a typical business firm, the cash system is affected by a variety of factors, and the particular factors affecting it at any one time are always changing. Unless management has a systematic approach for identifying, organizing, and evaluating the many factors that affect the firm's cash flow system, managing this crucial asset is virtually impossible. Before reading further, you should try to identify the activities that cause cash to flow into and out of your firm.

Taken literally, the term cash flow means any transaction or activity in which the firm engages that results in a change in its cash account. While these activities are varied, they can be placed in one of two categories: those that are associated with normal operations (purchasing, production, selling, and collecting), and those that result from all other financial or non-operating activities of the firm (borrowing or repaying loans, additional owner's investment or disinvestment, the purchase or sale of fixed assets, or extraordinary events such as a tax refund or fire loss). To gain a clear understanding of the concept of cash flow, it is necessary to distinguish between two categories: operating cash flows, and financial and non-operating cash flows..

Operating Cash Flows

Normal operations (those activities required to make or sell the firm's product or render its service) will, on a continuing basis, produce the largest volume of its cash inflows and outflows. The cash inflows that arise from these activities are:

- Cash sales.
- The collection of accounts receivable.

Operating cash outflows arise from:

- The payment for inventory purchases.
- The payment of accounts payable.

■ Those payments associated with other cash operating expenses, such as wages, payroll taxes, rent, and utilities.

It is important to note that the items listed above involve operating cash inflows and outflows, and are also recognized on the income statement as revenue or expense. For example, cash sales, wage payments, and payment of the firm's utility bill are all recognized by an accountant as either revenue or expense for a given period. Conversely, some items on the two cash flow lists do not appear on the income statement. For example, the collection of accounts receivable, or the payment of accounts payable are not recognized as revenue or expense items even though they affect cash flows. This is an important consideration since it is at the heart of the concept of cash flow from operations.

As with cash flow from operations, the financial and non-operating portion of the firm's cash flow system is created by a variety of transactions. Financial and non-operating cash inflows can arise from:

Financial and Non-Operating Cash Flows

■ Loans from creditors.

■ Additional investment by the owner.

■ The sale of fixed assets.

■ Nonroutine sources such as a tax refund or a non-operating income item such as interest income.

Financial or non-operating cash outflows result from:

■ The payment of principal or interest on debt.

■ Withdrawals (dividends if incorporated) by the owner.

■ The purchase of fixed assets.

■ Nonroutine uses such as the payment of a legal claim against the firm.

During its life span, a business experiences a variety of cash flows. Some are associated with operations, some result from financial transactions, and some from non-operating activities. While it is possible that financial or non-operating cash inflows may be the dominant source of funds for the firm at times, this condition can only be temporary. If a firm is to remain viable, cash flow from operations must be the major source of funds. Through time, cash flow from operations must be sufficient to pay out-of-pocket expenses, replace and add assets as needed, and provide a fair rate of return on invested capital. If cash flow from operations is not sufficient to maintain these three critical life-support systems, financial and non-operating cash inflows will not be available to a firm.

The Importance of Operations

For example, ask yourself if creditors would make loans to your firm without the prospect of sufficient cash flow from operations to make principal and interest payments on debt, or if it would be possible to attract additional owner's capital (taking a partner or selling more stock) without the expectation that operations will produce an acceptable rate of return on the investment. The answer is obvious: There would be no creditors or owners willing to provide funds to your firm. The message from this discussion then is clear:

On a continuing basis cash flow from operations is the most important source of funds for the firm. Without it there would be no other sources.

The Calculation of Cash Flow

Since you now know what is meant by the term cash flow, you must establish a method for measuring this critical indicator of a firm's financial health. One possible approach involves examining all of the firm's transactions in a specified time period, and isolating those that affect cash. This is accomplished by monitoring each accounting entry to s firm's cash account. This approach, however, has drawbacks. It involves an overwhelming mass of detail, and you would not get needed information in a form best suited to analysis.

A more efficient and, from a manager's viewpoint, more revealing approach to determining cash flow involves adjusting the income statement and balance sheet to a cash basis. Cash flow statements focus on what you should know: The reasons behind the change in a firm's cash position.

The following discussion on cash flow from operations, as well as that in the next chapter on the source and use of cash, details how the financial statements are adjusted to obtain cash flow. Available software models perform these adjustments automatically. (For information regarding software, see the card enclosed at the back of this book.) Tracing through the mechanics of the process simplifies learning and enhances your knowledge and understanding of a firm's cash system, and the factors that affect it.

The Concept of Cash Flow from Operations

Profit from operations is not cash from operations. The reason for the difference is simple: Cash flow from operations is affected by activities that appear on the income statement as revenues and expenses, and by activities that are shown on the balance sheet as current assets and current liabilities. In other words, cash flow from operations involves both income statement items and balance sheet items. Again, it would be worthwhile to try to identify these items for your firm before reading further.

Operating cash inflows consist of cash sales for the period, and the cash inflows resulting from the collection of accounts receivable. The receivables may arise from credit sales for this or some past period, but they represent cash inflows in the period that payment is received. On the other hand, cash sales are recognized as revenue on the income statement, but the cash flow from collected receivables is not (recall the example in Chapter 1 about the firm that sells only one product a year to Mr. Faithful). Because there are usually differences between revenue recognition by the accountant and the timing of cash inflows, the income statement may show more revenue and profit than cash flow from operations in some periods, and less in others.

Operating Cash Inflows

There are also disparities between the recognition of operating expenses on the income statement and the timing of the associated cash outflows. For example, the cost of producing or purchasing inventory is not recognized as an expense (cost of sales) on the income statement until the period during which the inventory is sold. This recognition may have nothing to do with the timing of the cash payments. Naturally, if inventory is purchased or produced, paid for, and sold in the same period there is no difference between the timing of the cash outflow and the recognition of the cost of sales expense on the income statement. At times this is the case, but more often the following will be true:

Operating Cash Outflows

- Inventory is purchased for cash in one accounting period and sold in another.

- Inventory is purchased on credit; the sale is made either in the same period or a later period; and the outstanding payable is paid in a period following that in which the sale was made.

When either of these conditions occur, there will be a difference between the cost of operations as shown on the income statement, and the cash outflows associated with operations.

Similar timing differences are associated with other operating expenses shown on the income statement and cash outflows. Recall, for example, the discussion of accrued expense items such as wage expense, interest expense, or tax obligations. Although these items can appear as expenses on the income statement in a given accounting period, the cash outflow will not occur until a subsequent accounting period. Also, the amount of depreciation expense shown on the income statement reduces revenue and profits for the period, yet there is no associated cash outflow.

The trick to calculating cash flow from operations is to prepare a statement that links income statement items with changes in those balance sheet items associated with normal operations. That is, the sales,

How Cash Flow from Operations Is Calculated

cost of sales, and operating expense items on the income statement should be adjusted for changes that occur in the inventory, accounts receivable, accounts payable, and accrual items on the balance sheet.

Trace through the mechanics of these adjustments using the financial statements of The Avanti Company shown in Chapter 1. At the end of that chapter, there was the increase in sales and net income shown on the income statement for 19X2, but some suspicions about the firm's financial position. Detailing the mechanics of cash flow from operations will not only enhance your understanding of the cash flow from operations statement, it will also provide insights into the factors that cause cash to flow into and out of a firm.

The Mechanics of Cash Flow from Operations

Avanti's income statement indicated growth in both sales and net income between 19X1 and 19X2. Sales grew to $340,000 and profits to $31,100. A quick glance at the balance sheet further substantiates the growth picture. Notice there was also a sizable increase in Avanti's asset base. Accounts receivable, inventory, and fixed assets all increased from 19X1 levels.

On the surface, the firm appears to be doing very well. Appearances, however, are sometimes deceiving. You may have learned from your own business experience that growth can be a very sharp two-edged sword. Growth can be rewarding, but it takes cash to finance growth in assets and sales, and the potential returns from growth can lag far behind the firm's need for immediate financing. In short, even the most profitable growth can severely strain a firm's liquidity position. Calculating the amount of cash flow from operations for Avanti in 19X2 will reveal why. These calculations appear on Avanti's statement of cash flow from operations, shown on the next page.

Adjusting for Cash Inflows from Operations

The first step in converting the income statement to a cash flow from operations statement is to adjust the sales figure to a cash basis. Consider for a moment the $340,000 sales figure that appears on Avanti's income statement for 19X2. If Avanti did not extend credit and made only cash sales to its customers, the entire $340,000 recognized as sales revenue would also be cash inflow for the period. But this is not the case. There is a large difference between the $340,000 of sales revenue, and the amount of cash inflow from sales that Avanti enjoyed.

The reason for the difference is credit sales. Notice that accounts receivable on the balance sheet increased by $28,822 from 19X1 to 19X2 ($25,778 to $54,600). Avanti extended more credit than it did last year. In doing so, the firm suffered a cash drain in the form of sales revenue not collected. While the amount of total sales increased from 19X1, cash flow from sales did not. A large portion of the sales increase, $28,822, came as increased credit that Avanti had to carry

Table 2.1

THE AVANTI COMPANY
Statement of Cash Flow from Operations
For the Period 19X1 to 19X2

Net Sales	$340,000	
Less: Increase in Accounts Receivable	(28,822)	
Net Sales Adjusted to a Cash Basis		$311,178
Cost of Sales	$194,500	
Plus: Increase in Inventory	31,958	
Less: Increase in Accounts Payable	(4,712)	
Cost of Sales Adjusted to a Cash Basis		(221,746)
Operating Expenses	$ 90,367	
Less: Depreciation Expense	(2,000)	
Less: Increase in Accruals	(1,410)	
Plus: Increase in Prepaids	5,000	
Operating Expenses Adjusted to a Cash Basis		(91,957)
Taxes Paid		(20,733)
Cash Flow (Cash Drain) From Operations		$(23,258)

The statement of cash flow from operations provides detailed information on the most important source of funds for the firm. By combining balance sheet and income statement data, the cash flow from operations statement highlights the critical operating factors that provide or drain cash during a given accounting period.

on its books. This increase in receivables not only strains the firm's cash position, but creates the need for financing. Obviously, while the firm's scarce cash is tied up in accounts receivable, it is not available for other uses.

To recognize the cash drain caused by increasing credit sales, the sales figure must be adjusted to a cash basis. On Avanti's cash flow from operations statement, the adjustment is made by subtracting the $28,822 increase in accounts receivable from the $340,000 sales figure.

Adjusting for Cash Outflows

To account for the effect of Avanti's other operating activities on cash flow from operations for the period, the income statement expense items must be adjusted for changes in the cost of sales, operating expenses, and cash flow from operations.

Adjusting Cost of Sales

Recall that the expense item "cost of sales" reflects the cost of those goods actually sold in a given accounting period. This cost is recognized on the income statement in the period of the sale, and not the period in which payment for the costs associated with purchasing or producing the inventory was made. If your firm's level of inventory (a current asset on the balance sheet) and accounts payable (a current liability on the balance sheet) do not change from the last period, then the cost of sales figure on the current income statement represents the cash outflow associated with this expense item. However, this is rarely the case for any firm. The effects of increases in inventory and accounts payable on cash flow from operations appear on Avanti's statement.

Cost of sales as shown on Avanti's 19X2 income statement was $194,500. If there had been no change in the levels of inventory and accounts payable between 19X1 and 19X2, this figure would represent both the expense and the cash outflow associated with cost of goods sold. But this is not the case. The balance sheet shows an increase in inventory from 19X1 to 19X2 of $31,958 ($24,167 to $56,125). This increase represents an additional outflow of cash that is not reflected on the income statement. Because the increase in inventory had to be paid for, the cash outflow associated with cost of sales is greater than the $194,500 shown on the income statement, greater by the increase in inventory of $31,958. To adjust the cost of sales figure for an inventory increase during the period, the amount of the increase is added to cost of sales.

Avanti's cost of sales figure must also be adjusted for the changes in accounts payable from 19X1 to 19X2. Notice from Avanti's balance sheets (Table 1.2) that accounts payable increased by $4,712 ($16,912 minus $12,200) between the two statement dates. This means that the company's ability to use trade credit allowed them to delay cash payment for inventory beyond the purchase date. By so doing, cash is retained in the business for the term of the credit period. Avanti is using its suppliers' funds just as Avanti's customers use its funds when they purchase on credit. The increase in accounts payable, therefore, means that the cash outflow associated with cost of sales is not as great as indicated by the figure on the income statement. In adjusting cost of sales to a cash basis, the amount of the increase in accounts payable is deducted from the cost of sales figure.

In arriving at cash flow from operations, the operating expense figure shown on the income statement is also adjusted for the cash effects of related activities. One such adjustment involves the depreciation expense figure. Since depreciation expense is a noncash deduction from revenue (recall the previous discussion on the depreciation process), the cash outflow associated with total operating expenses is not as large as shown on the income statement. To make the adjustment, depreciation expense is deducted from the total operating expense figure. On Avanti's cash flow from operations statement (Table 2.1), the depreciation expense figure of $2,000 is deducted from the total operating expenses of $90,367.

Adjusting Operating Expenses

The operating expense figure is also adjusted for any change in accruals payable (a current liability on the balance sheet). Since such items as accrued wages, accrued interest, and accrued taxes are unpaid obligations, any increase in accruals from year to year reflects cash retained in the business. (Recall the discussion of accruals payable in Chapter 1.) To the extent that cash payments are delayed, the cash burden of operating expenses is reduced. The increase in accruals of $1,410 experienced by Avanti between 19X1 and 19X2 is deducted from the operating expense figure shown on the income statement.

If prepaid expenses are included in the firm's transactions, the operating expense figure must be adjusted for any change in this current asset item. Prepaid expenses represent advance cash payment for service to be received by the firm in the future. For example, in the case of prepaid insurance, advance payment has been made in return for future insurance benefits. Even though advance payment is made, only that portion of the benefits assumed to be used in the period appear as an expense on the income statement. The unused portion remains as a current asset. If prepaid expenses increase from one year to the next, the cash outflow associated with operating expenses is greater than the figure appearing on the income statement by the amount of the increase. This was true in Avanti's case. Prepaids increased by $5,000, and the increase is added to total operating expenses on the cash flow from operations statement.

One last adjustment is required for income taxes. As you know only too well, the IRS does not deal in credit. Tax obligations must be paid in cash, and the income tax figure of $20,733 shown on Avanti's income statement (remember, the company is incorporated) represents a cash outflow. This figure is deducted from cash inflows from operations on the cash flow from operations statement.

Cash Flow from Operations

The cash flow from operations figure shown on Avanti's statement is determined by deducting Cost of Sales Adjusted to a Cash Basis — $221,746, Operating Expenses Adjusted to a Cash Basis — $91,957, and Income Taxes Paid — $20,733, from Net Sales Adjusted to a Cash Basis — $311,178. The result for 19X2 was $(23,258).

This result is startling! In the brief time it took to go from the company's income statement and balance sheet to the cash flow from operations statement, the picture changed from rosy to grim. While sales, profits, and assets were up for the period, cash flow from operations was a negative $23,258. This means that what is normally the most important source of funds for the firm was not a source at all. Operations caused a major drain on the firm's cash position — a drain that probably sent Avanti's management on several trips to the bank for financing. How could this have happened?

Interpreting the Cash Flow from Operations Statement

To find out why operations drained so much cash from the firm, let's examine more closely Avanti's cash flow from operations statement. Even the most cursory review of the statement provides an indication of the problem. Cash was drained by the increase or growth in working capital that accompanied the growth in sales. The large increase in accounts receivable reduced the cash inflow from sales, and the large increase in inventory increased the cash outflow for cost of sales. Remember, it takes money to finance inventory and accounts receivable. Dollars tied up in these two assets cannot be used elsewhere.

Avanti enjoyed sales growth, but inventory and accounts receivable grew at a faster rate than sales, and cash was drained off to support the increase. Whether the increase in receivables and inventory was prudent, or the result of poor management control, is something that Avanti management will have to investigate and decide. By having the information from the cash flow from operations statement, however, they now know where to look for answers.

While available software (see the card enclosed at the back of this book) performs the number crunching to automatically convert the balance sheet and income statement to a cash flow statement, it is extremely important for proper interpretation of the statement to be familiar with the logic behind the plus and minus statements. By doing so, you are better able to understand whether an increase or decrease in a particular account is having a favorable or unfavorable effect on your firm's cash flows. This is the type of information that you, as manager, should have.

The easiest way to become familiar with the remaining adjustments is to build on what you learned from the preceding discussion with your business experience and intuition. Consider the following examples:

- You know that an increase in receivables reduces cash flow from sales. It follows, then, that a decrease in receivables will increase the cash flow from sales. In the case of a decline in accounts receivable between two statement dates, the cash account not only benefits from the cash produced by sales and the collection of receivables in this period, it also benefits from the collection of receivables from past periods as well.

- An increase in inventory drains cash, and the cash outflow associated with the cost of sales is greater as a result. If inventory declines, however, the amount of the decrease is subtracted from cost of sales. The cash outflow associated with cost of sales is not as great as appears on the income statement because the firm has drawn down inventory that was paid for in some past period.

- The logic behind the treatment of accounts payable is also straightforward. In the Avanti example, an increase in payables is subtracted from cost of sales because cash is retained in the business. Conversely, a decrease in the level of payables means that these obligations have been paid. This causes cash to flow out of the business. To the extent that accounts payable have been reduced by cash payments, the cash outflow associated with cost of sales is greater than the figure shown on the income statement. Cost of sales would be adjusted to a cash basis by adding the amount of the decrease in accounts payable.

- Other cash adjustments to the operating expense figure include a decrease in the current liability accruals payable, a decrease in the current asset prepaid expenses, and a tax refund. A decrease in accruals payable is added to the operating expense figure. The logic behind this rule is exactly the same as that for a decrease in accounts payable. A decrease in prepaid expenses, which means a reduction in advance cash payments, is subtracted from the operating expense figure. A tax refund, which is a cash inflow, is deducted from the operating expense figure.

As you spend time examining cash flow from operations statements, it will become easier to interpret the results. The benefits from the time invested are well worth the cost. You will be in a position to:

- Identify, understand, monitor, and control the factors that affect your firm's cash flow from operations.

■ Manage your firm's cash flows more effectively.

■ Avoid the type of unpleasant shock suffered at Avanti.

Where to Now?

The cash flow from operations statement tells you what you need to know about the most critical component of your firm's cash flow system, but does not contain information on the financial and non-operating cash flows that also affect the firm's cash position. To obtain this information and complete the cash flow puzzle, you need one more statement — the *sources and uses of cash statement*.

Chapter 3
Financial & Non-Operating Sources and Uses of Cash

The cash flow from operations statement provides you with the most important piece of information about the firm's cash flow puzzle, but it does not include the financial and non-operating flows that are also a part of the cash system. Sound financial management requires that these cash flows be identified, evaluated, and controlled as well. To complete the treatment of cash flow analysis, this chapter will examine the source and use of cash concepts.

TOPIC	CONCEPTS DISCUSSED
The Balance Sheet	Why it is viewed as a statement of sources and uses of funds.
	Why changes in key balance sheet accounts are important to cash flow analysis.
Sources and Uses of Cash Statement	How to interpret the basic format of the statement.
	How to evaluate the financial and non-operating cash flows included on the statement.
	How to interpret the information provided by the statement.

The Concept of Financial and Non-Operating Cash Flows

In order to develop the concept of sources and uses of financial and non-operating cash flows and an understanding of the role they play in a firm's cash system, you must establish a more informative way of thinking about the balance sheet. In Chapter 1, the balance sheet was described as an accountant's measure of the financial position of a firm. Although accurate, this is an extremely limited view of the statement. It ignores the important role of the balance sheet as a source of financial information — information on what assets have been purchased, and how these investments were financed. This more practical view of the balance sheet focuses on the sources of funds that have been available to the firm, and how these sources were used.

The reasoning involved in this alternative picture of the balance sheet is simple. The equities portion of the balance sheet (liabilities and owner's equity) represents sources of financing — the amounts obtained from creditors and from the owners. The asset portion of the balance sheet reflects how this financing was used to invest in the various current and fixed items that constitute a firm's asset base. You know from experience that operating the business requires assets such as inventory, equipment, and buildings. The types of assets held by a firm and the amount of funds invested in each are the result of management's past investment decisions. Management decided how and where the funds available to a firm should be used and in what amounts. The result of these investment decisions is reflected in the asset section of a firm's balance sheet.

In order to make investment in assets possible, funds were needed. The equities portion of the balance sheet indicates where the financing came from, and in what amounts. These sources vary between short-term credit such as a 90-day bank loan, long-term credit such as a mortgage loan, and owner's financing provided in the form of paid-in capital and funds from operations retained in the business (not withdrawn as dividends). Considering the assets and equities portions of the balance sheet together, it is simply a source and use of funds statement. In short, increases in liability and owner's equity accounts represent sources of cash, and increases in assets represent uses of cash.

Focusing on Changes in the Accounts

In Chapter 1 it was suggested that year-end balance sheet values can be useful figures, but the changes that occurred in these values between the current and previous balance sheet are far more important. For example, the last chapter emphasized the importance to cash-flow-from-operations analysis of tracing changes in inventory, accounts receivable, accounts payable. Likewise, tracing changes occurring in fixed assets, liabilities, and owner's equity items between two balance sheet dates is the basis for analyzing the sources and uses of financial and non-operating cash flows. Understanding these changes can be an invaluable aid to management in answering important financial questions, such as:

- To what extent are your firm's investments financed internally with cash flow from operations, and to what extent do you rely on more risky outside sources?

- What percentage of externally raised funds comes from short-term debt, and what percentage from long-term debt?

- Is the amount of debt financing used excessive, and can your firm tolerate the financial risk involved with that level of debt?

- Is the amount of owner's withdrawals (dividends) reasonable in view of the firm's financing needs? Should more of the available funds from operations be retained in the business?

By now you probably have some idea of the various activities that generate financial and non-operating cash flows for your firm. So that the logic of the source and use of cash statement is crystal clear, you should examine each cash flow item and establish a simple set of rules for evaluating them. Before doing so, it would again be worthwhile for you to identify the financial and non-operating cash flows in your firm.

Cash may flow into the firm from the following four sources:

- **Cash flow from operations.** Remember, on a continuing basis this is the most important source of cash for the firm, and the one that makes all other sources possible.

- **An increase in any liability account excluding accounts payable and accruals.** (Changes in these two items were included in the determination of cash flow from operations.) Increases in liability items represent new borrowing and an obvious inflow of cash. For example, if you borrow from the bank, cash is increased by the proceeds of the loan, and the liability account, notes payable, will increase by the amount owed the bank.

- **An increase in the paid-in capital** (sale of capital stock if the firm is incorporated) **section of the owner's equity account.** This increase represents additional owner's investment and additional cash for the firm.

- **The sale of fixed assets.** If a fixed asset (such as a piece of equipment no longer used) is sold, the fixed asset account is reduced and cash is increased. Such transactions, although non-routine, still result in a cash inflow.

Cash flows out of the firm for the following uses:

- **Cash drain from operations.** This occurs when operations uses more cash than it generates. The condition results from operating losses or, as seen in Avanti's case, operating profits combined with the heavy cash drain from the rapid expansion of accounts receivable, inventory, or other assets.

- **The purchase of fixed assets.** This transaction, which appears as an increase in the appropriate fixed asset account, causes cash to flow out of the firm, either immediately or at some time in the future if financing is used to make the purchase. For example, if

Identifying Financial and Non-Operating Cash Flows

a new office building is purchased, the fixed asset account, buildings, would increase by the amount of the purchase price.

- **The repayment of debt**. When payment is made on a debt obligation, there is a decrease in the appropriate liability account in the amount of the payment. For example, if a 90-day bank note is repaid, the account, notes payable, is removed from current liabilities. This decrease reflects the outflow of cash.

- **Owner's withdrawals** (dividend payments). This transaction causes a reduction in the retained earnings section of the owner's equity account, and drains cash from the business.

These rules can be summarized as follows:

- Increases in liability and owner's equity accounts are sources of cash.

- Decreases in fixed asset accounts are sources of cash.

- Increases in fixed asset accounts are uses of cash.

- Decreases in liability and owner's equity accounts are uses of cash.

The statement which details the overall change in the firm's cash account is called the *statement of changes in financial position*. Fortunately, the format used to present the statement is flexible and can take whatever form best meets the needs of the situation. The important point is that all such statements are interpreted in virtually the same way.

Again, it should be emphasized that working through the rules used to prepare the statement requires a little time, but the effort is rewarding. Understanding these rules clarifies how and why a particular transaction or management decision affects the firm's cash system. This understanding is essential to the sound financial management of your business.

The Sources and Uses of Cash Statement

You will find that interpreting the sources and uses of cash statement is not a difficult task. To help get started, you can use Avanti's sources and uses of cash statement shown on Table 3.1. Remember, at last look, Avanti's management was trying to recover from the shock of seemingly profitable growth, and the reality of an operating cash drain. Before you look at the statement, it is important to note that:

Because it made exposition and learning easier, the cash flow from operations and the sources and uses of cash statements have been treated separately. In practice this should not be done. The two statements should be examined and evaluated together. The information that each provides complements the other; they are two parts of the

Table 3.1

THE AVANTI COMPANY
Sources and Uses of Cash Statement
For the Period 19X1 to 19X2

	Amount	**% of Total**
Sources of Cash:		
Increase in Notes Payable	$16,890	40 %
Increase in Installment Debt	25,668	60 %
Total Sources of Cash	$42,558	100 %
Uses of Cash:		
Cash Drain from Operations	$23,258	45 %
Increase in Fixed Assets	6,000	11 %
Decrease in Mortgage Payable	4,000	8 %
Payment of Interest Expense	3,300	6 %
Payment of Dividends	16,000	30 %
Total Uses of Cash	$52,558	100 %
Increase (Decrease) in the Cash Account	($10,000)	

The sources and uses of cash statement is the companion to the statement of cash flow from operations. It highlights the non-operating and financial cash flows that occur during a given accounting period. By combining the information from both statements, Avanti's managers have a complete picture of the factors that have given rise to changes in the firm's cash account over a given accounting period.

same financial puzzle. In fact, a well-prepared set of financial statements will include a combined cash flow statement with the balance sheet and income statement.

Interpreting the Sources and Uses of Cash Statement

Perhaps the most striking feature of the sources and uses of cash statement is its simplicity. The statement is divided into three main categories: sources of cash, uses of cash, and the increase (decrease) in the cash account. The sources of cash section details the activities which caused an increase in the firm's cash account during the period, while those that caused drains from the cash account appear under uses of cash. The increase (decrease) in cash is a summary figure which reflects the overall effect of, or difference between, the two sets of forces. Fortunately, the information provided by the statement is as easy to understand as the format. In evaluating the statement and its content, keep this fundamental financial principle in mind:

The firm should strive to strike a reasonable balance between the amount of investment in assets (rate of growth), the proportion of financing that is provided internally through cash flow from operations retained in the business or additional owner's capital, and the proportion that is financed externally from creditors. In short, management's investment, financing, and dividend/withdrawal policies should complement each other. When they do not, management is inviting financial catastrophe. For example, overreliance on debt financing creates financial risk the firm may ill-afford (remember that each dollar of debt represents a fixed cost that must be repaid); overexpansion of receivables or inventory drains funds and is usually indicative of poor credit control or lax inventory management; and excessive owner's withdrawals or dividends drains funds and dilutes the financial reserves necessary to see the firm through economic downturns.

To get a feel for how the sources and uses of cash statement is interpreted using this basic principle of financial balance, take a look at the results for Avanti.

A Picture of Unbalanced Growth

Recall that Avanti's income statements (Chapter 1) indicated sales growth and a profit increase for the period. On the other hand, the cash flow from operations statement (Chapter 2) revealed a large drain on the cash account caused by normal operations. The buildup in inventory and receivables had used more cash than operations could produce. A look at the uses of cash section of the sources and uses of cash statement further substantiates the picture of growth. From this statement we see that additional fixed assets were purchased in the amount of $6,000. Taken together, the cash drain caused by operations (which includes the increases in the current assets accounts receivable and inventory), and the expenditure to increase fixed assets amounted to 56% of total uses. How was this growth, along with the other uses of cash, financed?

The sources of cash section and the decrease in the cash account section of the statement provide the answer. Avanti's growth in assets as well as the other uses of cash were financed by borrowing against a portion of the firm's overall debt capacity (credit capability), and by reducing the firm's cash account. More than $42,000 was provided by creditors in the form of both short-term notes and long-term installment debt, and $10,000 was obtained by drawing down the cash account.

You may wish to verify that Avanti's cash account was reduced by $10,000 to help finance the activities undertaken during the year. To do so, momentarily return to Avanti's balance sheets in Chapter 1. Notice that the cash account declined by $10,000 between 19X1 and 19X2. Notice also that the amount of the decrease in the cash account shown on the sources and uses of cash statement is $10,000. This is not a coincidence. The fact that these two amounts are the same is exactly as it should be. The sources and uses of cash statement explains where cash came from and how it was used during the time spanning the two statement dates. By so doing, it also explains the amount of the change in the cash account between those two dates.

The question now arises regarding the wisdom of the financing policy employed by Avanti's management. While it is difficult to obtain a definitive answer to the question without the benefit of additional financial analysis, one item on the statement does stand out. Notice the item payment of dividends under uses of cash. As shown, dividend payments to the owners amounted to 30% of the total uses of funds. Under more normal circumstances dividends of this size may not be extravagant. In light of Avanti's healthy rate of growth and the corresponding need for financing to support it, however, this level of dividends should be questioned.

Growth requires financing, and some of this financing should come from funds retained in the business. In Avanti's case, large dividend withdrawals were made at a time when cash flow from operations was negative. This certainly aggravated the firm's need for funds. To meet this need, Avanti turned to its creditors. Borrowing to finance growth is not unusual for a firm with adequate credit capability. What is disturbing here is that Avanti, in effect, asked creditors to finance both a major portion of the firm's growth as well as dividend payments to its owners.

Creditors accommodated Avanti this year, but it is unlikely that this type of generosity will continue. It would be a rare creditor indeed who willingly assumed the responsibility for maintaining the lifestyle of the small business owners. If rapid growth is to continue, creditors would expect Avanti's owners to share a greater portion of the financing burden.

A Final Thought

When interpreting the sources and uses of cash statement, it is necessary to focus on both the particular items causing cash inflows and outflows, and on the relative importance of each. This latter piece of information is provided by the percent of total column. The values in this column represent each dollar amount expressed as a percentage of the total dollar amount in its respective category. For example, from Avanti's statement it is noted that cash drain from operations (45% of total uses) and increase in fixed assets (11% of total uses) combined for 56% of the cash used for the period. By focusing on these percentages you are able to place each source and use in its proper perspective, and to gain a picture of the extent to which balance exists in the firm's financial policies.

Where to Now?

The two cash flow reports provide information on the activities responsible for the flow of cash through the firm's cash system. This is the most important single piece of information that management should receive, yet it is not the only information required to analyze the firm's financial position and financial performance. To complete another part of the firm's financial puzzle, you need answers to questions such as:

- Are accounts receivable collected within a reasonable time period, or is the firm carrying excessive levels of receivables?

- Is inventory turned over at a satisfactory rate, or is the firm carrying excessive levels of inventory?

- Is the firm maintaining adequate profit margins and producing a fair return on assets and invested capital?

- Is the level of debt financing creating excessive risk for the firm?

Help in answering questions such as these is provided by financial ratio analysis. This is the third tool in the financial analysis arsenal and the subject of the next chapter.

Chapter 4
Financial Ratio Analysis

It was suggested in the previous chapter that only a comprehensive approach to financial analysis will provide all the clues necessary to solve a firm's financial puzzle. Information on cash flows is an important clue, but it is only one of several. The firm's balance sheet and income statement can offer additional insight into its financial performance. Again, the trick is knowing how to extract the appropriate information from these statements.

Financial ratio analysis can be a powerful tool for this purpose, and the table below briefly summarizes what this chapter covers regarding financial ratio analysis.

TOPIC	CONCEPTS DISCUSSED
Financial Ratios	How to compute ratios.
	What information ratios provide.
	How to interpret and use financial ratios.
Liquidity Ratios	Which ratios best measure your firm's liquidity position.
	How to analyze and use liquidity ratios.
Debt Ratios	Which ratios best measure your firm's debt position.
	How to analyze and use debt ratios.
	The meaning of financial risk.
Profitability Ratios	Which ratios best measure your firm's profit performance.
	How to analyze and use profitability ratios.

Initially, you may be surprised at the simplicity of the ratios themselves. They involve only the most basic of calculations, yet when used properly, ratios can improve the financial management of your firm by:

- Improving your understanding of financial relationships.

- Providing an appraisal of the firm's financial health.

- Identifying potential trouble spots that need your attention.

- Serving as a monitor of key financial indicators.

- Providing information for making projections and planning future courses of action.

- Providing information on how outsiders view the firm, its performance, and its prospects.

The Concept of Financial Ratios

Without the proper tools, interpreting the many dollar amounts shown on financial statements would be an impossible task even for the most gifted analyst. Numerous dollar values are confusing. Fortunately, ratio analysis eliminates this confusion.

One of the many important tasks that ratios perform is simplifying financial statement data by making comparisons. Financial ratios compare one financial value to another. Stated in formal terms, ratios take absolute values (dollar amounts) and convert them to relative values (percentages or index numbers). For example, assume that your bookkeeper reports that your firm earned operating income of $50,000 this period. Taken alone, this single, absolute value has little meaning. If compared to some measurable standard, however, the operating income figure can tell you a great deal about your firm's profit performance.

For example, you may compare the amount of operating profit for this year with the figure for last year. This could be done by calculating the percentage increase (rate of growth) in operating profit between the two periods. Profit growth is a much sought after goal. Or, you might divide the operating profit figure by the sales figure to determine the percentage operating profit margin for the period. Maintaining adequate profit margins means effective cost control and efficient operations. You may further reason that whether a $50,000 profit is desirable depends on the amount of investment that was required to produce it. If an investment of only $250,000 was involved, the $50,000 of profit represents a 20% return on investment — not bad. If, on the other hand, a $1 million investment was involved, the return of 5% is disappointing.

By comparing operating profit to other appropriate financial values, an otherwise hidden aspect of the firm's financial performance was uncovered. These comparisons involved calculating financial ratios.

A financial ratio is nothing more than a simple fraction in which the numerator and denominator consist of financial statement values. The fraction compares a balance sheet or income statement item in the numerator to a logically related balance sheet or income statement item in the denominator. Dividing numerator by denominator provides the ratio value. In the above example, the 20% return on investment was determined as shown below. Can you determine how the 5% return on investment was calculated?

Return on Investment = Operating Income ÷ Total Assets

Return on Investment = $50,000 ÷ $250,000

= 20%

Deciding Which Ratios to Calculate

Considering the many data items contained in a typical set of financial statements, a large number of ratio combinations are possible. Many of these, however, would be meaningless. For example, the ratio value produced by dividing interest expense from the income statement by total current assets from the balance sheet produces a result that is financial nonsense. It reveals nothing about the financial position of the firm.

The key to effective ratio analysis is not simply calculating a large number of ratios, but rather choosing financial relationships that provide useful information about the important facets of your firm's financial profile. This is accomplished by grouping related ratios. The most commonly used groupings or ratio categories include:

- Liquidity and activity measures.

- Debt usage (financial risk) measures.

- Profitability measures.

In the discussion that follows, the most important ratios in each category are identified, explained, and illustrated using the 19X1 and 19X2 data from Avanti's balance sheets and income statements (Chapter 1). The calculated ratio values are shown in Table 4.1. Working through the Avanti examples will be a major step toward developing the most important part of ratio analysis, the subtle art of interpreting ratio values.

Liquidity and Activity Measures

Liquidity, as used here, refers to the cash equivalence of the firm's current assets (cash, accounts receivable, and inventory). This group of ratios provides a rough measure of the firm's ability to meet short-term obligations as they mature, and to maintain the firm's normal operations. In general, the more liquid the firm's current assets, the closer the assets are to cash equivalents, and the lower the risk that creditors cannot be paid or operations will be strained or interrupted because of a cash crisis.

Activity, as used in the context of liquidity ratios, refers to the rate at which current assets such as inventory are converted (turned over) into sales, cash, or both in a given time period. The rate at which assets are turned over determines the firm's ability to generate liquidity (cash flow) and profitability. The primary liquidity and activity ratios are discussed in turn.

Current Ratio

The *current ratio* is calculated as total current assets divided by total current liabilities. It measures the dollar amount of current assets that are available to meet current liabilities. For Avanti, the current ratio value of 2 for 19X2 (calculated as total current assets of $118,725 divided by total current liabilities of $58,602) indicates that at the end of the year, Avanti had $2 in current assets for every $1 of current liabilities. Assuming that accounts receivable and inventory continue to turn over at normal rates (at times this may be a heroic assumption), the current ratio is interpreted by the size of the ratio value. In general, the larger the current ratio, the more liquid the firm. Conversely, a trend of declining current ratio values may signal deteriorating liquidity, and the need to investigate the reasons behind the decline.

Cash Flow from Operations as a Percentage of Net Sales Ratio

The *cash flow from operations as a percentage of net sales ratio* is calculated as cash flow from operations divided by net sales. The ratio value, which is a percentage, represents the amount of cash flow generated by operations per dollar of sales. For example, if net cash flow to sales for your firm was .15, this means that operations generated $0.15 (15 cents) in cash flow for each dollar of sales for the period. The larger this percentage value, the more cash per dollar of sales the firm has generated, and the more liquid and more efficient its operations. A rising trend for this value is the ideal. The ratio was not calculated for Avanti for 19X2 since cash flow from operations was negative.

Cash as a Percentage of Total Current Assets Ratio

The *cash as a percentage of total current assets ratio* is calculated as the dollar amount of cash from the balance sheet divided by total current assets from the balance sheet. In general, the larger this percentage, the higher the immediate liquidity level of the firm. It is important to note, however, that holding too much cash can be costly. Cash is a highly liquid, but low-earning asset. If excessive amounts of cash are held as liquid balances rather than invested in working assets, the firm may be less profitable than is otherwise possible. The cash to current assets ratio for Avanti in 19X2 of 2.5% was calculated as the ending cash value of $3,000 divided by total current assets of $118,725. Notice the decline in this ratio from the 19X1 level.

Table 4.1

THE AVANTI COMPANY

Selected Financial Ratios

For the Years 19X1 and 19X2

	19X1	19X2
Liquidity and Activity Measures:		
Current Ratio	1.8	2.0
Cash Flow from Operations as a percentage of Net Sales	NA	(6.8 %)
Cash as a percentage of Total Current Assets	20.7 %	2.5 %
Accounts Receivable as a percentage of Total Current Assets	41 %	46 %
Inventory as a percentage of Total Current Assets	38 %	47 %
Average Collection Period (in days)	32	58
Inventory Turnover (times per year)	6.1	3.5
Total Asset Turnover	1.06	1.02
Average Payment Period (in days)	54	64
Cash Cycle (in days)	37	97
Debt Measures:		
Times Interest Earned	18.3	16.7
Total Debt as a percentage of Total Assets	53 %	57 %
Profitability Measures:		
Gross Profit Margin	49.1 %	42.8 %
Operating Profit Margin	17.8 %	16.2 %
Net Profit Margin	10.2 %	9.2 %
Return on Investment	18.7 %	16.5 %
Return on Owner's Equity	22.6 %	23.1 %

This table contains the calculated value of key ratios for Avanti's most recent two-year period. The trend of the various liquidity and activity ratios provides insight into both the status of the firm's liquidity position and the factors that are affecting it; debt ratios indicate the degree of the financial risk to which the firm is exposed; and profitability ratios measure how effectively management is using the funds and assets available to the firm.

Receivables as a Percentage of Total Current Assets Ratio

The *receivables as a percentage of total current assets ratio* is calculated as the dollar amount of accounts receivable from the balance sheet divided by total current assets. Unless there is an intentional change in the firm's credit policy, the amount of receivables held by the firm should remain roughly proportional to the level of total current assets, and to the level of sales. A rising trend in the receivables percentage ratio usually indicates lax credit management, an impending strain on liquidity, and an adverse effect on profitability. Note that Avanti's receivables increased from 41% of current assets in 19X1 to 46% in 19X2 (calculated as $54,600 divided by $118,725). This buildup is part of the company's liquidity problem.

Inventory as a Percentage of Total Current Assets Ratio

The *inventory as a percentage of total current assets ratio* is calculated as the dollar amount of ending inventory from the balance sheet divided by total current assets ($56,125 divided by $118,725). As is true of receivables, the amount of inventory held by the firm should remain roughly proportional to the level of current assets, and to the level of sales. A rising trend for this percentage is also a danger signal. An excessive inventory buildup drains liquidity and adversely affects profitability. As shown on the table of selected financial ratios on the previous page, Avanti's inventory as a percentage of current assets increased from 38% in 19X1 to 47% in 19X2 (calculated as $56,125 divided by $118,725). This calculation provides further evidence of the major part of the company's liquidity problem.

Inventory Turnover Ratio

The *inventory turnover ratio*, and the two that follow, are often referred to as activity measures. They measure the rate at which various asset categories are turned over relative to the level of sales activity. Turnover or activity has a major impact on both the firm's liquidity position and its rate of profitability.

Inventory turnover is calculated as cost of sales from the income statement divided by ending inventory from the balance sheet. This ratio value represents the average number of times per period that inventory is purchased (or produced), and converted to sales. For example, if your firm's inventory turnover figure for the period was 4, this means that on average it takes approximately 90 days to convert an inventory item into a sale (360-day year divided by 4 times per year).

All other things being equal, the higher the turnover figure, the more liquid and more profitable your firm. Each time a dollar invested in inventory is sold, it completes the cash cycle from purchase (production) to sale to receivable to cash. Upon return, the dollar of inventory is accompanied by the firm's profit margin. The more times this cycle is completed (the higher the inventory turnover ratio), the larger the amount of profit margin that is returned, and the greater the level of profits for the firm. This ratio, therefore, is critical to the firm's financial health and should be monitored closely. It is an important part of a system of sound inventory control. A declining trend of inventory turnover values means slow moving or excessive inventory. Overstocked inventory traps the firm's scarce funds, depletes liquidity, adversely affects profits, and creates additional financing needs to carry the inventory.

From the table of financial ratios, we see that Avanti's inventory turnover slowed dramatically from 6.1 times in 19X1 to 3.5 times in 19X2 (calculated as $194,500 divided by $56,125). This finding is consistent with the liquidity problems evidenced on the cash flow from operations statement, and the inventory to current assets ratio discussed above. Management has all of the evidence necessary to indict inventory buildup as a major cause of Avanti's poor operating performance in 19X2. Now the company must begin the process of identifying the reasons why it happened.

The *average collection period (ACP) ratio*, which is also known as the *average days credit sales outstanding*, is calculated as (accounts receivable times 360) divided by net sales. It measures the average number of days that a credit sales remains on the books uncollected. In general, the shorter the time period (fewer number of days) that credit sales remain outstanding, the shorter the time period that the firm's scarce cash is tied up. A rising trend of ACP values is a danger signal.

Average Collection Period Ratio

ACP values that exceed the firm's credit terms usually reflect lax credit management and eventual liquidity problems. For example, if your firm grants credit terms of net 30 days and has an average collection period of 50 days, then it takes 20 days beyond the normal credit period to convert a credit sale into cash. During the lag between sales and collections, the firm's normal obligations continue and cash flows out of the business. Credit lags of this type are costly since financing must be arranged to compensate for the time scarce funds are locked into receivables.

As is true of inventory turnover, the ACP ratio should be closely monitored. Failure to control credit and the investment in accounts receivable has caused the demise of many firms, both small and large. Note that Avanti's average collection period almost doubled from 32 days in 19X1 to 58 days in 19X2 (calculated as $54,600 times 360 divided by $340,000). The problems indicated by the inflated ACP are consistent with those suggested by the cash flow from operations analysis, and by the ratio of accounts receivable to current assets.

Total Asset Turnover Ratio

The *total asset turnover ratio* measures the productivity of the firm's asset base. Productivity in this case means the dollars of sales that the firm is able to generate for each dollar invested in assets. All other things equal, the greater the number of sales dollars generated per dollar of assets, the more productive the asset base, and the greater the firm's earning power. The ratio values for Avanti show a slight decline in asset turnover from $1.06 of sales per dollar of assets in 19X1 to $1.02 in 19X2. As will be discussed later in this chapter, this decline contributed to the decline in Avanti's return on investment during the period.

Average Payment Period Ratio

The *average payment period (APP) ratio* is calculated as (accounts payable times 360) divided by purchases, and it measures the average number of days accounts payable are on the books before payment is made. In general, the number of days in the APP should be roughly equal to the terms offered by trade creditors. For example, if terms are net 30 days, then the firm's APP should be about 30 days.

A rising trend value for this ratio means the firm's rate of payments has slowed. Late payments suggest poor payment practices or a liquidity problem, or both. In either case, an increasing APP value indicates a potential problem with creditors — a problem that small firms can ill afford. Small businesses have very few financing options, and must jealously guard those (such as trade credit) that are available. Note from the table of ratios that Avanti's average payment period has swelled from 54 days in 19X1 to 64 days in 19X2 (calculated as $16,912 times 360 divided by $95,625). The company's obvious liquidity problems have forced its managers to risk jeopardizing creditor relations by delaying payments.

A Note on Working Capital and Ratios

A widely-used type of business financing is known as a *working capital loan.* Working capital refers to the investment in cash, accounts receivable, and inventory required to conduct normal operations. Many businesses experience seasonal increases in sales and, as a result, a temporary buildup in working capital. This temporary increase in cash, accounts receivable, and inventory creates a temporary need for financing.

For example, a department store has two distinct high-volume seasons: spring and the fall holidays. To accommodate these seasonal increases in sales, additional inventory must be purchased, larger than normal levels of accounts receivable must be carried, and more cash must be kept on hand to meet the higher level of transactions that occur. When sales return to normal, the funds invested in working capital are recaptured. Inventory is sold down, receivables are collected, and excess cash balances are reduced. During the interim, however, financing is required and it is management's responsibility to estimate the amount and the length of time these funds will be needed. The most thorough and effective approach to making this estimate is through the firm's cash budget (discussed in Chapter 7), but an approximation can be made using ratios and information on the level of expenses during the peak season.

The length of a firm's working capital period, or cash cycle, is determined by the average time required to turn over its inventory (purchase or produce and sell the inventory) and collect its receivables. This average time period can be measured using the inventory turnover and ACP ratios. For example, assume your firm's inventory turnover rate during the peak season is 4 times. This means that on average, funds are tied up in inventory for 90 days (360 divided by 4). Assume further that the average collection period during the season is 45 days. The combined value of 135 days represents the length of time that funds are tied up in working capital, and the length of time for which financing is needed.

If your firm has an established credit relationship with its supplier, some of its working capital financing is provided through the use of trade credit. Remember, if the firm can purchase goods and delay payment, it is, in effect, using the trade creditor's funds. The value of the APP ratio indicates the number of days for which trade creditors are supplying working capital needs. If the average payment period for your firm is 30 days, the length of the working capital period, the cash cycle, that must be financed from other sources is 105 days. This is calculated as:

Cash Cycle $=$ (Inventory Turnover in Days + ACP) – APP

Cash Cycle $=$ (360 ÷ 4 + 45) – 30
$\qquad = 105$ days

The number of days in the cash cycle, along with an estimate of the firm's average expenditures per day, can be used to make a rough estimate of the amount of working capital financing required during the peak season. Assume that from either an estimate based on operating expenses shown on the income statement (cost of sales plus operating expenses minus depreciation expense), or from actual cash outflows as shown in the firm's checkbook register, you determine that the firm incurred total cash outflows for operations in the amount of $100,800. Dividing this figure by 360 gives an approximation of the firm's average expenditures per day, $280. This is calculated as:

Average Expenditures per Day $\quad=$ Cash Operating Expenses ÷ 360

Average Expenditures per Day $\quad= \$100,800 ÷ 360$
$\qquad\qquad\qquad = \$280$

To obtain an estimate of the amount of working capital financing required to support the firm's cash cycle, simply multiply the cash cycle of 105 days by the average expenditure per day. For this example, the required amount of working capital financing is $29,400, which is calculated as:

Required Financing $=$ Cash Cycle x Average Expenditure Per Day

Required Financing $= 105$ x $280
$\qquad\qquad\qquad = \$29,400$

The cash cycle calculation also highlights the importance of trade credit as a source of financing. In this example, working capital needs totaled $10,800. Of this amount, trade creditors provided $2,400 in the form of delayed payment. Only the remainder of $8,400 must be raised outside the firm.

A Final Thought on the Cash Cycle

The cash cycle calculation is also a useful tool for depicting the effects that changes in the rate of inventory turnover, the ACP, or the APP have on the firm's cash position. Notice from the table of ratios that Avanti had an average cash cycle of 37 days in 19X1. In 19X2, inventory and receivables levels ballooned without a corresponding increase in sales. The result was a decline in the rate of inventory turnover, an increase in the ACP, and a dramatic 60-day increase in the cash cycle (37 days to 97 days). It is no surprise that Avanti's management had to make more trips than usual to the bank.

Debt or Financial Risk Measures

Debt ratios are intended to measure the degree of financial risk to which your firm is exposed. Risk means the uncertainty surrounding the occurrence of a particular event and financial risk refers to the uncertainty surrounding the firm's ability to meet its debt obligations. Debt financing involves contractual responsibilities for interest and principal. These payments must be made on established dates regardless of the firm's level of cash flows. Naturally, the more debt financing employed, the greater the amount of interest and principal payments that must be met, and the greater the risk that cash will not be available to meet them.

Debt financing is really a mixed blessing. On the one hand, the firm benefits from the use of funds acquired under specific and limited terms. Creditors agree to accept only the payments specified in the contract and, therefore, do not share in the earnings success of the firm beyond this amount. In return for this limited arrangement, creditors receive a legally binding claim on the firm's income and assets. Failure to meet the terms of the contract allows creditors legal remedy which includes the possibility of forcing the firm into bankruptcy.

This type of relationship is successful for both your firm and its creditors as long as borrowed funds can be invested in operations to earn a rate of return that is greater than the interest cost on the debt. When funds invested in operations generate compensatory cash flows, the firm's creditors and owners both benefit. Conversely, the mandatory payments and risk associated with debt financing hang over the firm like a guillotine. Debt financing must be used judiciously, and loan requests should be based on the level of cash flows estimated for planned operations. The risks for not doing this type of planning are too great. Chapter 8 discusses cash budgeting in greater detail, but for now, you must learn about two of the more prominent debt ratios.

The *times interest earned ratio* is most often calculated as net operating income from the income statement divided by interest expense from the income statement. Its value represents the dollars of operating income that were generated to meet interest charges that had to be paid. The more earnings your firm generates relative to mandatory interest charges, the bigger the financial cushion, and the lower the financial risk. For example, it is much safer for both the firm's creditors and owners if $10 in operating income is generated for each dollar of interest charges (a ratio of 10) as opposed to $2 in operating income per dollar of interest charges (a ratio of 2). Obviously, a declining trend of times interest earned values is a sign of increasing financial risk and a clear danger signal. The 19X2 times interest earned value for Avanti of 16.7 (calculated as $55,133 of operating income divided by $3,300 of interest charges) shows a slight, but not yet alarming, decline from 19X1.

Times Interest Earned Ratio

The *total debt as a percentage of total assets ratio* is calculated as total debt from the balance sheet divided by total assets or total liabilities and equity from the balance sheet. It measures the percentage of the firm's assets financed by creditors relative to the percentage financed by the owners. When the firm's asset base is financed with increasing amounts of debt (higher debt-ratio values), mandatory payment obligations are increased, and the degree of financial risk to which the firm is exposed increases. Note that the debt ratio for Avanti has increased from 53% to 57% in 19X2 (calculated as $190,270 divided by $333,725). This slight increase is not, in itself, necessarily alarming.

Total Debt as a Percentage of Total Assets Ratio

As a group, *profitability ratios* are the most important indicators of financial performance. They measure the efficiency with which the firm's assets and capital have been employed, and how effectively operations have been conducted. The more efficiently a business is run, the lower its cost of operations, the higher its profit margins, and the higher the level of profit generated. Likewise, the more sales a firm is able to generate per dollar invested in assets, the more efficiently those assets are employed, and the higher the return on investment a firm is able to generate. Profitability measures are, in effect, a report card on how well management has used the capital provided the firm by its creditors and owners. The ratios that measure profitability are gross profit margin, operating profit margin, net profit margin, return on investment, and return on owner's equity.

Profitability Ratios

The *gross profit margin ratio* is calculated as the dollar amount of gross profit from the income statement divided by net sales from the income statement. The ratio value, a percentage, indicates the amount of each sales dollar remaining after cost of sales has been deducted.

Gross Profit Margin Ratio

For example, Avanti's gross profit margin of 42.8% in 19X2 (calculated as $145,500 divided by $340,000) means that almost $0.43 (43 cents) out of each dollar of sales remained after about $0.57 (57 cents) was deducted as cost of sales. This was an alarming decline from the 49.1% figure for 19X1.

Gross profit margin is a critical measure of cost control and must be monitored closely. A declining gross profit margin means that less revenue is available from each sales dollar to cover operating expenses and profits. This occurs when inventory management and control measures are weak or nonexistent, or when inventory costs (cost of production for a manufacturing firm) rise faster than corresponding increases in selling price.

Operating Profit Margin Ratio

The *operating profit margin ratio* is calculated as net operating income from the income statement divided by net sales from the income statement. The ratio value, a percentage, reflects the amount of each sales dollar remaining after all normal costs of operations (cost of sales and operating expenses) have been deducted. Avanti experienced a slight decline in the operating profit margin from 17.8% in 19X1 to 16.2% in 19X2 (calculated as $55,133 divided by $340,000). As will be discussed below, the decline was caused by deterioration in the gross profit margin and not by an increase in operating expenses.

If the operating profit margin is deducted from 100%, the difference is the operating expense ratio. This percentage reflects the portion of each sales dollar required to cover operating expenses. For example, the operating profit margin of 16.2% for Avanti in 19X2 can be converted to an operating expense ratio of 83.8% (100% minus 16.2%). This latter figure means that cost of sales and operating expenses combined to absorb $0.838 (83.8 cents) from each average sales dollar. Expressed in either form, these measures are important indicators of cost control and, along with the gross profit margin percentage, should be monitored carefully. Deteriorating profit margins (increases in expense ratios) at any level must be investigated, the causes identified, and remedial action taken before the problem reaches the crisis stage.

Net Profit Margin Ratio

The *net profit margin ratio* is calculated as net income from the income statement divided by net sales from the income statement. It measures the percentage of each sales dollar remaining after all costs of operations, including taxes, have been deducted from sales. On a continuing basis, the net profit margin on sales represents the long-run capacity of a firm to generate owner's withdrawals (dividends) and produce satisfactory returns. For Avanti, the decline in net profit margin to 9.2% (calculated as $31,100 divided by $340,000) is further evidence of the alarming increase in the overall cost of operations.

A *common size income statement* is a traditional income statement converted to percentage form. As indicated by the common size values, each item on the income statement is represented as a percentage of sales. This is accomplished by dividing the dollar amount of a given income statement value by sales. For example, Avanti's cost of sales in 19X2 was 57.2% of sales for the period. It was calculated as:

Cost of Sales Percentage = Cost of Sales ÷ Sales

By depicting income statement expense items as percentages of sales, you have a useful tool for gauging its cost control efforts. The trend of expense percentages (or profit margin values) through time indicates where cost control problems may lie. To illustrate, examine Avanti's common size statements for 19X1 and 19X2 shown on Table 4.2.

As previously noted, both the gross profit and operating profit margins declined from 19X1 to 19X2. Without further investigation, it would be logical to conclude that the decline in both margins was the result of an increase in the cost of sales and in total operating expenses. However, a close look at these two categories of expense items for 19X1 and 19X2 indicates that this was not the case. Cost of sales increased dramatically over the period, but Avanti's managers controlled operating expenses very well. Total operating expenses declined from 31.3% of sales in 19X1 to 26.6% of sales in 19X2 as the result of a decline in all but the noncash expense item, depreciation. Through period-by-period comparisons of expense items expressed as percentages of sales, Avanti's managers gain an insight into the operating efficiency that is not available from absolute dollar amounts.

The *return on investment (ROI) ratio*, sometimes referred to as the measure of earning power, is most often calculated as net operating income from the income statement divided by total assets from the balance sheet. The ratio value is a percentage that reflects the dollars of income earned per dollar of invested capital. For example, the ROI figure of 16.5% for Avanti in 19X2 (calculated as $55,133 divided by $333,725) means that the firm was able to generate $0.165 (16.5 cents) for each dollar invested in assets (or for each dollar of total capital). The greater the return Avanti can generate per dollar of invested capital (a larger ROI figure), the more efficiently operations and assets (and the capital used to finance them) have been utilized, and the more profitable the firm. ROI is probably the best single measure of a firm's financial performance, and a rising trend is the ideal.

The *return on owner's equity (ROE) ratio* is calculated as net income from the income statement divided by owner's equity from the balance sheet. It is a measure of the dollars of net income earned per dollar of owner's capital (paid-in capital plus retained earnings), and reflects the efficiency with which the owner's invested capital has

Common Size Income Statement

Return on Investment Ratio

Return on Owner's Equity Ratio

Table 4.2

THE AVANTI COMPANY
Common Size Annual Income Statements
For the Periods 19X1 and 19X2

	19X1	19X2
Net Sales	100.0%	100.0%
Cost of Sales	50.1	57.2
Gross Profit	49.1%	42.8%
Operating Expenses:		
Wages & Salaries	11.2%	10.2%
Rent & Lease Payments	1.9	1.1
Utilities	1.8	1.5
Insurance	4.4	3.7
Advertising	2.1	1.5
Vehicle Operation & Maintenance	7.0	5.9
Accounting & Legal	0.8	0.7
Payroll Taxes	1.5	1.4
Depreciation	0.6	0.6
Total Operating Expenses	31.3%	26.6%
Net Operating Income	17.8	16.2
Less: Interest Expense	0.9	0.9
Net Taxable Income	16.9%	15.3%
Less: Income Taxes	6.7	6.1
Net Income	10.2%	9.2%

The common size income statement converts the dollar amount of the expense items shown on the income statement to percentages of sales. Trend values for these percentages provide Avanti management with evidence on the status of each profit margin item, and the effectiveness of overall cost control efforts.

been employed. Generating a satisfactory return is the reason an entrepreneur risks time, effort, and capital. If a firm does not generate a fair rate of return for its owners, there is no economic justification for its existence. In such a case, the owners would be do better investing time, effort, and money elsewhere.

Avanti's ROE figure of 23.1% in 19X2 (calculated as $31,100 divided by $143,455) represents a slight improvement over the 19X1 value. The reason can be attributed to the slight increase in net income, and to the increase in the use of debt financing (recall the debt ratio of 57%). Avanti management has decided to finance a large portion of its asset base with the more risky fixed cost funds of creditors rather than owner's invested capital.

Another Look at ROI

With your knowledge of return on investment, you can examine an alternative, more informative calculation of this crucial indicator. A firm's earning power, or ROI, is determined by the profit made on each sale, and the amount of sales dollars generated per dollar of investment in assets. Thus, ROI is a function of profit margin, which is a measure of the profit on each sales dollar, and asset turnover, which is a measure of the productivity of assets. In this form, it is calculated as follows:

ROI = Operating Profit Margin x Asset Turnover

ROI = (Operating Income ÷ Sales) x (Sales ÷ Total Assets)

Understanding the logic behind this calculation is important to understanding how your control over the investment in assets, such as inventory and receivables, and the cost of operations affects your firm's ability to generate earnings. Here is an example to help you better understand this logic.

Assume that Debi's Delites is a large retail food store. The firm leases its land and building and sells only for cash. Since its major fixed assets are leased and there are no accounts receivable, the firm's assets consist primarily of inventory. In this highly competitive industry, customers shop primarily on the basis of price, and the profit margins of food stores such as Debi's are extremely narrow. On average, the net operating profit margin for firms in this industry is between 5% to 7%. This means that about $0.93 (93 cents) to $0.95 (95 cents) out of each sales dollar goes to cover cost of goods sold and operating expenses, and only about $0.05 (5 cents) to $0.07 (7 cents) remains to cover income tax and contribute to profit. The question is: With this extremely narrow profit margin, how can Debi's generate a return on investment that justifies remaining in business? The answer is high asset turnover.

Remember, asset turnover means the number of sales dollars that are generated per dollar of asset investment. Since most of Debi's assets are concentrated in inventory, asset turnover in this case really means inventory turnover. For each dollar invested in inventory that Debi's converts to sales (turns over), a dollar and some pennies of profit margin are returned. While the profit margin returned on each sale is small (five to seven cents), a larger profit can be realized if inventory is turned (sold) many times. In fact, this is the case. Firms in this industry have inventory turnover ratios that average 15 times per year or more and, therefore, have satisfactory ROIs.

Conversely, firms such as a typical jewelry store have inventory turnover ratios of only one to one-and-one-half times per year. Successful firms in the industry, however, are able to generate compensatory ROIs by maintaining large profit margins on sales.

These insights underscore the importance of maintaining control over both the investment in assets and the cost of operations. For example, an excessive inventory or receivables buildup (no corresponding increase in sales) results in a decline in asset turnover and a decline in earning power. Likewise, deteriorating profit margins without an offsetting increase in asset turnover have a negative effect on ROI.

A Look at Avanti's Results

Note again from the financial ratios table (Table 4.1) that Avanti's ROI values declined from 18.7% in 19X1 to 16.5% in 19X2. By using our alternative calculation for this ratio, we can pinpoint the reasons for the decline.

ROI = (Net Operating Income ÷ Net Sales) x (Net Sales ÷ Total Assets)

19X1 ROI = ($51,172 ÷ $290,000) x ($290,000 ÷ $273,945)
19X1 ROI = 17.8% x 1.06
= 18.7%

19X2 ROI = ($55,133 ÷ $340,000) x ($340,000 ÷ $333,725)
19X2 ROI = 16.2% x 1.02
= 16.5%

Unfortunately for Avanti, the sharp drop in ROI is attributed to the decline in both profit margin and asset turnover. As shown by common size income statements for these two years, failure to control cost of sales caused the deterioration in gross profit margin. Analysis of the liquidity and activity ratios identified the excessive buildup in inventory and accounts receivable as the cause of the decline in asset turnover. If Avanti management is to improve the firm's financial health, it must regain control over these vital areas of the firm's operations.

Before evaluating Avanti's financial position using the ratio values shown on Table 4.1, you should review a few suggestions that will improve your efforts with ratio analysis.

How to Use Ratios

■ Meaningful information comes from a trend of values for each of the ratios employed. Ratio values for a single accounting period tell you very little about the direction of your firm's financial position. A single ROI value indicates something about financial performance for the period, but it is more important that you know how ROI behaved over a number of periods. For example, if ROI values are remaining relatively flat or declining during a period of economic growth, a potential problem area is indicated. Only a trend of values will provide this kind of insight.

The benefits of having a series of ratio values for consecutive time periods are not limited to information on past performance. Trend values may also signal impending changes. Most often, the major factors affecting a firm's long-run financial performance, such as economic, industry, and competitive pressures, do not fully impact a firm in one time period. The effects are felt gradually across several time periods. It is only through trend analysis that subtle changes in these factors may be detected with sufficient time to take remedial action.

■ To be effective, ratios should be used in combination with each other, and with the other tools of financial analysis. Individual ratios provide information on only one aspect of a firm's financial profile. To obtain all of the clues to a firm's financial puzzle, you must use all of the tools available. Information from various ratio values should be combined and compared with the insights provided by cash flow and cost-volume-profit analysis. This latter topic is the subject of the next chapter.

■ Ratio analysis does not provide definitive solutions. Ratio analysis will help identify problem areas and the avenues that must be investigated to remedy them. Solving the problems, however, is management's responsibility. This responsibility cannot be transferred to a mechanical tool.

For example, a problem area may be signaled by a declining trend in your firm's inventory turnover ratio. Assume that through further examination of the inventory as a percentage of total current assets ratios, gross profit margin figures, and cash flow analysis, you determine that the problem lies in an overstocking of slow-moving items. Although the tools of financial analysis supplied the information necessary to identify the problem, they do not provide an answer to the question: How can inventory management be improved? As manager of the firm, finding an answer to this question is your job.

- Ratio analysis is not a substitute for sound management judgment. Effective interpretation of ratio values requires an understanding of the financial relationships involved, a knowledge of the industry and markets in which your firm operates, a knowledge of your firm's operations, and your business experience. These are the qualities that make ratio analysis a powerful tool.

Evaluating the Ratio Results for Avanti

Even the most cursory examination of the results for Avanti shown on the table of financial ratios is alarming. Although Avanti has enjoyed growth over the past year, the information gleaned from the ratio values questions the wisdom of this growth. There appear to be more problem areas than strong points.

Liquidity and Activity Measures

Except for a slight increase in the current ratio, the liquidity and activity measures indicate a noticeable deterioration in the company's overall level of liquidity. Cash flow from operations was negative, and the ratio of cash to total current assets declined dramatically from 19X1. The problem can be traced to excessive inventory and accounts receivable. As indicated by the receivables and inventory to total current assets ratios as well as the ACP and inventory turnover values, the buildup in these two assets caused most of the liquidity drain. Apparently, the growth in sales has come at the expense of strict control over the firm's investment in working capital, and over its liquidity position. Avanti management must take immediate measures to avoid a liquidity crisis, and then carefully re-evaluate their growth strategy.

It is interesting to note how deceiving ratio analysis may be when limited to a single calculation. In spite of the serious decline in liquidity experienced by Avanti in 19X2, the current ratio increased. If the analysis were limited to this single liquidity measure, an analyst would be led to the conclusion that Avanti's liquidity position improved. By using additional tools of financial analysis, you discovered that the increase in the current ratio was attributed to an excessive buildup in receivables and inventory. As any experienced business manager knows, the accounts receivable and inventory portions of working capital are not always liquid. The inventory must be sold and the receivables collected before cash is realized. This appears to be the problem faced by Avanti.

Cost Control

As indicated by the common size statements shown on Table 4.2, profit margins have deteriorated from 19X1. The reason can be attributed to the sharp increase in 19X2 cost of sales. This increase is a clear danger signal, and the reasons behind the rise must be determined and corrected. Avanti management must determine answers to such questions as:

- Have inventory costs risen without a corresponding increase in selling price?

- Has the cost of providing service, including associated labor costs, risen without a corresponding increase in service charges?

- Have price reductions or promotions been used too extensively?

As indicated by the ROI analysis, the effects of inflated working capital and lax operating controls took their toll on profitability in 19X2. This decline is of particular concern because of Avanti's increasing reliance on debt financing. Notice that the times interest earned ratio has declined from the 19X1 level, and the amount of debt financing has increased. Increased debt financing, coupled with a drop in operating efficiency and a weakened liquidity position, may indicate an unacceptable increase in financial risk for the firm.

The Effects on Profitability

The ROE ratio does show a slight increase from 19X2. This occurred because of an increase in the absolute amount of net income from 19X1 to 19X2, and the increased use of debt financing. Again, this latter influence may represent an unacceptable increase in the level of financial risk to which Avanti is now exposed.

The information from ratio analysis, combined with that of cash flow analysis, has identified what could easily be potentially serious problems for Avanti. Fortunately, Avanti·management has received the information before these problems become insolvable. It is now management's responsibility to identify the reasons for the difficulties, and take the necessary remedial action.

Before leaving the topic of ratio analysis, it would be useful to identify some basic financial management principles that will improve your firm's financial ratios as well as its financial position. Remember, outsiders such as your banker use ratios to analyze the firm's historical and projected financial statements. It would be in your best interest to cast the most favorable financial picture possible. To accomplish this, consider the following:

Some Tips on Window Dressing

- Resist the temptation to rely too heavily on short-term debt financing. Financial statement values can be improved and financial risk reduced by replacing a prudent amount of short-term debt with more permanent financing. Short-term debt appears to have the advantage of lower interest rates, and its contract is usually easier to negotiate. Unfortunately, the payments on short-term loans come due all too soon, and there are no guarantees that the lender will refinance when they mature.

- Use debt financing judiciously. A rule of thumb often used by bankers to gauge debt levels for small firms is: For each dollar of debt financing management expects to borrow, there must be at least one dollar of equity financing to support it. This translates to a maximum debt to total asset ratio of 50%. Your banker views the owner's equity position as a margin of protection against financial difficulty. If you are concerned about the the risk exposure to your firm that debt financing creates, you should take a similar view.

- Save for a rainy day. Realize that cash flows retained in the business increase owner's equity, and provide a margin of safety against periods of adversity. Resist the temptation to take extravagant dividends and bonuses when times are good. A reasonable retention policy will provide added liquidity, ensure the financial strength necessary to weather the rough periods, and improve the appearance of your firm's financial statements.

- Monitor receivables and inventory levels closely. All experienced business persons, including your creditors, are aware of the serious problems created by the liberal extension of credit, and sloppy or nonexistent inventory control. Receivables must be monitored continuously to identify slow-paying customers, and a reasonable, but firm, collection policy must be maintained. Likewise, inventory turnover rates on products or product groups must be closely monitored to identify and weed out slow-moving items. Actions such as these will help both your firm's level of liquidity and its rate of profitability.

In short, the more effectively you manage your firm's financial resources, the more appealing will be the appearance of its financial statements. The best recipe for attractive financial window dressing is sound financial management.

Where to Now?

In this and the two previous chapters, you have examined tools of financial analysis that are applied directly to conventional accounting statements, the income statement, balance sheet, and cash flow statement. For some of the information needed for analysis, planning, and decision making, financial data must be organized in a format different from that of the traditional statements. Chapter 5 reveals how such changes are necessary to:

- Gain a clear understanding of your firm's cost structure.

- Gain a clear understanding of how your firm's cost and profits change at different levels of operations.

■ Determine the amount of profit contribution your products or product lines generate.

■ Determine the breakeven point for your firm.

The financial tools that provide this type of information are part of a subject referred to as cost-volume-profit analysis. It is the topic of the next chapter.

Chapter 5
Cost-Volume-Profit Analysis

The material in the previous chapters was developed around one dominant theme: The business is no stronger than the strength of its financial position. To achieve and maintain this strength, you must have a clear understanding of the impact that business decisions have on your firm's stock of financial resources. An important consideration in this regard is how the cost of operations, operating profits, and cash flows fluctuate as changes occur in your firm's level of sales or its volume of activity. Information on cost structure and cost behavior is part of the subject known as *cost-volume-profit analysis*.

TOPIC	CONCEPTS DISCUSSED
Variable and Fixed Costs	The meaning of variable and fixed cost, and how to identify these costs in your firm's costs structure.
	How these costs behave with changes in the volume of sales.
	The role of each type of cost in the decision process.
The Contribution Format Income Statement	How the contribution format income statement is prepared, interpreted, and evaluated.
	How this statement differs from the traditional accounting income statement.
	How the information from this statement is used for decision making.
Breakeven Analysis	The meaning of breakeven analysis, and how the breakeven sales point is calculated.
	How breakeven information is used for decision making.

This point is clearly illustrated in the following real-life example:

The owner/manager of a survey engineering firm was concerned about his firm's chronically poor performance. The firm had barely survived the 1981–82 recession and continued to struggle despite an upturn in the national and local economies. While the firm's contract work and revenues were increasing from the depressed level of the recession, a continued string of operating losses and meager cash flows threatened its existence.

Out of desperation, a financial consultant was hired. His financial analysis indicated that the direct costs of completing job contracts had risen faster than the increased revenues these jobs produced. In short, the firm's "true" profit margin had eroded. Management had not raised prices to offset the increasing costs of doing business, and had not been effective in controlling these costs.

When presented with these findings, the response of the firm's owner was disbelief. "That is impossible," he stated. "The income statement shows, and my accountant assures me, that the firm's gross profit margin is adequate." To convince the owner of the nature and severity of the problem, the consultant first explained the difference between cost of sales and gross profit as appears on the traditional accounting income statement, and the "true" costs to the firm of completing a job contract. He explained that the income statement shows only what the accountant defines as cost of sales. For this field engineering firm, cost of sales included only the small amount of supplies and materials used on a job. In reality, the true cost to the firm of performing a job contract includes all costs that vary with the revenues produced by that contract.

The consultant then asked the owner to identify the costs that vary directly with the typical contract work done by the firm. The owner identified the materials used on a job, the wages and related payroll taxes of employees directly involved in designing and performing field work, mileage and other variable costs associated with operating vehicles used on the job, the cost of preparing and printing survey maps and blueprints, the cost of subcontracted work, and the value of the owner's time spent in the field.

These costs were then calculated for two of the firm's recently completed contracts and compared to the revenues received for that work. The results were not the generous profit margins indicated on the firm's traditional income statement for these jobs, but rather a negative value which the consultant referred to as contribution margin. Not only had the two jobs failed to earn enough to cover direct costs and make a contribution to fixed overhead cost and profit, but they had literally cost the firm money to perform. Each job had cost more to complete than it brought into the firm.

As this sad but true tale makes clear, attempting to make business decisions and operate a firm without adequate information on the nature and behavior of its cost structure is courting disaster.

The cost structure of a typical business firm, when analyzed over a specific range of operations or a given planning horizon, normally consists of two distinct groups of costs: the dollar amount of one cost group varies or changes directly with changes in the level of activity, while that of the other group remains fixed or constant over a specified activity range or planning horizon.

Cost Behavior

You may have observed from your own business experience that as sales volume moves to higher or lower levels, the dollar amount of those costs directly related to sales changes to higher or lower levels. For instance, with an increase in sales a firm incurs the additional costs of carrying more inventory and accounts receivable, higher wage expense and payroll tax, and more sales commissions. As sales and the level of operations recede, these types of costs decline. Additional examples of costs that vary with sales in merchandising, manufacturing, and service firms are listed in the table below.

Variable Cost

Table 5.1 Examples of Variable Costs·

Type of Firm	Variable Cost Item
Merchandising	Cost of goods sold
	Sales commissions
	Freight-in
	Delivery expense
	Part-time employee wage cost
Manufacturing	Direct materials
	Direct labor
	Plant utilities expense
	Sales commissions
	Production bonuses
Service	Direct labor
	Subcontract work
	Supplies
	Vehicle mileage expense

This table contains examples of cost items that would normally classify as variable expenses in the indicated type of business firm. Variable costs are those that vary in total with changes in the volume of sales.

These are referred to as *variable costs* because they vary directly or proportionately with changes in sales over a given range of activity (for example, sales between $200,000 to $300,000) or a specific planning horizon (for example, one year). A direct or proportional change means that a given percentage increase or decrease in sales will cause the same percentage change in variable cost. For example, a 10% increase in sales results in a 10% increase in variable cost.

Fixed Cost

The dollar amount of other cost items, as opposed to variable cost, is unaffected by changes in sales over a specific activity range or planning horizon. This group of costs is referred to as *fixed* or, at times, *overhead costs*. Examples of these costs for the three types of businesses are listed below.

Table 5.2 Examples of Fixed Costs

Type of Firm	Fixed Cost Item
Merchandising	Rent
	Full-time employee wage cost
	Administrative salaries
	Depreciation on sales equipment
	Business license
	Insurance
Manufacturing	Supervisory salaries
	Leased plant or equipment expense
	Depreciation on plant and equipment
	Maintenance labor cost
	Administrative salaries
	Depreciation on office equipment
Service	Administrative salaries
	Supervisory salaries
	Business license
	Nonmileage vehicle expense
	Depreciation on equipment

This table contains examples of cost items that would normally classify as fixed expenses in the indicated type of business firm. Fixed costs are those that do not vary with changes in the volume of sales.

Understanding fixed and variable costs and the role they play in a firm's cost structure is essential to sound financial analysis, planning, and decision making. They determine how the cost of doing business, profits, and cash flows behave when sales and the level of operations change.

The Nature of Variable and Fixed Costs

The term *variable* as applied to variable cost refers to the total dollar amount of either an individual cost item or the entire group of items. This total is calculated as the number of units sold (or manufactured) times the amount of variable cost per unit. Total variable cost varies or changes with changes in activity.

Conversely, variable cost per unit remains constant or unchanged over a specific range of activity or planning horizon. Variable cost per unit is simply the amount of that cost associated with each unit of sales or dollar of service rendered. Variable cost, then, varies in total with changes in activity, but remains fixed on a per-unit basis.

For example, assume Avanti buys an inventory item for $50 and sells it for $100. The variable cost (cost of sales in this case) is fixed on a per unit basis at $50 (each item purchase cost $50), but total variable cost depends on the number of units sold. If one unit is sold, total variable cost (cost of sales) is $50 (one unit x $50 per unit). If two units are sold, total variable cost (cost of sales) is $100 (two units x $50 per unit). If 100 units are sold, total variable cost is $5,000 (100 units x $50 per unit). As sales increase, total variable cost (cost of sales) increases proportionately. The same would be true if sales decline.

It is important to note that the variable cost item, cost of sales, remained constant on a per unit basis. Over the entire sales range of one to 100 units, cost of sales remained constant at $50 per unit or 50% of selling price ($50 cost divided by $100 selling price). An increase in the number of units sold, however, caused a direct or proportional increase in total variable cost. Total variable cost varied directly with sales while the dollar or percentage unit cost figure was unchanged over the entire sales range.

Fixed costs, on the other hand, are those expense items that remain constant in total over a given range of activity or a particular planning horizon. By definition, these costs are not affected by changes in sales or operations. For example, Avanti's rent expense for the year is a fixed contractual amount, and must be paid regardless of the level of sales or volume of services performed.

An Example of Cost Behavior

The concepts of cost structure, cost behavior, and the relationship between fixed and variable cost can be expanded with another simple example. Assume you own a firm that produces and sells floppy diskettes. The diskettes sell for $2 each. From an analysis of historical cost data for your firm and from projections for materials and labor costs, you estimate that over the range of production and sales of

100,000 to 200,000 units (sales revenue of $200,000 to $400,000), variable production and selling costs will be $1 per diskette.

While total variable cost depends on the number of diskettes produced and sold, variable cost per unit will remain constant at $1 or 50% of selling price ($1 cost divided by $2 selling price). That is, for each diskette sold over the relevant range, variable cost per diskette is $1. You further estimate that fixed cost will be $50,000, and will remain constant at this amount over the relevant range. A summary of this data is shown in Table 5.3 below.

Table 5.3 Key Cost-Volume-Profit Data

Item	Amount
Relevant Cost Range	100,000 to 200,000 units
Selling Price per Unit	$2
Total Sales Revenue	$2 x number of units
Variable Cost per Unit	$1
% Variable Cost per Unit	50%
Total Variable Cost	$1 x number of units
% Total Variable Cost	50%
Fixed Cost	$50,000
Total Cost	Variable cost + fixed cost
Operating Income	Sales revenue – total cost

This table summarizes key cost-volume-profit data for a hypothetical manufacturer of floppy diskettes. This data is used in an illustration of how variable and fixed costs behave over a production range of 100,000 to 200,000 units.

Variable Cost and the Volume of Operations

If the diskette firm produces and sells 100,000 units, sales revenue is $200,000 and total variable cost is $100,000. Sales revenue is calculated as 100,000 units times the selling price of $2 per unit, and total variable cost as 100,000 units times the unit variable cost of $1. At this volume of operation, total variable cost is 50% of the selling price. This is calculated as $100,000 of variable cost divided by the $200,000 of sales revenue.

It is interesting to note the changes that take place when the level of production and sales increases. For example, if sales increase from 100,000 to 200,000 units (actually any increase within the relevant range produces the same effects), sales revenue increases to $400,000 (200,000 units x $2 selling price per unit), and total variable cost increases to $200,000 (200,000 units x $1 variable cost per unit).

Note, however, these subtle but critical points about variable cost behavior:

- Variable cost per unit remains constant at $1, or 50% of selling price over the relevant range (100,000 to 200,000 units).

- The dollar amount of total variable cost increases with increases in the volume of operations, but it is always 50% of sales revenue. When revenue is $200,000, total variable cost is $100,000 or 50% of sales ($100,000 variable cost divided by $200,000 sales revenue). At sales revenue of $400,000, total variable cost increases to $200,000 but is still 50% of sales ($200,000 divided by $400,000).

- As sales and production increase, the increase in total variable cost is proportional. This means that total variable cost changes at the same percentage rate as the change in sales. When sales revenue increases from $200,000 to $400,000 (an increase of 100%), total variable cost increases from $100,000 to $200,000 (also an increase of 100%).

% Increase in Sales = Change in Sales ÷ Original Sales
% Increase in Sales = ($400,000 − $200,000) ÷ $200,000
  = $200,000 ÷ $200,000
  = 100%

% Increase in Cost = Change in Cost ÷ Original Cost
% Increase in Cost = ($200,000 − $100,000) ÷ $100,000
  = $100,000 ÷ $100,000
  = 100%

This proportional change in sales and variable cost is exactly as it should be. If variable cost per unit remains constant at $1 or 50% of selling price, then total variable cost must be 50% of sales revenue at all levels within the relevant range.

- If production and sales were to decrease from 200,000 units to any lower level within the relevant range (for example, from 200,000 units to 100,000 units), total variable cost would decrease proportionately with the decline in sales. That is, the percentage decline in total variable cost would be the same as the percentage decline in sales. Note, however, that variable cost remains at 50% of sales revenue regardless of the level of sales within the relevant range.

To satisfy yourself that these relationships hold throughout the relevant range, make the same calculations using other changes in sales levels. For example, determine the outcome for a decline in sales from 200,000 units to 100,000 units, or an increase in sales from 100,000 units to 150,000 units.

Fixed and Total Cost, Operating Profit, and Activity

To complete the lesson on cost behavior, examine the effects of changes in activity within the relevant range on fixed cost, total cost (total variable cost plus total fixed cost), and net operating income (sales revenue minus total variable cost minus total fixed cost) for your diskette firm. Relevant, as used in this context, means the range of activity over which cost estimates are expected to hold. For the diskette firm, the relevant range is assumed to be sales between 100,000 and 200,000 units.

- At any level of production and sales within the relevant range, fixed cost remains at $50,000. By definition, total fixed cost does not change with changes in activity.

- Total cost (total variable cost plus total fixed cost) increases with an increase in sales and production. For example, at a sales level of 100,000 units, total variable cost is $100,000, total fixed cost is $50,000, and total cost is $150,000.

   Total Cost = Total Variable Cost + Total Fixed Cost
   Total Cost = $100,000 + $50,000
   $\qquad$ = $150,000

   If sales increase to 200,000 units, total variable cost is $200,000, total fixed cost is $50,000, and total cost is $250,000. Total cost increased with the increase in sales, but the increase is attributed solely to the increase in variable cost (from $100,000 to $200,000). Fixed cost did not change.

- While total cost increases with an increase in sales over the relevant range, the increase is not proportional. That is, the percentage increase in total cost is not the same as the percentage increase in sales. For example, when sales increase 100% from $200,000 to $400,000, total cost changes by only 67%, from $150,000 to $250,000.

   % Increase in Total Cost = Change in Cost ÷ Original Cost
   % Increase in Total Cost = ($250,000 − $150,000) ÷ $150,000
   $\qquad$ = $100,000 ÷ $150,000
   $\qquad$ = 67%

   The reason for the nonproportional change in total cost is the existence of fixed cost. Variable cost increases directly and proportionately with the increase in sales, but fixed cost remained unchanged.

- Net operating income increases with an increase in sales. When sales revenue is $200,000 (100,000 units), operating income is $50,000.

  Operating Income = Sales Revenue – Variable Cost – Fixed Cost
  Operating Income = $200,000 – $100,000 – $50,000
                   = $50,000

  When sales revenue increases to $400,000, operating income increases to $150,000.

  Operating Income = $400,000 – $200,000 – $50,000
                   = $150,000

  Note that the dollar amount of operating income increases for two reasons: higher sales volume means more dollars of margin (sales minus variable cost); and, fixed cost did not increase with the increase in activity.

- While net operating income increases with an increase in sales, the increase is nonproportional. The percentage increase in operating income is greater than the percentage increase in sales. For example, the increase in sales revenue from $200,000 to $400,000 is 100%. The increase in operating income from $50,000 to $150,000 is 200% [($150,000 minus $50,000) divided by $50,000]. Note that the reason the percentage change in operating income is greater than the percentage change in sales is the existence of fixed cost. While total variable cost increases with increases in sales, fixed cost remains constant.

- Unfortunately, nonproportional changes in total cost and operating income also work when sales decline. As sales volume drops, total variable cost declines but fixed cost remains unchanged. Remember, fixed cost is constant in amount over the relevant range, and the firm cannot escape it. It would be worthwhile for you to verify the accuracy of this statement by calculating the dollar and percentage effects of a decline in sales. For example, you may wish to verify that a decline in sales revenue from $400,000 to $200,000, a drop of 50%, results in a 67% drop in operating income.

Fixed Cost and Risk

This discussion of cost behavior leads to an extremely important financial principle: If the amount of fixed cost in a firm's cost structure is increased, or if fixed cost is substituted for variable cost (for example, by buying a building rather than renting, or by substituting machinery or equipment for labor), the potential for profit is increased but so is a firm's risk exposure.

Fixed cost, then, is a mixed blessing. If a firm has fixed cost associated with its operations, operating profits rise relatively faster (in percentage terms) than sales when sales are increasing. Also, the greater the amount of fixed costs associated with a firm's operations, the greater the percentage increase in operating profits with a given percentage increase in sales.

This bit of financial magic is known as *operating leverage.* It works to a firm's advantage when sales are rising, but to its disadvantage when sales are falling. When sales fall, operating profits fall at a faster rate. The percentage drop in operating income will exceed the percentage drop in sales.

Since fixed cost does not increase over the relevant range of operations, the burden of meeting these obligations is diminished as sales and associated cash flows increase. For example, the greater a firm's cash flow from operations, the easier the fixed payments associated with a mortgage loan are to meet. Conversely, the burden of fixed cost increases with a drop in sales and cash flow from operations. The mortgage loan, for instance, represents a legal promise to pay regardless of the level of activity. A firm cannot walk away from these types of fixed costs. Again, the financial principle is clear: Each additional dollar of fixed cost increases the firm's risk exposure.

It is essential that you make a careful evaluation of the firm's ability to support additional risk before decisions are made that increase fixed cost. If your firm is like most small businesses, financial resources are extremely scarce. This means that your firm lacks the financial strength to withstand large losses. Before making a decision involving the addition of fixed cost, consider this bit of financial wisdom: It is more important for the small firm to guard against downside risk than to gamble on upside potential.

Failure to appreciate the significance of this fundamental financial axiom has ruined too many small businesses.

Applying the Concept of Cost Behavior

Now that you are comfortable with the concept of cost behavior and the relationship between fixed and variable costs, you are no doubt wondering how they are used in analysis, planning, and decision making. The first application is *contribution analysis* using the contribution format income statement. The second is *breakeven analysis.*

The Contribution Format Income Statement

The contribution approach to analysis, planning, and decision making is an alternative approach to organizing the cost information found on the traditional accounting format income statement (see Chapter 1). The information produced by this technique is essential for a complete analysis of financial performance, and for a large number of planning decisions, such as:

- Adding a new product or product line.

- Product pricing and promotion.

- Structuring sales commissions.

- Expanding or dropping a product or product line.

The good news is that this powerful tool is neither hard to learn nor difficult to apply.

How the Contribution and Accounting Income Statements Differ

The unique feature of contribution analysis is an income statement that reflects cost behavior. Though this information is critical to financial analysis and planning, it is not supplied by the traditional accounting income statement.

You learned from the discussion of the income statement in Chapter 1 that the expenses deducted from sales revenue are organized by business function. For example, cost of sales includes all costs, whether fixed or variable, that provide for a firm's product or service. Likewise, operating expenses shown on the traditional income statement reflect the selling and administrative functions of a business without consideration of how these cost behave.

The traditional income statement approach to organizing costs limits the use of this statement for analysis and decision making because:

- There is no information on how costs are related to sales.

- There is no information on how costs change with changes in sales.

- There is no distinction between fixed and variable costs.

- There is no information on the contribution that each product or product line makes to fixed costs and profits.

Since fixed and variable costs are lumped together on the traditional income statement, cost behavior is ignored. The nature of a firm's cost structure and the degree to which these costs are sensitive to changes in the level of activity cannot be identified.

On the other hand, the contribution format income statement organizes costs, regardless of function, by relationship to sales. Cost behavior is the determining factor for location of a cost item on this statement. Those items that change with changes in sales are included in the variable cost category, and those items unaffected by sales changes are categorized as fixed costs. This organization of costs is illustrated by the 19X1 and 19X2 contribution format income statements for The Avanti Company shown on Table 5.4.

Note from Avanti's contribution statements and from the traditional income statements shown in Chapter 1 that the dollar amounts of sales and net operating income are the same on both sets of statements. Sales are shown as $290,000 and $340,000 for 19X1 and 19X2, respectively, and net operating income of $51,172 and $55,133 for these years. This is not a coincidence; these values result from normal operations of Avanti and the particular statement format employed will not alter that.

The critical and very valuable difference between the two statements is the manner in which the costs associated with operations are organized. The cost of sales and the operating expense items shown on the traditional income statements have been separated and reclassified on the contribution statement into their variable and fixed components. This difference is the key to the power of the contribution format. By categorizing costs into variable and fixed components, you are provided with information on cost behavior and product contribution.

The Concept of Contribution Margin

The focal point of the contribution format income statement is the contribution margin figure. Contribution margin is calculated as:

Contribution Margin = Sales – Variable Costs

This figure represents the amount of residual sales revenue available to contribute to fixed cost and profit. Each dollar of sales revenue creates variable cost that is directly related to sales. What remains from sales revenue after variable cost is a true measure of the profitability of a firm's products, and an indicator of its financial health.

Avanti's contribution statements indicate that while sales increased from 19X1 to 19X2, total variable cost increased even more. As a result, contribution margin declined from $118,900 to $112,400.

The Contribution Margin Ratio

A useful way to represent and evaluate contribution margin is through the *contribution margin ratio*. This key financial indicator is a simple percentage calculated as the dollar amount of contribution margin divided by the dollar amount of sales.

Contribution Margin Ratio = Contribution Margin ÷ Sales

This percentage represents contribution on a per-dollar basis. For example, if the selling price of one of a firm's products is $100 and the variable cost associated with that product is $60, the contribution margin per unit is $40 and the contribution margin ratio is 40%.

Contribution Margin Ratio = ($100 – $60) ÷ $100
= 40%

This figure represents the portion of each dollar of the product's sales that contribute to fixed cost and profit. After associated variable cost is

Table 5.4

THE AVANTI COMPANY
Contribution Format Income Statement
For 19X1 and 19X2

	19X1		19X2	
Sales	$290,000		$340,000	
Less Variable Costs:				
Cost of Sales	148,000		194,500	
Sales Commissions	12,900		19,200	
Vehicle Delivery Expense	10,200		13,900	
Total Variable Cost	$171,100		$227,600	
Contribution Margin (Ratio)	$118,900	(41%)	$112,400	(33%)
Less: Fixed Costs				
Wages & Salaries	19,600		15,500	
Rent & Leases	5,400		3,600	
Utilities	5.100		5,093	
Insurance	12,700		12,700	
Advertising	6,000		5,100	
Vehicle Expense	10,178		6,016	
Accounting & Legal	2,400		2,400	
Payroll Taxes	4,550		4,858	
Depreciation	1,800		2,000	
Total Fixed Cost	$ 67,728		$ 57,267	
Net Operating Income	$ 51,172		$ 55,133	

As shown on this contribution format income statement, costs are organized by relationship to sales. Those cost items that change with changes in sales volume are categorized as variable costs, and those that do not vary are identified as fixed costs. This approach to cost classification provides insight into how costs and profits behave as sales vary.

deducted from each of the product's sales dollars, $0.40 (40 cents) of contribution margin remains. Later in this discussion, you will learn that the number of times the firm can earn this 40-cent contribution determines the number of times the product must be sold to break even, or to earn some target level of operating profit.

Notice that Avanti's contribution margin ratio dropped from 41% in 19X1 to 33% in 19X2. This decline corresponds to the decline in the dollar amount of contribution margin for the period.

Interpreting the Contribution Format Statement

Now that you have learned how operating costs are organized on the contribution format income statement, interpreting and evaluating the information it provides is a simple task.

Notice from Avanti's contribution format statements that cost of sales, sales commissions, and vehicle delivery expense have been identified as variable. On the traditional income statements, both the fixed and variable components of these cost items are lumped together by function under their respective cost categories (cost of sales and operating expenses). By so doing, the true nature and behavior of these costs was hidden.

Also hidden by the traditional income statement, but made patently clear on the contribution format, is Avanti's true cost of producing sales and service. On the traditional statement, the cost of selling product and providing service to Avanti's customers is represented only by the cost of sales (cost of the goods sold) figure. On the contribution format statement, the true cost of these activities extends far beyond cost of sales. For each dollar of sales revenue, Avanti had to pay sales commissions and incur delivery expense as well as suffer the cost of the item sold and the service rendered. The vastly different effect of these two interpretations is made clear by comparing the gross profit margin shown on the traditional statement and the contribution margin shown on the contribution format.

The traditional income statements in Chapter 1 indicate that Avanti's gross profit (measured as sales minus cost of the goods sold) increased from $142,000 in 19X1 to $145,500 in 19X2. The contribution statements paint a more realistic, but unfortunately, less optimistic picture. From Avanti's contribution format statements, you can see that both the absolute amount of contribution margin and the contribution margin ratio declined. This condition is an indicator of a serious problem and should be a matter of grave concern to Avanti's management.

Investigate the reasons behind the deterioration of the contribution margin and contribution margin ratio by analyzing the behavior of the individual products that form Avanti's product line. The power of the contribution format income statement makes this type of analysis possible. This versatile statement can be prepared on an aggregate basis as shown for Avanti on Table 5.5, or it can be prepared for individual products or product lines as discussed below.

Before moving to Avanti's product contribution analysis, it is worth noting how the contribution format statement clarifies the relationship between variable cost, fixed cost, and sales. In spite of a large increase in sales between 19X1 and 19X2, Avanti experienced a significant decline in contribution margin over the period. Yet net operating income rose from $51,172 in 19X1 to $55,133 in 19X2. The question is, how could this happen? Since we now understand the concepts of cost behavior and cost structure, the answer is simple: The decline in contribution margin was offset by the decline in fixed cost.

If Avanti's management had relied only on an evaluation of the traditional income statement, the true nature of the problem (the decline in contribution margin) would not be revealed. If you recall, the traditional income statement showed an increase in both gross profit margin and net operating income. This created a false sense of well-being. The contribution format statement made clear the serious decline in product contribution that had taken place.

Analyzing Product Contribution

Since contribution format statements can be prepared for individual products or product lines, they serve as powerful tools for solving a variety of financial analysis and decision making problems. The focal points of the individual product or product line contribution statement are the percent of total sales that each product or product line represents, and the respective contribution margin(s) and contribution margin ratio(s).

- The *percentage breakdown of total sales represented by product or product line* reflects what is commonly referred to as sales mix or product mix. This key financial variable has a major impact on the firm's revenue and its overall financial performance.

- The *dollar amount of contribution margin* indicates the contribution made by each component of sales to total fixed cost (overhead) and operating profit. This key financial variable is a primary determinant of the firm's ability to generate cash flow and profit.

- The *contribution margin ratio* is a measure of efficiency. The larger this percentage value, the greater the contribution of the product or product line to overall financial performance.

These concepts are illustrated using Avanti's 19X1 and 19X2 product contribution statements which appear on Table 5.5.

Evaluating Product Contribution Statements

Interpreting the contribution statements for individual products or product lines is not difficult. It involves nothing more than using your business instincts to answer this question: If I were to prepare a contribution format statement for each of my firm's products or product lines, how would I prefer the results to appear? Ideally, you would want:

■ Each product in the product line to cover its associated variable costs with sufficient cushion to make a significant contribution to fixed cost (overhead) and profit.

■ The most profitable sales mix. That is, the products that generate the largest contribution margin ratios also make up the largest percentages of total sales.

Apply these two basic principles to Avanti's product contribution statements (Table 5.5).

Product Performance at Avanti

As shown on the product contribution statements, Avanti's product line consists of products A, B, and C. Notice that these products did not contribute equally to Avanti's cash flow and profit performance in 19X1. Although Product A accounted for only 30% of total sales in that year, it had the largest contribution margin ratio, 50%, of the three products. It contributed approximately $0.50 (50 cents) to total fixed cost and operating profit for each dollar of sales. At the other extreme, Product C generated 31% of total sales but contributed only $0.23 (23 cents) per sales dollar (a contribution margin ratio of 23%) to fixed cost and profit. Product B produced the largest amount of contribution margin, $54,400, because of the attractive combination of a large contribution margin ratio (48%) and a substantial portion of total sales (39%).

The sales mix and contribution margin ratio percentages highlight the impact of product mix and contribution on profits and cash flows. For example, note how Avanti's total contribution margin of $118,400 and net operating income of $51,172 would have increased if more units of product A or B would have been sold in place of Product C. In other words, if Avanti could have produced a sales mix more favorably weighted toward product A or B rather than Product C.

For instance, each 19X1 sales dollar of Product A contributed approximately $0.50 (50 cents) to fixed cost and operating profit as opposed to only $0.23 (23 cents) for Product C. If a dollar of Product A sales had been substituted for each sales dollar of C, then an additional $0.27 ($0.50 minus $0.23) of contribution would have been produced. It is obviously in Avanti's best interest to obtain a sales mix weighted toward higher margin items. Unfortunately, Avanti was not able to do this in 19X2 and, as a result, financial performance suffered.

Table 5.5

THE AVANTI COMPANY
Contribution Statements by Product
For 19X1 and 19X2

19X1

	Product A	Product B	Product C
Sales (% of Total)	$87,000 (30%)	$113,000 (39%)	$ 89,900 (31%)
Less: Variable Costs			
Cost of Sales	37,100	51,800	59,100
Sales Commissions	3,600	3,900	5,400
Vehicle Expense	2,600	2,900	4,700
Total Variable Costs	$43,300	$ 58,600	$ 69,200
Contribution Margin (Ratio)	$43,700 (50.2%)	$ 54,400 (48.2%)	$ 20,700 (23%)

19X2

	Product A	Product B	Product C
Sales (% of Total)	$90,000 (26.5%)	$105,000 (30.9%)	$145,000 (42.6%)
Less: Variable Costs			
Cost of Sales	40,895	58,300	95,305
Sales Commissions	5,476	4,700	9,024
Vehicle Expense	3,475	3,475	6,950
Total Variable Cost	$49,846	$ 66,475	$111,279
Contribution Margin (Ratio)	$40,154 (44.6%)	$ 38,525 (36.7%)	$ 33,721 (23.3%)

A contribution format income statement prepared by product or product line identifies the sales and related variable costs of the item in question as well as the percentage of total sales that item represents. This type of statement provides management with a powerful tool for analyzing the contribution to fixed costs and profit of individual items, and for the effect of sales mix on profit.

Identifying the Problem

With this insight, you can identify the reasons behind the decline in Avanti's total contribution from $118,900 in 19X1 to $112,400 in 19X2. (These figures are from Avanti's contribution format income statement, Table 5.4.)To do so, look first at the percent of sales figures on the 19X2 product contribution statement. Instead of increasing sales of the high margin items, products A and B, there was a significant increase in the sales of Product C. The share of total sales accounted for by this lowest-margin item increased to 42.6% while that of the two high-margin products declined to 26.5% and 30.9%, respectively.

Unfortunately for Avanti, poor sales mix was not the only culprit. The deterioration of total contribution margin is also attributed to a decline in the contribution margin ratios of both products A and B. Each of these products contributed less to fixed costs and profits than the year before. Notice that the contribution margin ratio for Product A declined to 44.6% while that for Product B declined to 36.7%. This erosion is, in all likelihood, a more serious and more difficult problem to correct than the unfavorable sales mix.

Avanti's management is faced with an important task. They must determine the reasons for this adverse turn of events, and then take immediate steps to correct the problem. There are a number of possible causes for poor sales mix and declining contribution margin. To identify the reasons for the poor sales mix, Avanti's management should look at such factors as:

- The focus and efficacy of its pricing policy.

- The amount of effort, focus, and efficacy of its promotion and advertising strategy.

- The balance between high-priced and/or high-quality, and low-priced and/or low-quality items in its product line.

- The product sales emphasized by its sales commission structure.

- The quality of its service.

The decline in contribution margin ratios can be caused by such things as:

- Poor cost control.

- Failure to adjust selling prices to cost increases.

- Too large a percentage of sales occurring at discount or sale prices.

- Poor purchasing and/or inventory control policies.

- Lost inventory through employee theft.

Unfortunately, there is no ready-made formula for identifying variable and fixed costs. Cost structures vary with different types of businesses, and using informed judgment, you must specify the variable and fixed items for your firm. The following guidelines will, however, simplify the identification process:

How to Identify Fixed and Variable Costs

- Begin with a thorough understanding of each expense item on your firm's accounting income statement. To accomplish this, you need nothing more than a facility with the principles discussed in the four preceding chapters and your knowledge of your firm's operations.

- To identify fixed cost items, ask yourself this question: If there were no sales or other activity over the relevant time period (usually one month or one year), or if the level of sales and operations change over this period (increase or decrease), would this cost item remain constant? If the answer is yes, the item is a fixed cost for that time period. For example, items such as rent expense, lease payments, supervisory or management salaries, and depreciation expense usually remain constant over a specific planning period or a relevant range of activity.

- To identify variable cost items, ask the same question. If the amount of the expense item changes with the level of sales or the volume of operations, then it is a variable cost. For example, items such as the cost of purchased inventory, labor expense, sales commissions, and income taxes (if the business is incorporated) usually vary with changes in sales or operations.

- It is important to remember that the concept of fixed and variable cost is related to time. They are short-run phenomena, and the fixed and variable designations only have meaning for a given time period or a given range of activity. In the long run, all costs become variable because everything is subject to change.

While most of your firm's operating costs will fall neatly into either the variable or fixed category over the relevant range, you may occasionally discover a cost item that contains both a variable and fixed component. When you ask yourself whether the cost continues at the same amount over the relevant time frame or sales range, or whether it varies with activity, you discover that it does some of each. A portion of the cost is fixed, and a portion varies with changes in the level of sales.

Dealing with Semi-Variable Cost

Semi-variable or mixed costs may include such items as utilities expense, telephone expense, labor cost (if both part- and full-time employees are used), and vehicle expense. For example, most of a monthly utility bill depends on actual consumption, a variable element. The bill also includes a minimum charge for having the service ready and available for use, a fixed element.

How is a mixed cost treated for analysis and planning? Technically, it should be divided into its fixed and variable components, and each component listed in the appropriate category on the contribution format statement. In the case of a semi-variable utility cost, for instance, the contribution statement would list "Utility Cost — Variable" in the variable cost section of the statement, and "Utility Cost — Fixed" in the fixed cost section.

Disaggregating or separating a mixed cost into its fixed and variable components involves examining the past behavior of the cost item over various levels of sales activity, and identifying the variable and fixed components. The following are a few helpful approaches to treating semi-variable cost items:

- If the semi-variable item is a relatively insignificant part of your firm's cost structure, make a judgment on whether it is primarily fixed or primarily variable. Designate the entire cost amount according to your judgment.

- If the fixed portion of the cost item is minor, treat the entire cost as variable. This will be the case for many mixed costs. For example, while the utility bill contains a fixed element, it is usually insignificant. In most cases, either this or the above approach will meet your analysis and planning needs.

- If either the mixed cost item itself or its fixed component is significant, or if the analysis requires more precision, a formal procedure can be used. Of the available disaggregating techniques, the Hi-Lo method is the most straightforward.

Treating Mixed Costs Using the Hi-Lo Method

Application of the Hi-Lo Method involves the following steps:

- Identify a representative time period (such as one year), or a relevant range of sales activity (such as sales between X dollars and Y dollars).

- List the historical sales values and associated mixed-cost amounts for the time period or range. For example, list the monthly sales values for the year and the monthly amounts of the corresponding semi-variable cost item.

- Choose the highest and lowest sales amounts from the range of sales values, and the amounts of the semi-variable cost item associated with the selected sales values.

- Subtract the lowest sales amount from the highest, and the lowest cost amount from the highest.

- Divide the difference in cost by the difference in sales to determine the formula for the variable component.

■ Apply the cost formula to either the highest or lowest sales figure to determine the variable component, and subtract this amount from the amount of the cost item to obtain the fixed component.

This procedure utilizes sales and labor cost data for Avanti's service department during a given seven-month period. Assume the following historical values have been observed:

Table 5.6 Seven-Month Sales and Labor Cost Data

Month	Sales	Labor Cost
January	$17,500	$3,200
February	17,000	3,150
March	15,000	2,900
April	16,500	3,000
May	19,000	3,500
June	18,000	3,200
July	16,000	3,000

This table contains data used to determine the fixed and variable components of the semi-variable cost item — labor — using the Hi-Lo Method.

This data indicates that labor cost increases as sales increase. This suggests that labor cost must contain a variable component. To separate the variable cost element from the fixed cost element, it is necessary to relate the change in sales to the change in labor cost. This is illustrated using the steps outlined above.

Table 5.7 High and Low Sales Levels and Associated Labor Cost

	Sales	Labor Cost
Highest sales level observed and associated labor cost	$19,000	$3,500
Lowest sales level observed and associated labor cost	15,000	2,900
Difference	$ 4,000	$ 600

The data shown on this table is used to illustrate the steps required to separate the fixed and variable components of a semi-variable cost using the Hi-Lo Method.

Variable Cost Rate = Difference in Cost ÷ Difference in Sales

Variable Cost Rate = $600 ÷ $4,000

= $0.15 of labor cost per $1 of sales

Using this variable cost rate formula, the variable component of labor cost can be calculated at any sales level. For example, at a sales level of $15,000 the variable cost portion of labor cost is $2,250. This is calculated as follows:

Variable Cost Rate = $0.15 of labor cost per $1 of sales

Variable Cost Rate = $0.15 x $15,000 of sales
$$= \$2,250$$

Given the amount of variable component, the fixed portion of labor cost can be calculated. This is accomplished by deducting the variable cost element from either the high or low amount of labor cost. The following illustration uses the highest sales value and associated labor cost figure. For practice, you may wish to verify the $650 shown below by calculating the fixed cost element using the $15,000 sales level and the associated $2,900 labor cost.

Fixed Cost Element = Total Labor Cost – Variable Cost Element

Fixed Cost Element = $3,500 – ($0.15 x $19,000)
$$= \$3,500 - \$2,850$$
$$= \$650$$

Since both the fixed and variable elements have been isolated, labor costs can be expressed as $650 plus $0.15 per sales dollar. This expression is referred to as the cost formula. For analysis or planning purposes, the $650 would be listed on the contribution format statement as "Labor Cost — Fixed" and the amount of the variable component would be calculated as .15 multiplied by sales.

A Final Word on Contribution Analysis

Before moving to the discussion of breakeven analysis, one important point should be re-emphasized. The financial statements you receive from your accountant have been prepared in accordance with traditional accounting principles. While the format of these statements meets your accountant's reporting needs, it is not always suitable for decision making. Modifications to the way financial information is organized are often necessary to meet the needs of a particular decision. One such modification is the contribution format income statement.

As with other financial calculations, the mechanics of converting the traditional income statement to a contribution format can be performed manually or with available computer software. You, however, must do the analysis and render the judgments necessary to separate your firm's operating cost items into fixed and variable categories. While this analysis requires a little of your time, the benefits produced from the analysis far outweigh the costs of the time invested. By making the analysis, you gain valuable insight into the nature of your firm's operations, its cost structure, and how individual costs behave. More often than not, these insights are as valuable to sound financial management as the actual data gathered.

The second major tool in the cost-volume-profit arsenal is *breakeven analysis*. This concept, although simple, has a number of valuable applications for analysis, planning, and decision making. To obtain a firm grasp of this concept, it is useful to begin with a discussion of what must be done to cover the variable and fixed costs associated with your firm's normal operations.

Breakeven Analysis

Recall that variable cost is that category of expenses directly related to sales. Thus, each time a dollar of sales revenue is generated, the firm automatically incurs a given percentage of variable cost. To cover the variable cost, the amount of sales revenue must be equal to or greater than the amount of variable cost incurred. For example, if variable cost is $1 per unit or $1,000 in total, the selling price per unit must be at least $1 and sales revenue must be at least $1,000. If sales revenue is equal to variable cost, contribution margin is zero. If the amount of revenue is greater than variable cost, a positive contribution margin is generated.

Covering Variable Cost

The ability of a firm to meet total fixed cost depends on two critical factors: the size of the contribution margin, and sales volume. In order to generate contribution to fixed cost, a firm's contribution margin must be positive (greater than zero). That is, sales revenue must exceed variable cost. The larger the margin of sales over variable cost, the more dollars available to contribute to fixed cost.

Covering Fixed Cost (Overhead)

In addition to positive contribution, sales volume must be sufficient to generate an amount of contribution margin that is at least equal to fixed cost. For example, if fixed cost totals $1,000, there must be sufficient sales to generate $1,000 of contribution. If sales revenue produces a contribution margin just equal to fixed cost, a firm breaks even. Total sales revenue equals total cost (total variable cost plus total fixed cost). If sales revenue produces a contribution margin that exceeds fixed cost, a firm earns operating income. The larger the margin of contribution over fixed cost, the greater the amount of operating income earned.

A simple example using your hypothetical diskette firm will clarify the above points. Recall that this firm sold diskettes for $2 each, had variable production, selling, and administrative expenses of $1 per diskette, and fixed costs of $50,000. Using an abbreviated contribution statement format, this data would appear as shown in Table 5.8.

An Illustration of Cost Coverage

Note from this data that each time a diskette is sold, two events take place: $2 of sales revenue is generated, and $1 of variable cost is incurred. The result is a contribution margin of $1 per unit sold (a contribution margin ratio of 50%). This means that each time a diskette is sold, $1 of margin is available to contribute to the fixed cost burden of $50,000.

Table 5.8 Contribution Format Statement Data for Fixed and Variable Cost Coverage

Selling Price per Unit	$2.00
Less: Variable Cost per Unit	1.00
Contribution Margin per Unit (Ratio)	$1.00 (50%)
Total Fixed Costs	$50,000

The contribution format statement data for the hypothetical diskette manufacturer shown here is used as an illustration of the concept of fixed and variable cost coverage — the foundation for breakeven analysis.

If 1,000 diskettes are sold, $1,000 of total contribution margin is generated, thereby reducing fixed-cost burden to $49,000 ($50,000 minus $1,000). If 50,000 diskettes are sold, $50,000 of total contribution margin is generated and fixed costs are covered ($50,000 of contribution margin equals $50,000 of fixed cost). At this volume of sales, operating income is zero and your firm has reached the breakeven point. This is illustrated using the abbreviated contribution format statement shown below. As this illustration suggests, breakeven is simply the point where total revenue equals total cost or, alternatively stated, the point where total contribution margin equals fixed cost.

Calculating Breakeven

We can now determine how breakeven sales volume is calculated. Breakeven sales volume is simply fixed cost divided by the contribution margin ratio. Applying this formula to your diskette firm involves dividing the $50,000 of fixed costs by the 50% contribution margin ratio. This calculation is shown on Table 5.9.

Table 5.9 Contribution Format Statement Data for Breakeven Point

Sales	$100,000	(50,000 units @ $2.00)
Less: Variable Costs	50,000	(50,000 units @ $1.00)
Contribution Margin	$ 50,000	
Less: Fixed Costs	50,000	
Operating Income	$ -0-	

The contribution format statement data for the hypothetical diskette manufacturer shown on this table is used to illustrate the concept of the breakeven point.

Breakeven Sales Volume = Fixed Cost ÷ Contribution Margin Ratio
$$= \$50,000 \div .5$$
$$= \$100,000$$

The data on Table 5.9 verifies this calculation. The $100,000 of sales revenue creates $50,000 of variable cost and a $50,000 contribution margin. This amount of contribution is exactly equal to the amount of fixed cost at this volume of operations and net operating income is zero. Your firm is at the breakeven point.

What Happens After Fixed Costs are Covered?

It is useful to continue the illustration by asking the question, what happens as the firm generates sales beyond the breakeven level? You may already see that once the breakeven sales volume is reached, each additional $1 of sales revenue produces one dollar of operating income. At the point of breakeven sales volume, total fixed cost has been covered. Each sale thereafter incurs only variable cost. Since contribution margin is $1 per unit ($2 revenue less $1), the $1 of contribution goes directly to operating profit.

This can be illustrated using the abbreviated contribution statement and assumed sales of 50,001 units.

Table 5.10 Contribution Format Statement Data for Sales Beyond the Breakeven Point

Sales	$100,002	(50,001 units @ $2.00)
Less: Variable Costs	50,001	(50,001 units @ $1.00)
Contribution Margin	$ 50,001	
Less: Fixed Costs	50,000	
Operating Income	$ 1.00	

The contribution format statement data for the hypothetical diskette manufacturer shown on this table is used in an illustration of how sales beyond the breakeven point affect profit.

Using Breakeven Analysis

While there are a number of applications for breakeven analysis, most are related to the question of risk exposure, as the following two examples illustrate.

1. Assume that your diskette firm is considering a new advertising and promotion campaign. This strategy would raise fixed costs for the year from the existing level of $50,000 to $75,000. The new breakeven sales volume associated with this higher level of

fixed cost is $150,000. This figure is calculated by dividing the proposed level of fixed costs of $75,000 by the 50% contribution margin ratio. This pertinent data associated with this decision appears in the table shown below.

The increase in the breakeven sales volume from $100,000 to $150,000 means your diskette firm must generate an additional $50,000 of sales revenue to meet its new cost level. Through breakeven analysis you are able to isolate the key variables in the decision, and identify the critical question that must be answered. Before implementing the promotion campaign, you must satisfy yourself that the potential sales and profits created by the advertising campaign are worth the risk of raising the breakeven sales volume by $50,000. That is, will the additional advertising produce sales revenue sufficient to cover the additional cost, and provide a satisfactory return on the required investment.

Table 5.11 Breakeven Analysis Data After Increase in Fixed Cost

	Current	Proposed
Selling Price per Unit	$2.00	$2.00
Variable Cost per Unit	1.00	1.00
Contribution Margin	1.00	1.00
Contribution Margin Ratio	50%	50%
Fixed Cost	$ 50,000	$ 75,000
Breakeven Sales Volume	$100,000	$ 150,000

The contribution format statement data for the hypothetical diskette manufacturer shown on this table is used to illustrate how breakeven analysis can be employed to evaluate the risk exposure associated with a decision that would increase fixed cost.

---

2. Assume your diskette firm is also considering, independent of the proposed promotion campaign, a decision to manufacture the labels and packaging for the diskettes in-house rather than contracting the work as is now being done. You estimate that producing the labels and packaging would increase variable costs from $1 to $1.10 per diskette. This would lower the contribution margin from $1 to $0.90 per unit and reduce the contribution margin ratio to 45%. This decline in the contribution margin ratio increases the breakeven sales volume to $111,111 ($50,000 divided by .45). This pertinent data for this decision is summarized in Table 5.12.

Table 5.12 Breakeven Analysis Data After Increase in Variable Cost

Selling Price per Unit	$2.00	$2.00
Variable Cost per Unit	1.00	1.10
Contribution Margin	1.00	90
Contribution Margin Ratio	50%	45%
Fixed Cost	$ 50,000	$ 50,000
Breakeven Sales Volume	$100,000	$111,111

The contribution format statement data for the hypothetical diskette manufacturer is used to illustrate how breakeven analysis can be employed to evaluate the risk exposure associated with a decision that would increase variable cost and reduce contribution margin.

The decision to move production in-house raises variable cost and increases risk. Your firm would have a higher breakeven sales level, and would be locked into production responsibilities. On the other hand, in-house production gives the firm full control over the quality of the product. Again, through breakeven analysis you are able to identify the important considerations associated with the decision. You must now ask yourself if the benefits from having full control over production are worth the added risk of increasing breakeven sales by $11,111 and reducing operating flexibility.

In both these decisions, breakeven analysis made it possible to identify, isolate, and focus on the important questions surrounding risk. Since risk taking is a subjective consideration, only you can decide whether the risk in these decisions is appropriate for the firm.

The Question of Risk

In making this choice, you must carefully consider the firm's ability to withstand adversity. This important consideration is brought into perspective by asking this question: What happens to the firm if plans go awry? That is, will your firm be able to generate the cash flows necessary to cover the cost of operations in the event of the "worst case" scenario?

When financial resources are extremely scarce, the potential for withstanding adversity is severely limited. It is clear, then, that protection against downside risk is more important to the long-term financial health of the firm than an over-ambitious grasp at upside profit potential.

Where to Now?

With the background provided by this chapter, you are now in a position to investigate the most critical piece to a firm's financial puzzle: sales revenue. Sales revenue is a function of both sales volume and sales mix, and you must understand the behavior of both. Analyzing sales behavior is the subject of the next chapter.

Chapter 6
Sales Analysis

Sales is the catalyst that imparts life to a business, and is the ultimate regulator of all its activities. It is sales or the prospect of sales that sparks and determines the extent of all the undertakings decided on by you, the business manager. Decisions on the amount of inventory to purchase or produce, the number of employees to hire, and the type of fixed assets to acquire are made because of sales. Without this vital force, these decisions are but a meaningless exercise.

Because of this vital role, the sales figure requires scrutiny beyond the mere tracking of period-by-period dollar amounts. The summary sales figure that appears on your firm's income statement is the result of the workings of an intricate network of component parts. To understand sales behavior, you must understand each component. The systematic breakdown, monitoring, and analysis of sales is an important part of what is known as *sales management*.

A sound program of sales management consists of three activities: converting sales forecasts into realistic sales goals or objectives; recording and tracking sales activity; and analyzing the data. The principles of financial planning and goal setting, and the art of sales forecasting are the topics of Chapter 8. Analyzing sales data is the subject of this chapter. The following is an outline of those topics that will be covered.

TOPIC	CONCEPTS DISCUSSED
Sales Analysis	What is sales analysis and why it is important?
	Steps in the sales analysis process.
	How sales analysis is related to planning.
	The techniques used in sales analysis.
	The benefits produced by effective sales analysis.
	Guidelines for effective sales management.

What Is Sales Analysis?

Sales analysis is simply the breakdown of the total sales figure into its component parts so that the performance of each can be evaluated. By tracing sales revenue to the individual components — products, product lines, market segments, customers, territories, or salespersons — you are in a position to identify trouble spots and take remedial action before problems reach crisis proportions. On the other hand, confining sales analysis to the evaluation of summary sales figures is analogous to sailing a ship in the vicinity of icebergs: The greatest danger comes from what is *not* visible, not from what is visible.

For example, a total sales figure 10% greater than that of last year is a seemingly healthy situation. If, however, sales of a firm's most profitable product are down 10% during this period, there is cause for concern, not jubilation. Likewise, if sales to a firm's most important customer have declined, but the weakness is disguised by sales to less important customers, there is also cause for concern. In both cases, reliance on the total sales figure obscured an underlying problem area. Only through careful analysis of the components that determine total sales can potential disasters be detected and averted.

Without a systematic, ongoing approach to recording and analyzing your firm's sales, you risk failure to:

- Distinguish between high- and low-volume products.

- Distinguish between profitable and unprofitable products or product lines.

- Match sales effort with the profit potential of various products or product lines.

- Identify customers providing satisfactory and unsatisfactory sales volume.

- Recognize changing or emerging trends in consumer preferences.

- Identify strong and weak store locations, market segments, or sales effort.

In short, without an effective sales analysis program you risk not having a clear understanding of what makes your business run, and what factors are important to its success.

Testing Your Sales Knowledge

If you have any doubts about the value of sales analysis to the planning, decision making, and control process, it would be interesting to determine how many of the following questions you can answer about your firm's sales. Do you know:

- Which are the strong and weak products, product lines, market segments, or territories (locations)?

- What are the latest performance measurements for products, product lines, salespersons, territory, or store location?

- What is the sales trend and market position for each product, product line, territory, or store location?

- What is the sales cost and contribution margin of each product or product line?

- Who are the firm's most important customers, and what percentage of total sales and contribution do they contribute?

- How effective is the firm's overall marketing effort?

Only through effective sales analysis can unequivocal answers to questions such as these be obtained.

Sales analysis is an ongoing process consisting of two equally important steps:

Steps in the Sales Analysis Process

1. Recording sales activity by individual sales component.

2. Monitoring and analyzing the data on individual components to detect the strengths and weaknesses in sales activity.

Total sales are separated into specific components for analysis, depending upon the needs of your firm. Most often, the components analyzed are individual products, product lines, customers, market segments, locations, or salespersons, or some combination of these. To perform the analysis, data for the selected components is recorded and tracked in terms of sales dollars, unit volume, or some measure of profit such as contribution margin or gross profit margin.

For example, data on the contribution margin generated by individual product, product line, store location or customer, or by units sold by each salesperson may be recorded, monitored, and evaluated. This type of analysis increases understanding of the factors that contribute to sales performance, and provides information on:

- Which products or product lines are selling and which are contributing the most or the least to overall profits.

- Who buys your firm's products, and which customers contribute the most to overall profits.

- Which locations produce the most or least sales, and which are the most or least profitable.

- Which salespersons are the most and least productive.

The benefits of effective sales analysis are not limited to measuring progress and spotting areas that require corrective action. Sales analysis also provides the information, background, and understanding that

Sales Analysis and Planning

is vital to your operational and financial planning effort. A sound sales analysis program will help you:

- Generate more realistic sales forecasts and sales goals.

- Identify the sales mix that will maximize expected revenues.

- Determine the most efficient allocation of advertising and promotion expenditures.

- Find the most efficient commission system for sales personnel.

- Recognize the most efficient allocation of sales personnel.

To gain insight into how sales analysis is performed, trace through one of Avanti's experiences in 19X2.

What Avanti Learned About Sales Analysis

Prior to 19X2, sales analysis at Avanti was limited to the evaluation of two indicators: the difference between total planned sales and total actual sales, and the difference between the actual and targeted sales-growth rates. While summary information should be included in the sales analysis process, it is not enough. As Avanti management discovered from the events of 19X2, they had to rethink their approach to this important management function.

During 19X2, total sales increased to $340,000 from $290,000 the previous year. Since this 17% increase exceeded the 10% growth rate targeted in management's operating and financial plans, the business appeared to be doing well; however, as seen in Chapter 2, that euphoria was short-lived. Additional analysis revealed that profits had increased by only 7.7% during the year, and cash flow from operations for the period was negative. At that point, Avanti's management was determined to find out what went wrong.

Identifying the Problem

The investigation quickly identified Avanti's problem as poor analysis and control. Managers did not generate information that allowed them to recognize problem areas in time to take corrective action. They had relied on the firm's annual income statement for sales information, and in so doing had neither separated nor tracked sales by component. Recognition of the problem led to the monthly compilation of sales analysis reports. The first of these is shown on Table 6.1. This sales analysis report provides information on product contribution.

Even a cursory examination of this data indicates that the problem of sagging profits and cash flow is attributed to the dramatic change that took place in Avanti's sales mix. Sales mix had shifted from high-margin products to low-margin products. To see this more clearly, examine the data on the sales analysis report that, unfortunately, Avanti's management did not see until after the fact.

Table 6.1 Sales Mix and Contribution Analysis (By Product Group)

Product Group	19X1		19X2	
	% of Sales	% Contribution Margin	% of Sales	% Contribution Margin
A	37%	50%	26.5%	50%
B	39%	48%	30.9%	48%
C	24%	<u>23%</u>	42.6%	<u>23%</u>
Weighted Avg. Margin =		37.3%		24.7%

The sales and contribution margin data on this sales analysis report is organized by product group. Organizing this data in this manner allows you to evaluate the profit contribution of individual products or product lines, and the impact of sales mix on total profits.

As shown in the first column of Table 6.1, Avanti has three product groups in its product line: Group A, Group B, and Group C. The "% of Sales" columns for each year indicate the percentage of total sales represented by each product group. The "% Contribution Margin" columns show the percent of each sales dollar remaining after its variable costs have been deducted. For example, in 19X1 product group B accounted for 39% of total company sales (39 cents out of each average sales dollar), and generated an average contribution margin of 48 cents per sales dollar. Obviously, Product B made an major contribution to Avanti's total sales and profit performance in 19X1.

The 19X1 data also reveals another critical point: 76% of Avanti's sales in that year came from the combination of product groups A and B (37% for Product A plus 39% for Product B). These two product groups also combined to produce an average contribution margin of almost $0.49 for each sales dollar ($0.50 for A and $0.48 for B). Group C, on the other hand, with a meager contribution margin of 23%, accounted for only 24% of total sales. In short, Avanti's sales mix was weighted favorably toward the products that generated the most profit and cash flow. As a result, Avanti enjoyed an overall or weighted average contribution margin of 37.3%. This means that the average sales dollar produced contribution margin of 37.3.

Compare the 19X1 figures with those of 19X2. Notice that in 19X2 Avanti experienced a major change in sales mix. The combined share of total sales for the high-margin product groups A and B shriveled to 57.4%, while Group C, the low-margin product, increased to 42.6%.

A Little Detective Work

This shift in sales mix from high-margin to low-margin items spelled disaster for Avanti's profits and cash flow. Despite the increase in overall company sales for 19X2, the unfavorable shift in product mix reduced overall contribution margin to a dismal 24.7%. Each average sales dollar in 19X2 generated substantially less contribution to fixed costs, taxes, and profits than 19X1 sales dollars. The message from this experience is clear:

If Avanti's aggregate sales data had been broken down into separate product/margin components, and the data analyzed on a regular basis (each month for example), this unfavorable trend would have been detected early. Early detection would have put Avanti's management in a position to take the necessary remedial action before the problem reached crisis proportions.

Alternative Approaches to Sales Analysis

While sales analysis by product is a vital part of effective sales management, it is often necessary to include other sales components in the effort. It may be useful to examine sales and contribution by customer, location, market, or territory as well as by product. For example:

- A merchandising or manufacturing firm interested in identifying its most important customers would track sales and profit contribution by individual customer.

- A service firm interested in identifying the type of service most often required by its several largest customers would track specific service revenues by customer.

- A retailing firm interested in comparing the performance and contribution of each of its store locations would track sales and profit contribution by location.

- A manufacturing firm interested in identifying product sales and profitability by market territory would track product sales and total contribution for each territory.

In addition to the study of sales by individual component (one-way analysis), it may also be useful to analyze paired combinations of sales variables (two-way analysis). For example, you may wish cross-tabulations of such information as the percentage of a product's total sales purchased by each customer; the percentage of a product's total contribution margin generated by each customer; or the percentage of a product's total sales or margin generated by each store location. To get a feel for reports such as these, look at several of the combinations now used by Avanti.

Avanti's Monthly Sales Reports

Avanti's management, now fully aware of the need to stay abreast of developing trends, prepares sales analysis reports on a monthly basis. First among these reports is the breakdown of the contribution margin for product groups A, B, and C. This breakdown is shown in Table 6.2, and the summary of sales by customer for the month of April, 19X3 is shown in Table 6.3.

Table 6.2 Product Contribution Breakdown

Product Name/Number	Contribution Margins
Group A:	
A1	60
A2	50
A3	40
Group B:	
B1	50
B2	48
B3	46
Group C:	
C1	26
C2	23
C3	20

The data on the product contribution breakdown report identifies the contribution margin of each product within a given product group. Routinely performed one-way analysis of this type (profit contribution by product) allows Avanti's management to monitor the performance and contribution of individual components of overall profits.

Since Avanti has only one location and its management is not interested in sales by geographic area, the monthly analysis reports focus on sales and contribution margin by product and by customer. The following is an examination of the one-way and two-way analyses used by Avanti management.

One-Way Analysis: By Product

To meet Avanti's needs, the one-way analysis tables are arranged to provide sales and contribution margin data for each product and customer. These appear in two reports for the month of April, 19X3 shown in tables 6.4 and 6.5.

The product sales analysis report (Table 6.4) displays the pertinent information that Avanti's management needs to track product performance. The first column of the report lists each product in Avanti's product line (note that if a large number of products are involved, the report could be prepared using product lines rather than individual products). The "Dollars of Sales" and "% Total Sales" columns summarize

Table 6.3
THE AVANTI COMPANY
Sales Summary
For the Month of April, 19X3

Product Name	Customer Name	Date of Sale	Sales $ Amount
C1	Swan Bicycle	04/03/X3	$ 2,000
A3	Marie, Lisa	04/03/X3	750
A1	Almond, Greg	04/05/X3	1,000
B2	Trip Bicycle	04/10/X3	10,000
B1	Morris Repairs	04/14/X3	2,000
C1	Morris Repairs	04/14/X3	1,500
A3	Dennis, Charles	04/19/X3	750
C1	Gallagher, Kenny	04/21/X3	400
C1	Rainbow Bicycle	04/21/X3	3,500
A2	Rally Bicycle	04/23/X3	8,000
A1	Twelve-Speed Drive	04/25/X3	1,000
A1	Hamsley, Andy	04/26/X3	1,000
B3	Slayton, Gary	04/26/X3	600
C3	Swan Bicycle	04/27/X3	3,000
A1	Swan Bicycle	04/27/X3	11,000
C2	Trip Bicycle	04/29/X3	5,000
B1	Brewer, Debi	04/31/X3	700

The sales summary report organizes sales data by product. The information is used in subsequent one-way and two-way analyses of sales performance.

total sales for each product, and the percentage of total sales represented by each. The calculation of these values is straightforward. Total product sales is obtained by summing the individual sales for that product during the period, and the percentage value is calculated as total product sales divided by total sales.

For example, the $2,700 of Product B1 sales for the month is obtained by adding all sales amounts for B1 appearing in the sales summary (Table 6.3). As shown in the summary, B1 sales consist of $2,000 of sales to Morris Repairs, and the $700 sale to Debi Brewer. In Table 6.4, the percentage of total sales for B1, 5.2%, is obtained by dividing the $2,700 of B1 sales by the $52,200 of total sales for the month.

The values in the % Total Sales column of Table 6.4 are of particular interest to Avanti's management. They serve as measures of the firm's sales mix for the period. An examination of this column for Avanti reveals that sales mix is again shifting toward the more desirable, high-margin products. Product A1 (with a contribution margin of 60%) accounted for 26.8% of sales for the month, Product B2 (with a margin of 48%) accounted for 19.2% of sales, and A2 (with a 50% margin) accounted for 15.3%.

Avanti's product analysis report also provides information on the total dollars of contribution margin generated by each product, and the percentage of total contribution that each product represents. The values in the Dollars of Margin column are calculated by multiplying the Dollars of Sales value for a each product by that product's contribution margin. (Recall that the contribution margins for Avanti's products were shown on Table 6.2.)

For example, the $8,400 of contribution for the month produced by Product A1 is obtained by multiplying its sales of $14,000 by its contribution margin ratio of 60%.

Total Contribution = Total Sales x Contribution Margin Ratio

Total Contribution = $14,000 x 60%

$\qquad\qquad$ = $8,400

The % Total Margin values are obtained by dividing the Dollars of Contribution for each product by the total dollars of contribution for the month. In the case of Product A1, the 36.4% was calculated as $8,400 divided by the $23,100 of total contribution for the month.

The percentage contribution values are important indicators of the profitability of a firm's sales mix. Note that in Avanti's case, the three best sales performers for the month (A1, B2, A2) produced almost 75% of the total contribution for the month. Apparently, Avanti's management's program designed to influence the sale of high-margin items is producing rewards.

Table 6.4
THE AVANTI COMPANY
Monthly Sales Analysis Report (By Product)
April, 19X3

Product Name	Dollars Of Sales	% Total Sales	Dollars of Contribution	% Total Contribution
A1	$14,000	26.8 %	$8,400	36.4 %
A2	8,000	15.3	4,000	17.3
A3	1,500	2.9	600	2.6
B1	2,700	5.2	1,350	5.8
B2	10,000	19.2	4,800	20.8
B3	600	1.1	276	1.2
C1	7,400	14.2	1,924	8.3
C2	5,000	9.6	1,150	5.0
C3	3,000	5.7	600	2.6
Totals	$52,200	100 %	$23,100	100 %

This table provides examples of two common forms of one-way sales analysis, sales by product, and contribution margin by product. Routinely performed one-way analyses of these types allows management to evaluate the performance and contribution of individual components to overall sales and profits.

Avanti's customer sales analysis report is shown on Table 6.5. With the exception of the focus on customers rather than products, the information produced by this report is identical to that of the product analysis report. Total sales and total contribution for each customer, or for major customers if a large number are involved, are determined using the information from the monthly sales summary (Table 6.3) and the product contribution breakdown (Table 6.2). All calculations are made in the same manner as those used to prepare the product analysis report.

The value of analyzing sales by customer lies in the information afforded management on key customer purchase patterns. As is the case with many small firms, a small percentage of Avanti's customers account for a large percentage of its business. The product analysis report indicates that Swan, Trip, and Rally accounted for about 77% of sales and 76% of profits for the month. Obviously, the planned and actual purchase pattern of these contributors is critical information and should be closely monitored.

The information contained on the one-way reports used by Avanti can be arranged in a number of possible formats. The only rules governing the selection of a particular format are the relevance of the information, and management's preference for presenting it. For example, the percentage of total sales or total margin figures contained in the one-way reports (by product and by customer) can be combined into a single two-way analysis. An example of such a report appears on Table 6.6. The product and customer sales analysis report shows percentage of total sales values cross-tabulated by product and by customer. These percentages are calculated in the same manner as those contained in the one-way reports. A cross-tabulation of this data, however, is often more convenient to use and evaluate since key variable combinations are easily identified.

This chapter has emphasized the need to include sales analysis as a normal part of your management process. Sales and the factors that determine this important variable are not static. A firm's markets are in a continual state of change: new competitors enter the market while others leave; competitors alter strategy and products to gain advantage; customer needs and loyalties change; and new economic, legal, and social trends evolve. These dynamics will favor some of s firm's products, will hurt some, and require major changes in others. It is only through a systematic approach to sales analysis that fundamental changes can be detected in time for you to implement corrective action.

One-Way Analysis: By Customer

Two-Way Analysis

Sales Management Do's and Don'ts

Table 6.5

THE AVANTI COMPANY
Monthly Sales Analysis Report (By Customer)
April, 19X3

Customer Name	Dollars Of Sales	% Total Sales	Dollars of Contribution	% Total Contribution
Debi Brewer	$ 700	1.3 %	$ 350	1.5 %
Charles Dennis	750	1.4	300	1.3
Kenny Gallagher	400	0.8	104	0.5
Andy Hamsley	1,000	1.9	600	2.6
Greg Almond	1,000	1.9	600	2.6
Lisa Marie	750	1.4	300	1.3
Morris Repairs	3,500	6.7	1,390	6.0
Rainbow Bicycle	3,500	6.7	910	3.9
Rally Bicycle	8,000	15.3	4,000	17.3
Swan Bicycle	16,000	30.7	7,720	33.4
Gary Slayton	600	1.2	276	1.2
Trip Bicycle	15,000	28.8	5,950	25.8
Twelve-Speed Drive	1,000	1.9	600	2.6
	$52,200	100 %	$23,100	100 %

This one-way analysis table, sales by customer, provides management with information on key customer purchase patterns.

Table 6.6

THE AVANTI COMPANY
Monthly Sales Analysis Report (By Product and Customer)
April, 19X3

Customer Name	A1	A2	A3	B1	B2	B3	C1	C2	C3	% Total Sales
Debi Brewer				1.3%						1.3%
Charles Dennis			1.4%							1.4%
Kenny Gallagher							0.8%			0.8%
Andy Hamsley	1.9%									1.9%
Greg Almond	1.9%									1.9%
Lisa Marie			1.4%							1.4%
Morris Repairs				3.8%			2.9%			6.7%
Rainbow Bicycle							6.7%			6.7%
Rally Bicycle		15.3%								15.3%
Swan Bicycle	21.1%						3.8%		5.8%	30.7%
Gary Slayton						1.2%				1.2%
Trip Bicycle					19.2%			9.6%		28.8%
Twelve-Speed Drive	1.9%									1.9%
Total Percent	26.8	15.3	2.8	5.1	19.2	1.2	14.2	9.6	5.8	100%

This two-way analysis table, sales by product and by customer, provides management with information on key combinations of variables that influence overall sales and profits.

Guidelines to Improve Sales Analysis and Management

Listed below are guidelines that will improve the sales analysis and sales management process.

- **Resist the Temptation to Rely on Overall Sales.** While overall sales volume is easier to compile and evaluate, it provides only a narrow view of performance. To make effective plans and decisions, you must understand the factors that affect sales performance. This understanding comes from knowing the details that are hidden in summary sales values.

- **Set Individual Sales Goals.** Your firm's sales forecast should be translated into measurable targets or goals for individual sales components, and sales analysis should focus on the timely measurement of progress toward these goals. In Avanti's case, monthly sales goals are set for each product, and monthly reviews are conducted to determine progress toward these goals. Significant deviations between the expectations as reflected in the sales goals, and the actual performance measured through sales analysis is the signal for management action.

- **Keep Appropriate Sales Records.** Effective sales analysis requires good sales data. This means sales records that reflect the sales relationships most important to the business. If sales by product, customer, location, or any other breakdown or combination is most important, then sales should be recorded, monitored, and evaluated on that basis. You must determine the factors that are relevant to your business, and once determined, you must make certain that the appropriate records are maintained and evaluated. You cannot lose sight of the fact that sales is the most important of all your firm's variables.

- **Sales Records and Analysis Should Be Timely.** The purpose of tracking and analyzing sales is to spot deviations from expectations in time to take remedial action. In general, the time lapse between review periods depends on the amount of fluctuation in a firm's sales pattern. The more stable the sales pattern, the longer the permissible interval between analysis dates. A reasonable approach would start with monthly review periods and adjust as the data indicates the need to do so.

- **Analyze Sales Data.** The most convenient source of sales analysis data is the sales invoice. This document usually contains information on customer name, quantity ordered, price, geographic location, and salesperson, among other items. Summary data can be obtained by combining invoices. Other sources of sales information include cash register tapes, sales summary sheets, and customer records. In addition to these sources, it is useful to have accounting records that identify contribution margins by product as well as traditional gross profit margins.

- **Be Aware of the 80%-20% Principle.** The pattern of sales in business firms often approximates what is referred to as the 80%-20% principle: A large portion of overall sales or profits (the 80%) is determined by a small portion of your customers, products, or territories (the 20%). If this is true, then you should devote the largest portion of your control efforts to the 20% group. Conversely, the group that makes only negligible contributions to sales and profits should receive only minimal attention. Products that fall into this marginal category should also be the subject of periodic survival tests. If there is no valid reason that offsets a product's poor performance, it should be a candidate for elimination.

- **Sales Analysis Does Not Give Specific Answers.** As with any management tool, sales analysis can help spot trouble signs and specific areas requiring investigation. Sales analysis does not, however, solve problems or substitute for management judgment. It is only an analytical tool. In Avanti's case, a sound approach to sales analysis would have identified the change in sales mix in 19X2 at an early date. Determining the underlying reasons for the change, and the actions required to correct the problem were, as always, Avanti management's responsibility.

A Final Thought

The dominant themes of this chapter as well as the entire analysis section of this book have been the need for timely information and your active involvement in monitoring and evaluating this information. The source of good information is a well-designed set of records. Some of these records, such as the balance sheet, income statement, and cash flow statement, are or should be supplied by your accountant. Others, such as ratio values, contribution format statements, and sales analysis data, must be prepared for each specific use. While this preparation can be done manually, the task can be automated and simplified using a well-designed set of computer models. For information regarding financial models software, see the card enclosed at the back of this book.

Where to Now?

This chapter concludes the section on financial analysis. Up to this point, you have been exposed to the principles and techniques used to evaluate a firm's financial position and its financial performance. Now it is time to investigate the principles and techniques used to establish a firm's financial future.

This author believes that planning is the most important of all management activities. Planning can mean the difference between your firm's successful financial performance, a mediocre existence, or its failure. It is an activity that you can learn to do, and do well.

Introduction to Financial Planning

The previous chapters focused on the tools used to analyze the complex interaction of the numerous forces that combine to regulate a firm's financial performance, and the strengths and weaknesses that determine its financial condition. This information is essential for measuring a firm's rate of financial progress — where it has been and where it currently stands. It is also essential to the second step in a program of sound financial management: financial planning. Financial planning is the process through which a financial blueprint of where a firm is expected to go and how it plans to get there is prepared.

The Second Ingredient of Sound Financial Management

The subject of finance deals with money and credit, and financial planning deals with planning for the acquisition and use of these limited resources. It is the twofold process of evaluating the financial consequences of a firm's strategic and operating plans, and preparing a financial plan to support these activities.

The Role of Financial Planning

In order for a business to operate profitably, to grow, and to be prepared for adverse developments or unexpected opportunities, you must have detailed information on how your stock of financial resources affects operating decisions. Financial planning provides this critical information as well as the financial controls needed to manage those resources efficiently. In short, without effective financial planning, there is no true financial management of your firm.

What you will learn about financial planning is outlined in the table below.

TOPIC	CONCEPTS DISCUSSED
Planning	What is planning and why is it important?
	The information needed for and steps involved in preparing strategic and operating plans for your firm.
Financial Planning	What is financial planning and its role in the overall planning process of your firm.

Part Two

TOPIC	CONCEPTS DISCUSSED
Financial Planning (continued)	The steps in the financial planning process.
	How sales forecasts are prepared and used in the financial planning process.
Cash Planning	The role of cash planning in the financial planning process.
	The information needed for and steps involved in preparing a cash budget.
	How to use the information produced by the cash budget.
Profit Planning	The role of profit planning in the financial planning process.
	The information needed for and steps involved in preparing pro forma statements.
	How the information from pro forma statements and breakeven analysis is used in the financial planning process.
Planning Worksheets	A step-by-step, how-to guideline for preparing your firm's financial plan.

The Benefits from Sound Financial Planning

There is no question that financial analysis and planning, if done properly, requires some of your valuable time. If you are like most small business managers you are probably thinking, "More demands on my time is the last thing I need." But the benefits produced by financial analysis and planning are well worth the time invested. The information gained from these activities allows you to:

- Uncover potential problems before they reach crisis proportion. This gives you the time to develop solutions and map alternative courses (actions) before emergency conditions force unpleasant choices.

- Generate financial information about the business that serves as a standard for gauging your firm's performance relative to management's expectations and to other firms.

- Identify and become familiar with the key factors that determine the success and well-being of the business. Many small business managers become so immersed in day-to-day operations that they lose an overall perspective of the business, its customers, markets, and competitors. By doing financial analysis and planning, you are forced to maintain this critical perspective.

- Formulate and test alternative strategies and operating plans. In other words, the impact of planned activities can be tested before the fact.

- Present the business in a professional manner to those outside parties interested in your firm's financial health. For example, prospective creditors, such as bankers, use the tools of financial analysis to provide answers to questions about the credit risk the firm represents. By using the same tools as the banker, you gain insight into how creditors perceive your firm. Being forewarned and forearmed when approaching a bank for a loan is no small blessing. What's more, approaching a bank with a well-developed set of plans goes a long way toward convincing the banker that your firm is in the hands of capable management and is, therefore, a worthy loan candidate.

In short, the benefits from financial analysis and planning translate into a well-managed, efficient business that is in a position to maximize its financial potential.

A Final Thought

Financial planning is a two-step process: 1) developing the information, assumptions, and projections on which plans are prepared; and 2) translating the information, assumptions, and projections into dollar values. The first step is by far the most important in the process. It requires a combination of good information about a firm's external and internal environment, and the sound judgment of a knowledgeable management.

As is true of financial analysis, the second step in the financial planning process involves number crunching. This task can be done manually, or it can be automated and simplified by using computer models. See the card enclosed at the back of this book for more information on financial models software.

Where to Now?

Chapter 7 details principles and guidelines for conducting the planning process in a small firm. This overview provides the foundation for the two most important steps in financial planning: cash planning and profit planning. These critical steps are covered in detail in chapters 8 and 9. Chapter 10, Planning Worksheets, consists of a series of questions that lead you through a how-to approach to financial planning.

Chapter 7
Financial Planning

During the early 1980s, the U.S. economy was plagued with the dual horrors of spiraling inflation and severe recession. Statistics for this period indicate a failure rate for small firms equivalent to that experienced during the Depression years of the 1930s. For those firms able to survive, this period probably represents only a vague, unpleasant memory; but for those that did not, what remains is a painful lesson in mismanagement.

Certainly, some of the small firms that failed were victims of circumstances beyond the control of management. Unfortunately, most were victims of their own shortcomings.

These firms were not prepared for the worst case scenario and therefore unable to react and adjust to adverse developments. In short, their managers did not plan.

Planning is the most basic, yet the most important of all management functions. Without planning, a firm is like a ship at sea without charts and a navigational system. Its course is determined by random events over which the captain and crew have no control. Sound planning provides a firm with realistic objectives, and the course it must take to achieve them. Below is an outline of topics that will be covered in this chapter.

TOPIC	CONCEPTS DISCUSSED
Planning	What planning is and why it is necessary.
	The benefits of planning.
	The basic steps in the planning process.
Financial Planning	What financial planning is and why it is necessary.
	How financial planning is related to overall planning.
	The tools used in financial planning.

Why You Should Plan

If you were to survey typical small business managers for their views on planning, you would uncover more reasons why planning is not done than why it is done. The two most common excuses offered for this failing are expressed in the statements cited below. How many times have you said or heard a fellow business person say:

"Planning is not worth doing because change occurs so quickly that events never work out according to plan."

While this statement is partially true, it is also the strongest testimonial to the need for systematic planning. Unquestionably, the future is uncertain, and it is a rare coincidence when actual events occur exactly as forecast. Yet, the only intelligent way to deal with this uncertainty is to make informed forecasts for different sets of possible events (alternative futures), and develop alternative plans to meet these possibilities. Such an approach forces management to prepare a firm for the unexpected. Taking the time to plan for "what if" situations minimizes the possibility that managers will be unprepared to deal with adverse developments.

"I'm too busy with day-to-day operations to spend valuable time planning for the future."

This unfortunately is also a true statement for many small firm managers. Burdened with all or most of the responsibilities associated with operating the business, a manager's schedule is often pre-empted by day-to-day problems. When this occurs, the manager is caught in a vicious cycle. Failure to plan creates an endless stream of routine problems, and fighting these "brush fires" leaves little time for planning. Without a well-conceived set of plans, activities become poorly focused, or worse, become random. When this happens, managers usually lose control of the firm. Conversely, taking the time to plan alternative courses of action for alternative sets of conditions prepares the firm for the unexpected as well as the expected. Advance preparation reduces both the number of brush fires that occur as well as the amount of time that must be spent putting them out when they do occur.

Ironically, while these statements are used as justifications for not planning, they are the very reasons why a formal approach to planning is necessary. While it is true that planning alone cannot guarantee success for your firm, it is also true that lack of planning drastically increases the probability of its failure. By not planning, you are betting that your firm will succeed solely on the basis of luck or circumstance. Considering the time, effort, and capital you have invested in your business, do you want to take such an enormous gamble?

Planning has been described as a hard "look within," a broad "look around," and a long "look ahead." The "look within" refers to an objective appraisal of the amount and quality of resources that are owned or can be obtained. Resources are the financial, physical, human, and intangible assets necessary to operate the business. These include such things as cash, credit capability, equipment, management and staff expertise, employee know-how, patents, location, or the reputation of your firm. Available resources set the upper limit on what your firm can achieve.

"Looking around" means identifying and understanding the environment in which your firm operates. Environment refers to your firm's economic, social, legal and competitive surroundings, and the key factors associated with these surroundings that affect its success. Examples include:

- **Economic factors**, such as the rate at which the economy is growing, the direction of interest rates, the expected rate of inflation, unemployment rates, gross national product, or labor costs.

- **Market and competitive factors**, such as new product developments, the level of disposable income in your firm's target market, a change in strategy of a major competitor, or changes in consumer tastes and preferences.

- **Social factors**, such as the population growth rate, the percentage of consumers over a certain age, or changes in the public's values, preferences, and attitudes.

- **Political factors**, such as a change in tax laws, or new environmental restrictions.

A long "look ahead" means the need to make informed forecasts for different possible combinations of critical factors, and to develop alternative plans to meet these possibilities. To find out how these three components of planning are combined to form a systematic approach to the planning function, study the sections below.

While the specifics of planning will vary from firm to firm, good planning involves certain basic steps that are common to all organizations. Effective results from planning can be achieved if you approach the process systematically, perform the steps in logical sequence, and conduct the planning effort on a continuous basis. Steps in the planning process include:

1. Prepare a Forecast.

Sound plans cannot be developed without a realistic forecast of the conditions your firm should expect to face during the planning period.

Forecasting is simply the art of using past and current information to make reasonable assumptions about the future. As suggested by this definition, the key to effective forecasting is good information — information about the environment in which your firm operates, and the factors that are critical to its success.

Since demand for your firm's products or services is dependent on the level of purchasing power in the market it serves, the first step in forecasting is understanding the chain of events that determine economic activity in that market. Economic data and forecasts for specific areas are often published by or readily available from a number of sources, such as:

- **Research bureaus of college and university schools of business.** Academic institutions often monitor economic trends and publish forecasts for a variety of economic indicators on the national, state, and local level.

- **State or area planning and development commissions.** These agencies are a prime source of information on economic growth, and employment and income levels for state and local market areas.

- **Special interest groups, such as the state and local chambers of commerce, realtor associations, and industrial development authorities.** These agencies often collect and monitor data and make forecast local economies.

- **Informal sources, such as loan officers at financial institutions or local taxing authorities.** These groups are usually a valuable source of data and information on the local economy.

- **Industry sources, such as trade journals or trade associations.** These agencies publish economic status reports, forecasts, and changing trend information for their specific industry. The trade publications that are pertinent to a particular business should be must reading.

What is gleaned from these sources should be supplemented with your own experience and observations about the economy and your firm's industry and markets. An excellent device for recording and storing these observations is a personal economic diary. The diary need be nothing more than your informal notes of the occurrence, impact, and results of economic events that affect your firm's market. By logging these events and relating them to the firm's sales performance, you have compiled a convenient database of information that helps you understand the key factors affecting your business. A simple example will clarify the forecasting process.

Assume you are a residential contractor operating in a market area in which the primary determinants of economic activity are a local air force base and a state college. The large payrolls and subsequent expenditures of the base and college personnel, and the expenditures of college students are the key to the level of economic activity in the area. These expenditures create demand for goods and services, jobs, and income.

Assume further that from your reading of industry publications and business news you have learned that the demand for residential housing in a given market area is heavily dependent on population changes, the level of employment and income, the availability of housing, and the level of interest rates. Given their importance to the success of your business, you wish to monitor changes in these factors along with changes in the level of activity at the base and college. This can be accomplished with your economic diary.

The diary can be used to record your notes on unfolding events, such as:

- Shifts in interest rates;

- New building permits in the area;

- Changes in employment rates and income levels in the area;

- The rate and type of personnel changes (officer versus enlisted) at the base; and

- Changes in student enrollment and faculty positions at the college.

By relating changes in these key factors to home sales in the area, you gain an understanding of what affects demand for housing. With this background, you are in a position to gather or interpret information as it becomes available (e.g., expected personnel levels at the base, expected enrollment at the college, a change in the direction of interest rates), and make realistic forecasts of future market conditions and home sales.

Armed with informed expectations, you are in a position to develop plans that prepare the firm for these possibilities. Instead of being the victim of surprises, you are ready to take advantage of them.

2. Set Attainable Objectives.

Objectives should be clearly formulated, realistic, measurable goals. By having established objectives for your firm, you ensure that:

- Activities are organized, coordinated, and directed toward some commonly understood target.

- There are measurable standards for the business by which actual performance can be compared and evaluated.

An example of the statement of objectives for a hypothetical small firm similar to Avanti is given in Table 7.1 below.

Table 7.1 Statement of Objectives

Activity	Objective
Finance	Achieve a 20% return on investment.
	Maintain a gross profit margin of 48%.
	Reduce operating costs by 5%.
Marketing	Achieve average annual sales growth of 6%.
	Capture an additional 10% of the local market for our product line over the next three years.
	Improve the sales mix of our products with a shift to higher margin items.
Personnel	Recruit and train a productive salesperson during the next year.
	Develop and implement a sales bonus system.
Personal	Introduce my son into the business and begin his training for my succession.
	Retire by age 60.
	Spend at least 10 more hours per week with my family.

This table contains examples of objectives for a typical small firm. By having clearly formulated, realistic, measurable objectives, management is able to direct all activity toward common goals, and to measure actual performance against predetermined standards.

To establish realistic objectives, you must have a clear understanding of your firm's opportunities, capabilities, and limitations. This requires knowledge of the firm's external environment, its internal operations, and its available resources. Without this knowledge, goal statements are meaningless. For example, if the firm whose objectives were stated above operated in a market that was highly competitive and economically stagnant, the objectives for sales growth and return on investment would be difficult if not impossible to achieve.

3. Identify Available Resources.

Reliable estimates of the amount and quality of available resources are necessary to determine what can reasonably be attained by your firm. This step in the planning process involves nothing more than simply taking stock of your business. You must identify the financial, physical, human, and intangible assets it owns or is capable of acquiring. To do so, you have to be a financial Sherlock Holmes and piece together information from a number of sources, including:

- The tools of financial analysis, which will provide a wealth of information on your firm's financial position, and the trend of its key financial indicators.

- Your firm's banker or other creditors, who can provide an indication of its current and future credit capacity.

- Professional appraisers, technicians, or engineers, who can provide estimates, when necessary, on the quality, economic life, and productivity of your firm's physical assets.

- Trade journals, government publications, and specific engineering journals, that can provide estimates on the nature and rate of technological changes that affect your industry or your firm's assets.

- Your employees, whose proficiency can be determined from your own evaluations, the opinion of a hired consultant, or comparisons with published productivity data or the experience of similar firms.

4. Develop Plans.

The plans you develop for your firm should take two basic forms: strategic and operating. A strategic plan is broad in scope, covers a long time frame, and establishes the basic mission, purpose, and overall direction for your firm. It involves making decisions on how, where, and when the major resources will be deployed to establish your firm's products, markets, and risk exposure. There are several approaches to developing a strategic plan, but one very effective method involves providing answers to a series of searching questions, such as:

- What is the basic mission of your firm — what is its purpose, what can it reasonably be expected to accomplish, and what must be done or changed to accomplish it?

- What is the basic philosophy of your business — do you emphasize price, quality, service, customer satisfaction, convenience, etc., and is this philosophy still appropriate? What relationship do I want with my employees, customers, creditors, etc. and what policy changes would improve these relationships?

- What image does your firm now project — prestige, service, quality, price, reliability, etc., and is this what you want it to project?

- How do your customers, suppliers, employees, and competitors regard the business? Are their perceptions and opinions consistent with your concept of the firm's mission, philosophy, and image?

- What is the basic business of your firm? Is this approach to doing business still appropriate, or are things changing to the extent that your basic business must be re-evaluated and changed?

- What products or product lines are necessary to conduct this business, and what would be necessary to meet changing needs?

- Are the resources of your firm adequate to conduct this type of business effectively? If not, what is required? Does your firm have the financial capability to obtain these resources?

- What changes are taking place (economic, competitive, social, or legal) that will have a significant impact on your business in the future?

- What will be the basic business of your firm in the future (e.g., one year, three years, and five years from now), and what resources will be required for its operation? Will the firm have the financial capability to obtain these resources?

- What are the strengths and weaknesses of your firm, and what must be done to correct the weaknesses and build on the strengths? Will the firm have the financial capability to overcome weaknesses and build on strengths?

- What markets does your business serve, and what markets will be served in the future? What changes must be made to move into future markets?

- Who are your customers and is this customer base stable or changing? Which additional customer groups can be attracted, and what must be done to attract them?

- Who will be your customers one, three, and five years from now? What products or services will be required to serve these customers?

- Where do you want your firm to be one year, three years, and five years from now? What must be done to get there?

Operating plans are the detailed programs that specify how your firm will achieve its objectives. Operating plans, as opposed to strategic plans, are narrow in scope, cover a short time frame of usually one year, and are prepared for each individual segment of your firm's operations. These plans usually take the form of budgets such as marketing, production, personnel, and cash budgets.

A budget is simply an operating plan expressed in terms of numbers. The numbers represent specific targets the firm expects to meet, the contribution that each part of the business makes toward meeting them, and the expenditures required to carry out the plan. When the separate budgets have been finalized, they should be coordinated into an overall, or master, operating plan.

Since all activity in your firm is predicated on sales, the operational planning process starts with your estimate of a reasonable range for total sales for the upcoming budget period. Given the sales estimate, budgets can be established for each segment of your firm's operations. For example, the personnel budget reflects estimates of manpower and training needs; the purchasing budget details estimated inventory and physical asset requirements; the marketing budget reflects estimates of when, where, and how much advertising and promotion is required to support the sales estimate; and the cash budget and pro forma statements detail the amount and timing of the financing required to implement planned activity.

An important part of the operational planning process is financial planning. Through financial planning, the various operating budgets as well as the comprehensive master budget are evaluated to determine if the financing necessary to implement planned activity is available or can be obtained. Through financial analysis and planning, an estimate is made of the amount of financing that will be generated internally from operating cash flows, and the amount that must be raised externally through trade creditors, lenders, or additional owner's capital. If sufficient financing cannot be obtained, planned operations must be scaled to a level consistent with available funding.

When operating plans have been determined to be financially feasible, the planning period of one year is divided into short budget intervals such as months or weeks. Short budget periods make it convenient to schedule activities, monitor progress toward objectives, take remedial action before crises develop, and alter plans when conditions have changed significantly.

5. Develop Alternatives.

Although the forecast and plans you prepare represent the best estimate of future conditions (the most likely case) and intended activity, you must act as if forecasting error is inevitable. Unfortunately, in an uncertain world this will be the case. Regardless of how informed the forecast and meticulous the plans, the future cannot be known with complete certainty.

The way to deal effectively with forecasting error is to consider alternative conditions and alternative responses to these conditions in advance. To do so, you employ what is referred to as "what if" or scenario analysis. This technique involves preparing estimated ranges for forecast variables and planned activity.

For example, you may prepare three sets of forecasts and plans. One set would reflect the most likely or expected conditions; the second, the most optimistic; and the third, the most pessimistic. The advance preparation provided by this approach eliminates the likelihood of unpleasant surprises. You have contingency plans that can be implemented as changes are signaled.

6. Monitor Results.

As suggested above, the planning process does not end when budgets are prepared. In fact, control, a critical phase of the management process, is just beginning. Control means comparing actual results for a given budget period with what was planned. When major deviations between actual and planned activities are discovered, it must be determined whether remedial action can correct the problem, or whether actual conditions are so different from forecast conditions that a change in plans is necessary. Through control, you stay abreast of changes as they develop and provide the time necessary to implement alternative responses in an orderly fashion.

The Benefits from Planning

At this point you may be wondering, "All this sounds good, but if I am going to invest valuable time and effort into planning, what is the payoff?" The answer is: bottom-line benefits.

It has been shown repeatedly that firms, both small and large, engaged in formal planning produce better returns (ROI) than those that do not plan on a systematic basis. Increased ROI is reflected in improved profit margins, improved asset turnover, or some combination of both. This means greater cash flows and long-run profits for the firm.

What is it about planning that creates better performance? Good planning produces benefits, such as:

- All of your firm's activities are coordinated and focused toward commonly understood goals.

- Planning forces you to identify and monitor the behavior of the factors that are critical to your firm's success. Doing so minimizes the possibility that day-to-day pressures will cause you to lose sight of what is important for the business.

- Preparing plans produces measurable goals and objectives that make it possible to evaluate progress. By knowing where your firm should be going and the progress it is making, you know where and when either remedial action or a change in plan must take place.

■ Preparing forecasts and plans is the only effective approach to dealing with uncertainty. The planning process forces you into "what if" questioning of possible alternative futures. Dealing with contingencies before the fact allows quick response to change, and eliminates panic solutions to crisis situations. There is a lot of truth to the old management adage, "If a manager is continually fighting brush fires, there is no management of the firm."

In short, good planning improves the performance of your firm, reduces its risk exposure, and makes you a more competent manager. It is this combination that produces tangible, bottom-line benefits.

Financial planning is the process through which the operating plans of your firm are converted into estimates of the financial resources required to carry them out. The process consists of three crucial steps: 1) translating operating plans into their financial consequences through the preparation of a cash budget or pro forma financial statements; 2) using these tools to estimate the amounts and timing of the financing that will come from internal and external sources; and 3) preparing a financial plan that schedules when and where external financing will be obtained.

What Is Financial Planning?

As you may suspect, financial planning for your firm is not very different from the process of planning and managing your household finances. Because the funds in the household cookie jar are limited, there are limits on the expenditures that can be made and the number of wants that can be satisfied. Yet competing demands are placed on these scarce funds by various family members who have seemingly unlimited wants and their own ideas on how money should be spent. In order to maximize the total family benefits that can be obtained from available funds, expenditures must be carefully planned.

A similar situation exists in your business. Available financial resources serve as the basic raw material for operating the business. Since your firm's stock of financial resources is limited, there is a limit on the level of competing or alternative operating activities that can be financed. Careful planning is required to ensure that funds are used wisely. The more efficiently available financial resources are allocated among competing spending opportunities, the greater the number of needs that can be satisfied, and the more improved your firm's cash flows and profits.

Financial planning is a system within a system. It is both an important part of your firm's overall planning effort, and a self-contained process consisting of a series of coordinated steps. These are:

How Financial Planning Is Done

1. Prepare a Sales Forecast.

While the suggestion that financial planning starts with a sales forecast may come as a surprise, it is true. All activity in a firm is predicated on sales or the prospect of sales. Without sales there simply is no activity — purchases of inventory and equipment are not made, labor is not hired, and there are no cash flows. It is the anticipation of sales activity that gives rise to operating plans, the necessity for financing, and management of the resulting cash flows.

2. Evaluate Plans for Financial Consequences.

Before strategic and operating plans are implemented, a careful assessment should be made to determine whether the resources required to fulfill expectations will be available. Even the most well-designed plans are unattainable paper estimates without the necessary financing. To be realistic, plans must pass the test of financial feasibility.

The two most important tools used for this purpose are the cash budget and pro forma financial statements. The cash budget is the principal tool used in the short-term financial planning process. It is the vehicle through which planned operations are translated into a period-by-period estimate of cash inflows and outflows. The completed cash budget for a given planning period provides you with a picture of the cash flow consequences of planned operations. Armed with this information, you are able to estimate and plan for the amount and timing of the cash flow from operations that will be available to meet financing needs, the amount and timing of funds that must be raised outside your firm, and the repayment schedule for any external financing used.

Pro forma statements are financial statements (balance sheet and income statements) that reflect assumed rather than historical events. For planning purposes, the assumptions used to prepare the statements are a firm's strategic and operating plans. The resulting pro forma statements provide a financial profile of a firm. This profile shows the impact that planned operations will have on a firm's financial performance and financial position. Together, the cash budget and pro forma statements provide the information necessary to formulate a firm's financial plan.

3. Formulate a Financial Plan.

A firm's financial plan is a blueprint or program detailing expected financial flows. It should consist of:

- An analysis of how the required financing will be used to support planned operations. This includes details on planned expenditures for both working capital (increases in inventory, accounts receivable, payroll, etc.) and fixed assets (buildings, equipment, vehicles, etc.).

- An estimate of the amount and timing of the cash flow from operations needed to meet financing needs. Available cash flow is cash flow from planned operations less expected owner's withdrawals.

- An estimate of the amount and timing of external financing that will be needed to supplement available cash flow from operations.

- An analysis of the types of external financing to be raised. This includes an estimate of the maturity of the financing needed (short-term versus long-term), and the type and proportions of financing needed (debt versus owner's equity).

- A detailed schedule showing how and when external financing will be repaid.

- A negotiated commitment from the suppliers of the required external financing.

- An estimate of the profitability and financial position of a firm as a result of planned operations.

The financial plan is simply a business plan, either operating or strategic, converted to financial requirements. Remember, an important part of financial planning is assessing the financial feasibility of planned operations. The financial plan is the finalized expression of this process. The cash budget and pro forma statements are the tools used to make the assessment and to provide the information required to prepare the financial plan. See chapters 8 and 9.

Since the financial planning process begins with and depends on the sales forecast, you need to take a closer look at this important activity.

Sales Forecasting

Forecasting is the art of estimating future sales for the period or periods in your planning horizon. Good sales forecasting is a two-step process: 1) establishing an initial forecast value or values; and 2) adjusting the forecast to reflect expected conditions. The initial forecast is fine-tuned using your experience, judgment, and knowledge of the environmental factors that affect your firm's sales.

The starting point for the sales forecast is a realistic estimate of future sales. This estimate is usually obtained from historical sales data. In many cases, what has happened in the past provides some indication of what may happen in the future. When this is true, initial sales estimates can be obtained by extending or extrapolating from a trend of historical sales values.

A trend is simply a line of average relationships. Through the averaging process, fluctuations in sales caused by any seasonal or random factors affecting a firm are eliminated, and the sales pattern is represented as a smoothed line, or trend line. Though the trend line ignores variations in a firm's sales pattern such as normal seasonal fluctuations in activity, it does offer a reasonable starting point for the forecast.

The second step in the sales forecasting process involves adjusting the projected trend line for your estimate of the future set of conditions (economic, industry, competitive, etc.) that will affect sales for the firm. A projected trend is simply a mechanical extrapolation of an averaged set of historical conditions; conversely, a forecast is an informed estimate of the future. Unless it is reasonable to assume that past conditions will again prevail over the entire planning horizon, any projected trend values should be adjusted to reflect expected conditions. The adjustments include consideration of such factors as:

- **Expected Economic Conditions.** The trend line should be adjusted to reflect an estimate of how the expected direction of the economy (recession, prosperity, etc.) will affect a firm's industry and markets. Reputable forecasts by professional economists are widely published in a variety of business, industry, and trade association periodicals. A consensus of these forecasts will serve as a good working estimate of the short-term (up to one year) and long-term (one to three years) direction of the economy.

- **Expected Direction and Intensity of Key Variables.** Sales estimates should also be adjusted for expected changes in the key factors that affect a firm. For example, if your firm's sales are sensitive to interest rates, as was the case in the example of the residential construction firm, the initial sales estimate should reflect expected changes in interest rates.

- **Seasonal Influences.** Extrapolated or projected trend values are the result of a smoothing or averaging process. Often, this smoothing process removes evidence of seasonal or other rhythmic fluctuations that occur in a sales pattern. If your business is subject to seasonal variations, the projected trend line should be adjusted up or down for these seasonal influences. For example, if your firm's sales during the spring and summer seasons are above average and the fall and winter months are below average, projected trend values would be adjusted up for seasonal peak months, and down for the slower periods.

- **Anticipated Changes in the Firm's Markets.** Any anticipated changes in competitive conditions in the market for the firm's products or services must be reflected in the sales estimate. For example, if events such as new product developments, the encroachment of new competition, changing demographics, or a changing customer base are anticipated, they must be factored into the initial sales estimate.

■ **Planned Changes.** The sales estimates must also be adjusted for the influence that strategic and operating plans will have on a firm's sales. For example, if you plan such actions as a major promotion and advertising campaign, the introduction of new products or product lines, or a change in location, the impact of these factors on the sales forecast must be taken into consideration.

A Useful Approach to Projecting Sales

The tools available for projecting historical sales range from naive trend calculations to sophisticated mathematical or computer models. (See the card enclosed at the back of this book for more information on financial models software.) The most straightforward approach to generating a trend of forecast values is to assume that historical values from some previous time period will repeat themselves in the future. For example, if actual sales for the first three months of 19X2 had been $1,000, $2,000, and $3,000, the initial forecast values for the first three months of the 19X3 planning horizon would be $1,000, $2,000, and $3,000.

A more effective approach to generating the initial forecast value(s) is the smoothed-trend technique. This requires nothing more than basic arithmetic and, if so desired, a pocket calculator.

The smoothed-trend technique is a simple averaging process that produces an extrapolated or extended trend line from a series of historical data. The new forecast (trend) value for each period is calculated as the sum of the previous forecast figure and a smoothing value, multiplied by the amount of error in the previous forecast. The smoothing value is any number between 0 and 1, and the forecast error is the difference between the last actual value and the last forecast value.

New Forecast Value = Previous Forecast Value + Smoothing Value
x (Last Actual Value – Last Forecast Value)

For example, assume the owner of a taxicab service is forecasting the number of passengers that will be carried by the firm's cabs next week. If the forecast of the number of passengers last week was 1,000, the actual number carried was 1,050, and the smoothing value .5, then the forecast value for the upcoming week would be calculated as:

New Forecast Value = 1000 + .5 x (1050 – 1000)
= 1000 + .5 x (50)
= 1000 + 25
= 1,025 passengers

The value of the smoothing value in this example, .5, was chosen arbitrarily. In practice, the smoothing value must be decided by the planner. Unfortunately, there is no rule of thumb by which the choice can be made; the appropriate smoothing value depends on the given historical data series. Values close to 1, such as .7, .8, or .9 exhibit wide fluctuations in the values. Conversely, smaller values such as .2, .3, or .4 provide a smoother trend if there is little fluctuation in the series.

Calculating a Smoothed Trend

Assume that the monthly sales data for your firm's forecasting process is contained on Table 7.2, below. Actual or historical data appear in the second column of the table, and sales forecasts based on a .5 smoothing value in the third column. Assume further that it is now December 19X2, that your forecasting and planning horizon is for the year 19X3, and that your operating and financial plans require monthly sales forecast values. To learn how the forecast figures were calculated, look at the first two months of data from the following table.

Table 7.2 Smoothed-Trend Forecasts with a .5 Smoothing Value

Month	Historical Sales	Forecast Value
January 19X2	$4,189	$ –
February	3,390	4,189
March	3,840	4,060
April	4,077	3,950
May	4,280	4,013
June	4,410	4,147
July	4,100	4,278
August	3,800	4,189
September	4,105	3,995
October	4,390	4,050
November	4,473	4,220
December	4,525	4,346
January 19X3	–	4,436

This table contains hypothetical sales data which is used in an illustration of the "Smoothed-Trend" forecasting technique.

It would be impossible to calculate a forecast value for February because there is no previous forecast value for January 19X2 from which to calculate forecast error (last historical value minus last forecast value). In order to have a starting point for the forecast, therefore, the first historical value is substituted for the first forecast value. In this example, the first actual value, $4,189 from the January 19X2 Historical Sales column is copied to the second row, February, in the Forecast Value column. Given this proxy for the initial forecast value and the actual sales value for February when it becomes available, the forecast for March 19X2 can be made using the smoothed-trend calculation.

March Forecast Value = Previous Forecast Value + Smoothing Value
                           x (Last Actual Value – Last Forecast Value)

March Forecast Value = $4,189 + .5 x ($3,930 – $4,189)
                     = $4,189 + .5 x ($-259)
                     = $4,189 + ($-129)
                     = $4,060

When the actual March 19X2 sales figure ($3,840) is available, the forecast value for April 19X2 can be made.

April Forecast Value = $4,060 + .5 x ($3,840 – $4,060)
                     = $4,060 + .5 x ($-220)
                     = $4,060 + ($-110)
                     = $3,950

Each of the remaining forecast values on Table 7.2 were derived in the same manner. Note, however, that only one monthly forecast value, January, is available for the 19X3 planning horizon. The reasons for this are 1) the absence of actual or historical values after December 19X2, (December was assumed to be the month during which forecasting and planning for 19X3 is taking place) and 2) the simple smoothed-trend technique is capable of generating values for only one period in advance. This limitation does not pose a serious problem for the required initial forecast since the trend line is easily extrapolated. To learn how to extend the trend line for the remaining 11 months (or whatever number of periods desired), there is another, simpler calculation.

For each additional period the trend line must be extended, add to the latest forecast value the difference between the latest forecast value and the previous forecast value.

Extrapolating the Trend Line

Extended Forecast Value = Last Forecast
                          + (Last Forecast – Previous Forecast)

Using this calculation, the trend value for February 19X3 is:

February Forecast Value = $4,436 + ($4,436 – $4,346)
                        = $4,436 + $90
                        = $4,526

Trend-line values for the remaining periods would be calculated using the same procedure. For example, the trend value for March 19X3 is:

March Forecast Value = $4,526 + ($4,526 – $4,436)
                     = $4,526 + $90
                     = $4,616

Things to Remember

Two important points concerning the extrapolated trend line should be kept in mind. First, the accuracy of the trend line can be improved if it is recalculated when new actual data becomes available. In the illustration above, for example, the forecast for February 19X3 can be recalculated and the new trend line extended when actual sales for the month of January are tabulated.

Second, remember that a mechanical projection is not the forecast, it is only the starting point for the forecast. It is a figure or figures with which you can work to produce the forecast. The initial forecast must be adjusted for both expected conditions, and the normal seasonal factors affecting your firm.

A Final Thought on Planning

A systematic approach to financial planning will provide, in addition to the benefits already discussed, convincing answers to the often penetrating questions posed by your firm's banker when responding to a loan request. How many times, for example, have you heard your banker ask questions, such as: For what specific purposes are the funds needed? Exactly how much do you need? For how long will you need the funds? How and when will you be able to repay the loan? What happens if things do not work out as planned? Sound strategic, operational and financial planning provide the information necessary to answer these questions. Having solid plans for alternative sets of conditions sends a clear message to your banker: The financial reins of your firm are in the hands of competent management.

Where to Now?

Since much of this book deals with the subject of cash flow, it may come as no surprise that the first financial planning concept to be explored is the cash budget. Cash flow is the lifeblood of any firm, and the cash budget is the most effective tool for planning and controlling cash flows. Hopefully, it will become the mainstay of your planning effort.

Chapter 8
Cash Planning with the Cash Budget

While the accounting concept of net income is a good indicator of long-term financial progress, a firm's financial health is dependent on cash flow. In view of the importance of cash flow, cash planning is a critical management function. It provides answers to questions such as:

- During what periods will your firm experience cash deficits, and when will it enjoy surplus cash?

- Will planned activity require financing?

- If financing is required, what amount is needed and when must these funds be available?

- What proportion of the required financing will be generated internally, and what proportion must be raised outside the firm?

- What is the impact on your firm's cash position and financing requirements if the most optimistic or the most pessimistic set of conditions occur during the planning horizon?

To understand why cash planning is so important to your business, consider what can happen if cash planning is not done and unexpected cash shortages occur. In this situation, you are faced with the unpleasant choices of slowing down cash outflows, dipping into available financial reserves, or obtaining emergency financing.

The typical method of slowing outflows during periods of cash shortage is to delay payments to trade suppliers. This can be a costly alternative. Late payments may prompt suppliers to delay inventory shipments, or place your firm on a "cash only" basis. The result would be lost sales or costly production delays, or both. Slow payment practices may also become known to other lenders, credit rating agencies, or even your firm's customers. This would damage your firm's credit rating, its ability to borrow, and customers may be lost to competitors, if they question your firm's financial stability.

If your firm attempts to obtain emergency financing under crisis conditions, the wrong message is signaled to lenders. First, the lender may be reluctant to grant a loan to relieve a crisis created by management shortcomings. Second, if granted, the loan would only be made under highly restrictive terms and prohibitive interest costs. Third, and most important, the lender would have little confidence in your ability to plan. This would adversely affect your firm's ability to obtain financing in the future.

Alternatively, if emergency reserves are depleted, your firm's financial strength is reduced. This makes you more vulnerable to further financial shocks, and can also have an adverse affect on your credit rating and ability to borrow.

Cash planning is the tool that minimizes the likelihood of difficult choices such as these, and will be discussed in greater detail in this chapter.

TOPIC	CONCEPTS DISCUSSED
Cash Planning	What is cash planning, and what benefits does it produce?
	The tools used for long- and short-term cash planning.
	The information produced by cash planning.
The Cash Budget	What is a cash budget?
	How to choose the cash budget format and estimate cash flows.
	What information the cash budget provides, and how to interpret this information.
	How to deal with the uncertainty associated with cash budgeting.

What Is Cash Planning?

Cash planning is simply the two-stage process of estimating and planning the firm's expected operating and non-operating cash flows over a specific time horizon. This process is the essence of financial planning. Cash forecasting provides you with the opportunity to examine the impact that operating plans will have on your firm's cash position, to identify the amount and timing of financing needs, to make advance preparation for obtaining needed financing, and to maintain control over cash flows as they occur.

The Time Frame for Cash Planning

The planning horizon over which cash projections are made is divisible into either long or short time frames. Extended planning horizons, which are characterized by greater uncertainty and involve broad-based strategic and operating plans, require only rough approximations of financing needs. These estimates may be made with projected, or pro forma, financial statements. This approach to long-term financial planning is the subject of the next chapter.

Over short planning horizons (one year or less), forecasting error is typically reduced, and operating and cash plans can be formulated with sufficient detail to implement and control scheduled activities. Cash forecasts and plans take the form of detailed cash receipts and disbursement statements. These statements, known as *cash budgets*, are typically prepared for each of the meaningful subperiods or budget intervals (weeks or months) that constitute the short-term planning horizon (usually one year).

Cash planning is the most vital management activity in which you can engage. The following benefits are derived through cash planning.

The Importance of Cash Planning

- You are provided with a clear understanding of the key factors affecting your firm and its cash position.

- You remain alert to changes that impact your firm's cash position.

- You are in a position to formulate more convincing financing proposals.

- You gain the experience and judgment required to improve the quality of the overall planning effort.

Each of these stated benefits are explored in greater detail below.

Cash planning forces you to identify, evaluate, and monitor the variables that are vital to your firm's success. The insights provided by this involvement increase your understanding of the business. The more you know about the nature and behavior of the factors affecting your firm and its operations, the more effectively all activities, including cash flows, can be forecasted, planned, and controlled.

Understanding the Behavior of Key Variables

For example, financial analysis focuses attention on a firm's cash cycle. As discussed in Chapter 4, the cash cycle is the length of time elapsed between the purchase and payment of inventory (raw materials or merchandise inventory), and the eventual receipt of cash from the collection of accounts receivable. With an understanding of the cash cycle, you are in a position to evaluate and plan for the cash flow effects of changes in sales, inventory, production procedures, receivables levels, and payment practices. Understanding your firm's cash cycle also provides help in deciding the maturity structure of the financing needed to support it.

Changes in the economic, competitive, and social environment in which a small firm operates provide the opportunity for success as well as the possibility of failure. Your task is to anticipate and capitalize on

Monitoring the Environment

change. Through a formalized approach to cash planning, you are forced to monitor factors that lead to changes in your firm's environment. This information enables you to develop realistic assumptions about alternative futures, and to perform meaningful "what if" analysis. Understanding and planning for change is the only rational way to deal with and take advantage of its impact.

Preparing Sound Financing Proposals

The *cash plan* is an important part of the financing process. First, the cash planning exercise puts you in touch with the realities of a loan request. Cash forecasting and planning provide a clear understanding of the amount of funds needed, the specific purposes for which the funds will be needed, the length of time for which the funds will be needed (maturity of the loan), and how the financing will be repaid. These issues are of key concern to any prospective lender.

Second, a sound cash plan increases your credibility. Lenders are acutely aware of the small firm manager stereotype — overburdened and administratively deficient. This image is substantiated when a loan request is poorly prepared and undocumented. On the other hand, lender confidence in the firm's manager is bolstered when a sound, well-documented, detailed cash plan accompanies the loan request.

Controlling Cash

A cash plan also serves as the standard against which actual operations can be measured. By comparing actual cash flows from operations to budgeted cash flows, you can measure your firm's progress, and determine where adjustments, if any, are needed. These efforts ensure that scarce cash resources are utilized as efficiently as possible.

Cash planning and control are companion activities. Through cash planning, you identify and plan for the factors that are vital to your firm's success. Control is a learning experience. By identifying the reasons for major differences between actual cash flows and expectations, you increase your understanding of how key factors impact your firm. Increased understanding means a better cash forecast, and an improved cash forecast means a better cash plan.

The Nature of the Cash Budget

The *cash budget* is a period-by-period estimate of the amount and timing of the cash flows produced by planned operations. It usually covers a planning horizon of one year, which is divided into shorter subperiods or budget intervals, such as months or weeks.

Cash budget estimates include both operating and non-operating cash flows. As discussed in chapters 2 and 3, operating cash flows are those associated with normal operations of a firm. Non-operating cash flows consist of all other cash-related investment, financing, and dividend activity.

Both operating and non-operating cash projections are combined as either cash inflows (receipts) or cash outflows (disbursements). Cash inflows consist of any transaction that causes cash to flow into the firm. These include:

- The cash receipts produced by normal operations — cash sales and the collection of accounts receivable.

- The cash receipts arising from non-operating sources, such as the sale of a fixed asset, a tax refund, or income earned on investments.

Cash outflows include:

- The cash disbursements associated with normal operations: payments to trade creditors (accounts payable), payments for cash operating expenses, and tax payments.

- The cash disbursements associated with investment, financing, and dividend activities: interest and principal payments associated with debt obligations, fixed asset purchases, and owner's withdrawals (dividend payments).

The last section of the budget details the beginning cash balance, total cash for the period, the minimum cash balance requirement set by managers, and the cash shortage or surplus for the period. Each of these budget sections will be discussed in detail.

A Word on Estimating Cash Flows

It is important to note that accrued revenue and expense items that appear on the traditional income statement (see Chapter 1) are not included on the cash budget. The cash budget is a forecast of cash inflows and outflows, and cash flows are often unrelated to revenue and expense items in the short run. The following set of rules should help distinguish between the two concepts when preparing your firm's cash budget:

- The depreciation expense figure shown on the traditional income statement is a noncash expense item that is not included on the cash budget. Recall that a check is never written to pay depreciation expense.

- Cash sales appear as a cash inflow on the cash budget; credit sales do not appear on the cash budget. A credit sale is not a cash flow until the receivable is collected. Thus, only the estimated collection pattern on accounts receivable appears as cash inflows on the cash budget.

- Purchases made for cash appear as a cash outflow on the cash budget; purchases made on credit (accounts payable) do not. A purchase made on credit does not become a cash flow until payment on the account is actually made. Thus, only the estimated payment pattern on accounts payable appears as cash outflows on the cash budget.

- Total debt payments (interest and principal) appear on the cash budget in the period in which the payment will be made. Note that the traditional income statement shows the interest portion of the payment as an expense of the period, but not the portion attributed to the repayment of principal.

- The cash flows associated with cost of sales and normal operating expenses are treated on the budget as cash outflows for the period in which they are expected to be paid. The accrued expenses that appear on the traditional income statement are not included on the budget. Recall that an accrued expense item, such as accrued wages or taxes, is the accounting recognition of an obligation of an expense that has been incurred but not paid.

The rule for choosing cash flow items to include on the budget can be simplified: A cash flow is any activity that causes the cash account to increase or decrease. It is these estimated cash activities that are data for the cash budget.

Preparing the Cash Budget: Choosing the Budget Format

Selecting an appropriate cash budget format requires decisions on the number of cash flow classifications to be used, the length of the planning horizon, and the number of subperiods or intervals into which the planning horizon will be divided.

Cash Flow Categories

There is no universal formula for establishing the degree of aggregation or detail in the cash flow items selected for display on the cash budget. The number of cash flow categories selected is a matter of judgment, and should be determined by the size and importance of the item involved, and the needs of the planner. For example, if tracking the individual items that make up a firm's utility expense (telephone, electricity, gas, etc.) is not important for cost control, then these items can be lumped into one cash outflow figure (utility costs) on the budget. If, on the other hand, power usage is a closely monitored component of production cost, or telephone expense is a important component of sales cost, then these items would be put into separate outflow categories to facilitate cost control.

The Length of the Planning Horizon

The choice of an appropriate planning horizon for the cash budget is usually made by default. Since the cash budget is the vehicle through which operating plans are converted to financial requirements, the planning horizon of the cash budget should coincide with that of the operational planning effort. Most often this is equivalent to a firm's fiscal year.

The choice of an appropriate subperiod or budget interval is also a matter of judgment. It is determined by the amount of cash flow expected by a firm, and the stability of its operations. The greater the amount of cash that flows through a firm, the more important it becomes to carefully plan and monitor cash activity. Thus, the larger the volume of cash flows, the shorter the budget interval should be. Likewise, as volatility or uncertainty in a firm's operations increases, shorter budget intervals are needed to plan and monitor cash flows. In the case of most small firms, however, monthly budget intervals are usually appropriate.

The problem of choosing appropriate subperiods for the cash budget planning horizon is best resolved by using an approach known as *progressive budgeting*. This technique is based on two simple principles:

- The nearer the period being forecast, the shorter the budget interval should be.

- Budgeting is done on a continuous basis by dropping from the budget the subperiod most recently completed, and adding a new forecast subperiod to the end of the planning horizon.

For example, assume your cash budget planning horizon covers your firm's fiscal year, which begins in December. The most immediate forecast periods, December, January, and February, would be treated as monthly estimates. The remaining nine months may be aggregated into three quarterly totals.

As business for each of the first three months (December, January, and February successively) is actually completed, that month would be dropped from the budget and cash flow estimates for the most distant quarter (January, February, and March) added to the end of the planning horizon. When the first three monthly periods have been completed, the upcoming quarter is divided into monthly estimates, and the last three months aggregated into quarterly totals.

Through this approach, the upcoming quarter is always expressed in monthly intervals, and successive quarters are continuously rolled through the planning horizon. This "rolling" or progressive approach to budgeting provides three important benefits from the planning effort.

- First, by doing cash budgeting on a continuous basis, cash planning remains a management priority.

- Second, continuous involvement in cash planning keeps you alert to any changes in the trend of factors affecting cash.

- Third, the up-to-date information gleaned from comparing forecast and actual cash flows for the most recently completed subperiod puts your firm in a position to either react to adverse events before the crisis stage is reached, or to take advantage of

Budget Intervals

developing opportunities. (Recall the discussion of management control in the previous chapter.)

Getting Started

Technically, the cash budgeting process begins with a sales forecast and an estimate of the collection pattern on accounts receivable. For the first-time planner, however, it is probably wise to begin by examining the past. This means organizing historical cash flows for one or more fiscal periods into the subperiods of your selected cash budget format.

Plugging historical cash flows into their proper budget classifications provides several important benefits, such as:

- You learn how to collect cash flow data for budget preparation.

- You gain valuable experience on how to interpret the cash budget.

- You increase your insight into how cash flow items behave, and what factors determine this behavior. This understanding improves the quality of the cash forecast, and makes the task considerably easier.

- You learn how to maintain cash control. This means comparing actual cash flows for a completed budget interval with forecast cash flows, and identifying the reasons behind major deviations.

Estimating Cash Inflows: Forecasting Sales

The major challenge in cash budget preparation is producing realistic estimates of cash inflows from cash sales and the collection of accounts receivable. Since both projections depend on sales, the cash budgeting process begins with a forecast of this key variable. It is important to note, however, that such estimates are only a starting point for the sales forecast. They should be adjusted for anticipated changes in conditions surrounding a firm or its environment, and for the impact of planned operations.

Estimating the Cash Flow Produced by Cash Sales

Following completion of the sales forecast, estimates of the proportion of sales that will be made for cash, and the collection pattern of accounts receivable must be made. The basis for these estimates is the firm's historical pattern of cash sales, and its collection experience.

The cash sales estimates are made by applying an expected cash sales percentage to the forecast sales figures for each subperiod in the budget. The estimated cash sales percentage is easily established using the following steps:

- Select a representative sample of historical sales figures for the periods that correspond to the subperiods in your cash budget. For example, if your budget spans an entire year in monthly intervals, compile historical sales figures by month for the years, quarters, or seasons that correspond to those in the planning horizon.

- Identify the amount of sales for each period that were made for cash, and convert these amounts to percentages. That is, divide the dollar amount of cash sales for each period by total sales for that period.

  Cash Sales Percentage = Dollars of Cash Sales ÷ Total Sales

- Average the percentages and use the average as the forecast cash sales percentage. That is, total the percentage values from like periods and divide by the number of periods in that total.

  Forecast Cash Sales Percentage = Total Cash Sales Percentages
  ÷ Total Number of Periods

Historical sales data is obtained from sales records. If your firm has an in-house accounting system, the necessary information can be gleaned from the sales journal. If not, the data is available from such sources as customer receipts, cash register tapes, or the sales summary sheets.

Estimating the Cash Flow Produced by Receivables

The estimated cash inflow from the collection of accounts receivable is determined by applying collection pattern percentages to the forecast sales values for each period. These percentages represent the proportion of a given period's sales that is expected to be collected in each subsequent period. For example, an estimated collection pattern of 30%, 50%, and 20% means that 30% of sales from a given month should be collected in that month; 50% in the month following the month of sale; and 20% in two months following the month of sale.

The collection pattern percentages can be established using information from your firm's historical sales and receivables records, and a technique known as the *payments pattern approach*. The payments pattern approach uses customer receipts data to determine the percentage of customers that pay at various times after the date of sale. For example, if your cash budget is divided into monthly intervals, you would compile historical credit sales by month, and then use customer payment records to identify the percentage of a given month's credit sales that have been collected in that and subsequent months.

The collection pattern percentages are easily established using the following steps:

- Select a representative sample of historical credit sales figures for periods that correspond to the subperiods in your cash budget. For example, if your budget spans an entire year in monthly intervals, compile historical sales figures by month.

It is important to keep the following point in mind when amassing the historical credit sales figures to be evaluated: If your business is seasonal or sales fluctuate significantly during the year, the pattern of credit sales and collections will not be the same for each month. It is important that collection pattern percentages represent similar periods. For example, the percentages used to estimate collections for June, the first quarter, or the fall holiday season should be derived from their historical counterparts.

- Historical credit sales for each period should be separated into individual customer components. This must be done to identify the percentage of customers that pay at various times after the date of sale. In order to keep the data manageable, you can usually combine the accounts that represent only a minor portion of your firm's business into one total amount. The behavior of larger accounts should be tracked separately.

- Trace individual customer payments made on credit sales (customer purchases) for a given month. These payments would then be converted to percentages of that month's credit sales.

To illustrate these steps, examine Avanti's credit sales for the month of May. During this month, sales and service revenues totaled $28,500. Credit sales were $25,365, or 89% of the total, and cash sales made up the remaining $3,135, or 11% of the total. The breakdown of credit sales by customer is shown on Table 8.1.

Table 8.1 The Avanti Company's Credit Sales for May

Customer	May Purchases
Peacock's Paint Centers	$10,600
Debi D's	5,300
Azalea City Rental	4,200
Mecca Corporation	3,800
All Other Credit Sales	1,465
Total Credit Sales for May	$25,365

The customer purchases data in this table is used to illustrate the "Payments Pattern Approach" to estimating accounts receivable collection pattern percentages. The Payments Pattern Approach uses customer purchases and payment data to determine the percentage of customers that pay at various times after the date of sale.

Further analysis revealed the following customer payment pattern on credit sales made in May. Note that the dollar amounts represent collections on sales originating in May. Remember, the goal is to associate payments with a given month's sales.

Table 8.2 Customer Payments on Purchases Made During May

Customer	May	June	July	August
Peacock's Paint Centers	$ -	$ -	$10,600	$ -
Debi D's	-	5,300	-	-
Azalea City Rental	-	3,500	700	
Mecca Corporation	-	-	2,800	1,000
All Other Credit Sales	1,300	165	-	-
Total Payments	$1,300	$8,965	$14,100	$1,000
Percentage of May Sales	5%	35%	56%	4%

This table organizes payment data for purchases made during May by the firm's key customers. Organizing payment data in this manner allows managers to associate payments with credit sales for a given month.

The collection pattern for May sales is indicated by the percentages in the last row of the table. The 5% figure ($1,300 divided by $25,365) represents either the proportion of cash sales for the month, or the proportion of credit sales that were made and collected in that month. The remaining percentages reflect the monthly lag in collecting credit sales for May. The 35% ($8,965 divided by $25,365) figure represents the proportion of May's sales collected one month from the date of sale; the 56% figure ($14,100 divided by $25,365) represents the proportion collected with a two-month lag; and the 4% figure ($1,000 divided by $25,365) represents the proportion collected with a three-month lag.

To obtain the collection pattern percentages that will be used in preparing the cash budget, Avanti's management would collect data from additional historical periods; make the collection pattern calculations; and average these percentages. This procedure is illustrated in Table 8.3.

The months used in these calculations were chosen by Avanti's management because they reflect similar seasonal influences. The collection pattern percentage for each category is a simple arithmetic average of the six values in that category. That is, the six sample percentages were added and the total divided by six. These percentages will be used to project cash receipts for the second and fourth quarters of the budget. Avanti management feels that these quarters have similar seasonal influences.

Table 8.3 Collection Pattern Percentages

Month	Current	1-Month Lag	2-Month Lag	3-Month Lag
May 1989	5 %	35 %	56 %	4 %
June 1989	2	52	46	-0-
November 1989	6	51	38	5
May 1988	4	36	55	5
June 1988 .	4	49	45	2
November 1988	3	58	47	2
Total	24 %	281 %	287 %	18 %
Collection Pattern	4 %	47 %	48 %	3 %

This table contains a sample of purchase/payment percentages taken for representative months in the firm's fiscal years. The averages of these collection pattern percentages are used to estimate cash inflows from the collection of accounts receivable when preparing a cash budget.

Avanti's collection pattern data reveals two points worthy of note. First, Peacock's Paint Centers appears to be one of Avanti's large customers: the purchase amount in May for this customer represents almost 42% of credit sales for that month ($10,600 of $25,365). As is true with all of the firm's large customers, the payment practices of Peacock's should be closely monitored. Second, the payments pattern for May is atypical. While this divergence poses no problem when May data is combined with two other months to obtain quarterly projections, this unique payments pattern must be taken into consideration when cash flow forecasts are made for the individual month of May.

Benefits Derived from Payment Pattern Analysis

Performing the analysis to obtain collection pattern information produces several important benefits: Managers obtain the information necessary to do cash budgeting; they gain an understanding of the nature and behavior of credit accounts that is not obvious from aggregate accounts receivable data (this knowledge is essential to sound credit management); and they are forced to keep abreast of the payment practices of large customers. Since these accounts can easily determine a firm's financial health, they should be monitored on a continuous basis.

Estimating Cash Outflows: The Nature of Cash Outflows

Estimating cash outflows is the easier part of the cash forecasting process. Although outflows vary over long time frames, in the short run most are the result of events and plans that are already in place. This means that the majority of cash flows are either fixed in amount, or predetermined by managers for short budget intervals.

Some of a firm's cash outflows are fixed by contract during the budget horizon and pose no forecasting problem. Cash expense items, such as loan payments, rental or lease payments, insurance costs, and management salaries are known with virtual certainty over near-term budget intervals.

Other cash outflows, although not set by contract, are also known to managers with reasonable certainty in the short run. For example, payroll costs vary with the level of activity over long time frames. During short budget intervals, however, management schedules employee hours; payroll costs are therefore known in advance and are relatively easy to estimate. This is also true of the cash outflows associated with such items as the payment for purchases, advertising costs, owner's withdrawals (dividends), and expenditures for fixed assets.

The remaining category of cash outflows can usually be estimated from historical patterns. For example, such items as telephone and other utility expenses, vehicle costs, office supplies, and a variety of miscellaneous operating cash outflows can be extrapolated from historical trends.

Compiling Cash Outflow Data

The key to making realistic forecasts of cash outflow is having an intimate knowledge of the timing of your firm's obligations and its payments practice. This information can be obtained from several sources, including your firm's operating plans, cash payments journal or check register, and monthly income statements.

- Operating plans establish the events and activities that will cause cash to flow through your firm.

- The cash payments journal or check register provides a detailed description of historical cash outflows by type of payment.

- The nonaccrued expense items shown on monthly income statements provide the basis for estimating particular categories of cash outflows. Often, the amount of such monthly expense items as utilities, advertising, rent, and vehicle costs are reasonable approximations of actual cash outflows.

Again, it is worth noting that the best method for organizing historical cash outflow data for analysis is the cash budget format. By using the cash budget for this purpose, you gain a feel for the pattern of the firm's cash outflows, the activities that cause cash to flow through your firm, and the art of cash budgeting.

Deciding the Size of the Minimum Cash Balance

The final issue to be decided in preparing a cash budget is the size of the cash balance required to protect against unforeseen, adverse developments and forecasting error. If business firms operated in a world of perfect certainty, such contingency balances would not be needed. In this ideal world, you would know exactly the timing of all cash flows, and activities would be scheduled so that cash inflows and outflows are perfectly synchronized.

So much for fairy tales. In the real world, you must deal with risk and uncertainty. There is no guarantee that cash inflows will occur exactly at the time needed to meet upcoming obligations. To protect against the risk of financial embarrassment, forecasting error, and unforeseen developments, you should carry a cash balance that exceeds projected operating needs. The size of this contingency balance must be sufficient to allow you to sleep worry-free, but yet not so large that your firm is foregoing earnings because of excess liquidity.

By now you are now probably asking the obvious question: What is an appropriate size contingency balance, and what size balance is too large? Unfortunately, there is no precise answer. The size of the contingency balance needed to protect against uncertainty depends upon the stability of the business and its cash flow pattern. If operations and cash flows are relatively stable and reasonably predictable from period to period, only minimal contingency balances are required. If operations and cash flows fluctuate dramatically from period to period, larger balances must be kept.

Cash balance requirements for both operating needs and contingencies can be estimated from a combination of historical cash flow patterns, your experience, judgment, and attitude toward risk. Historical cash flow patterns organized in a cash budget format provide a wealth of information on cash balance needs. Careful study of the degree of fluctuation in the net cash flow figures (cash inflows minus cash outflows) produces realistic guidelines for establishing your firm's cash balance needs. The information gleaned from historical data should be tempered with your judgment and attitude toward risk.

It is important to note that while contingency balances are a necessary protection against unforeseen adverse developments, it is in your best interest to keep these balances at the minimum level required. Cash and its equivalent are low earning assets. If cash assets are held in excess of your firm's liquidity needs, dollars are withheld from investment in working assets that can produce higher returns.

Sound budgeting practices are the keys to maintaining appropriate contingency balances. As you become more proficient with the art of cash budgeting, the accuracy of cash forecasts will increase. Increased accuracy means better estimates of the cash balances that must be kept to meet both operating needs and to provide for contingencies.

To gain insight into the cash budgeting process, examine The Avanti Company's budget for the planning horizon covering 19X3. Its management decided that after the unpleasant surprises of 19X2 (see chapters 1 and 2), there must be a better way to run the business. Careful study of the planning principles convinced them that the benefits offered by a formal approach to financial planning far outweighed the small effort involved.

The Cash Budget Worksheet

Avanti's cash budget worksheet for the first six months of the 19X3 budget period is shown in Table 8.4. Technically, the worksheet is not a part of the cash budget, and it does not have to be completed to produce a cash budget. The worksheet is, however, an extremely practical device and its use is advised.

Information from the Cash Budget Worksheet

The calculations associated with estimates of cash sales, the lagged collection of accounts receivable, and the payment for inventory purchases are usually made on the worksheet. Making these detailed calculations on the worksheet instead of the cash budget itself provides two advantages: 1) the important pattern of cash inflows from collections, and outflows associated with inventory purchases are clearly highlighted; and 2) by removing arithmetic detail from the cash budget, you can focus on informative summary figures.

Note these important points about Avanti's cash budget worksheet:

- The sales figures for May and June are actual, not projected, values. These historical sales values are included on the worksheet because collections from their credit components will occur during months that are in the planning horizon. If Avanti's expected receivables collection pattern had covered three months, actual sales for April would also have been included on the worksheet.

- The sales figures for July through December, the first six months of the cash budget horizon, are projected values.

- The historical and projected sales figures serve only as reference values for the calculation of cash inflows. Only cash sales and the collections associated with credit sales are included in the cash budget. Note the important difference between the concepts of cash flow as used in preparation of the cash budget, and revenue as used in the preparation of the traditional income statement.

- The estimated cash inflows from credit sales are calculated by applying the estimated cash sales percentage and the customer payment pattern percentages to the appropriate sales figures.

- Estimated inventory purchases and the resulting cash payments to suppliers reflect Avanti's purchasing and inventory policy and the credit terms it is offered.

Table 8.4

THE AVANTI COMPANY
Cash Budget Worksheet
First Six Months of 19X3 Budget Period

	Actual Values		Projected Values					
	May	June	July	Aug	Sept	Oct	Nov	Dec
Net Sales	$26,000	$30,200	$20,000	$20,000	$29,000	$35,600	$46,200	$52,800
Collections:								
Cash Sales (5%)			1,000	1,000	1,450	1,780	2,310	2,640
1-Month Lag (20%)			6,040	4,000	4,000	5,800	7,120	9,240
2-Month Lag (75%)			19,500	22,650	15,000	15,000	21,750	26,700
Cash Flow From Sales			26,540	27,650	20,450	22,580	31,180	38,850
Other Cash Inflows			-0-	-0-	3,000	-0-	-0-	-0-
Total Cash Inflows			26,540	27,650	23,450	22,580	31,180	38,850
Purchases		11,400	11,400	16,530	20,292	26,334	30,096	11,400
Payment for Purchases			11,400	11,400	16,530	20,292	26,334	30,096

This table contains an example of a cash budget "Worksheet." Calculating the key cash budget variable values on the worksheet removes confusing detail from the budget itself.

As indicated on Table 8.4, Avanti's management has estimated that 5% of sales each month will be for cash, and the remaining 95% will be credit sales. They have further estimated that an average 20% of credit sales will be collected one month after the month of sale, and 75% collected two months after the month of sale. Applying these percentages to the actual and forecast sales values produces the estimated monthly cash inflows from sales.

For example, the $26,540 projected cash inflow from sales for July is calculated as follows:

The cash sales figure of $1,000 is determined by multiplying the sales estimate for July of $20,000 by the expected 5% cash sales percentage.

Cash Sales = Projected Sales x Cash Sales Percentage

Cash Sales = $20,000 x .05

        .   = $1,000

The lagged one-month collection figure for July of $6,040 is determined by multiplying the June sales figure of $30,200 by the 20% collection rate.

One-Month Collection Lag = Last Month's Sales x Collection Percentage

One-Month Collection Lag = $30,200 x .20

                                 = $6,040

The lagged two-month collection figure for July of $19,500 is determined by multiplying the May sales figure of $26,000 by the 75% collection rate.

Two-Month Collection Lag = 2 Months Prior Sales x Collection Percentage

Two-Month Collection Lag = $26,000 x .75

                             = $19,500

Note that both the one-month and two-month lagged collection figures for July reflect credit sales made in June and May. While July is the first month of the planning horizon for the cash budget, May and June are historical (actually completed) months that are not in the budget horizon. This point is made to emphasize the fact that the cash budget reflects estimates of the timing of actual cash flows, not the transactions that gave rise to them.

Cash inflows from sales for each of the remaining months in the budget horizon are calculated in the same manner. For example, the estimated cash inflow from sales of $38,850 for December is calculated as:

December Sales of $52,800	x .05	=	$ 2,640
+ November Sales of 46,200	x .20	=	9,240
+ October Sales of 35,600	x .75	=	26,700
			$38,850

Calculating Cash Inflow from Sales on the Worksheet

The cash flow from sales and any other expected cash inflows comprise the total cash inflow figures for this six-month segment of the budget horizon. These summary figures are moved to Avanti's cash budget for the appropriate months.

Calculating Payments for Purchases on the Worksheet

The other major section of Table 8.4 contains the calculation of the anticipated payments for inventory purchases (accounts payable). Payments for purchases are a function of Avanti's inventory and purchases policy, the credit terms offered by the firm's suppliers, and the firm's payment practice.

In Avanti's case, inventory purchases are based on expected sales. To allow ample time for shipment, purchases are made one month in advance of the month the goods must be on hand to meet anticipated sales. For example, the projected inventory needs for August would be purchased in July.

To determine the dollar amount of purchases, Avanti's management applies the average cost of sales percentage to the projected sales figure for next month. As discussed in Chapter 4, the average cost of sales figure is obtained from historical income statements by calculating cost of sales as a percent of sales. The calculations associated with Avanti's purchases policy are illustrated with an example from the worksheet.

If Avanti management felt the cost of sales percentage (cost of sales divided by sales) for 19X3 would average the same as that experienced in 19X2, 57%, purchases made in July to accommodate sales in August would total $11,400.

Estimated Purchases = Projected Sales x Cost of Sales Percentage

Estimated Purchases = $20,000 x .57
                = $11,400

Given Avanti's policy of purchasing estimated inventory needs one month in advance, purchases are made prior to the month of sale. Notice, however, that payment is not made for these purchases until one month later, August. This lag reflects the credit terms extended to Avanti. Since Avanti purchases under 30-day terms and intends to pay suppliers accordingly, the $11,400 of purchases will be paid for in August. This re-emphasizes the fact that for cash budgeting, it is not the transaction that matters but rather the timing of the resulting cash flow.

Insights Provided by the Worksheet

The cash budget worksheet highlights the impact that the lag in the collection of receivables has on cash inflows. Notice from the figures that Avanti anticipates a heavy seasonal buildup in sales from September through December. While these sales create accounting revenue that will appear on the income statement, most of the cash inflows from this seasonal buildup do not occur until January and February. This cash flow lag creates a cash drain that must be financed.

The cash budget prepared by Avanti for fiscal 19X3 appears on Table 8.5. As an aid to interpreting the budget, view it as if it contained two major sections. The first section — net cash flow — consists of the expected operating and non-operating cash flows that determine net cash flow for each period. The operating and non-operating cash flows include the total cash inflow figures calculated on the worksheet, and the various associated cash outflows. Included in cash outflows are the payments for purchases figures which were also calculated on the worksheet. The net cash flow figure provides a period-by-period indication of the cash required to support anticipated operating activity.

The Cash Budget Format

The items that appear below net cash flow make up what is referred to as the financing section of the cash budget. This section reflects the impact that operations are expected to have on the firm's financing needs over the budget horizon.

Viewing the cash budget as a combination of two sets of activities, the operating cash flow section and the financing section, will highlight the three key variables on which management must focus: net cash flow, required financing, and excess cash.

Net cash flow is simply total cash inflows minus total cash outflows. This value reflects the net impact of planned operations on a firm's cash position. If net cash flow is positive, inflows are expected to exceed outflows. A negative value has the opposite interpretation.

Interpreting the Cash Budget — Net Cash Flow

Note that net cash flow for Avanti is positive in July ($3,562) and August ($5,652), negative from September through December, positive for January ($27,232) and February ($25,622), and negative from March through June. The positive values indicate surplus cash from operations, and the negative values reflect the cash drain caused by the anticipated seasonal buildup in sales, receivables, and inventory.

The time pattern of net cash flow and its component inflows and outflows provides important information about the seasonal nature, if any, of a business. As indicated by Avanti's cash budget, the firm experiences major seasonal influences during the fall and spring quarters. Knowing the timing of seasonal peaks and troughs allows Avanti's management to plan for the heavy financing needs these periods create, and for the investment of surplus cash during slack periods.

The portion of the budget appearing below net cash flow displays when financing will be needed and when excess cash will be available. Calculation of the key figures of this section involve nothing more than simple arithmetic.

Interpreting the Cash Budget — Financing Section

The total cash figure is determined by adding the beginning cash balance to net cash flow. Avanti's budget indicates that total cash will be positive for July ($8,562), August ($14,214), and September ($3,556); negative for October (-$1,734), November (-$4,466), and December (-$13,560); and positive for the last six months of the budget horizon.

The minimum balance required represents the size of the contingency balance established by management. Recall that the contingency balance is management's estimate of the minimum level of cash needed to protect against forecasting error and unforeseen events. Avanti's management has established a balance of $5,000 as the floor below which they do not want the firm's cash account to fall.

The minimum balance required plays an important role in the determination of the firm's financing needs or its cash surplus. The minimum balance required is subtracted from total cash to obtain the estimate of required financing or excess cash. If total cash exceeds the minimum balance required, the firm is expected to have surplus funds for the period. The amount of the surplus is the positive difference between the two values. Note that this is the case for Avanti in July and August. Excess cash in July ($3,562) is the difference between $8,562 and $5,000, and in August ($9,214) the difference between $14,214 and $5,000.

July Excess Cash = Total Cash – Minimum Balance Required

July Excess Cash = $8,562 – $5,000

$\qquad = \$3,562$

As shown on the cash budget, Avanti also expects to enjoy cash surpluses from January through June.

If the minimum balance required is larger than total cash (a negative value), the difference is the amount of required financing for that period. For example, the required financing value for September ($1,444) was calculated as follows:

Required Financing = Total Cash – Minimum Balance Required

Required Financing = $3,556 – $5,000

$\qquad = \$(1,444)$

The cash budget indicates that financing will also be required in October ($6,734), November ($9,466), and December ($18,560).

The Information Produced by the Cash Budget

The key to a clear understanding of the information provided by the cash budget is the three key budget variables: net cash flow, required financing, and excess cash. These cash budget items demand careful scrutiny.

The net cash flow figures for the 19X3 planning horizon highlight the highly seasonal nature of Avanti's business. The negative cash flow values for September through December, and for March through June signal the increase in activity that should occur during these periods. The strain on working capital is so great during the September – December period that external financing is required to continue operations.

The total amount of financing needed to support the seasonal buildup during the fall quarter is indicated by the largest financing required value. In Avanti's case, it is $18,560, and this amount is reached during the month of December. In order to cover the expected cash deficits from September through December, Avanti's management would make financing provisions for at least $18,560 prior to the fall quarter.

Avanti is also expected to experience negative net cash flows for the March through June period (-$9,498, -$1,690, -$5,532, and -$12,354, respectively). There is, however, an important difference between this peak season and that of the September – December period. The large cash runoff in January and February resulting from the collection of credit sales made from September through December produces excess cash. These surpluses are sufficient to compensate for the March – June net cash flow deficits. As a result, outside financing is not needed and Avanti should enjoy an excess cash position from January through the end of the fiscal year; at that time, they anticipate a cash balance of $10,220.

If you had prior doubts about the value of financial planning and cash budgeting, the insights provided by Avanti's cash planning efforts should remove those doubts forever. There simply is no better vehicle than the cash budget for detailing the effects of planned operations and the impact of seasonal influences on the cash position of the firm. Imagine what life would be like at Avanti without the information provided by the budget. Both Avanti's cash position and its management would be in a constant state of turmoil. This is certainly not the situation you want for your firm.

Something Extra from the Budget

Interpreted properly, the cash budget also provides insight into the maturity (short- or long-term) of any indicated required financing. The key figure in this regard is the final total cash figure for the budget horizon. In Avanti's case, this was the June figure of $10,220.

Because the ending value is positive, the financing raised by Avanti must cover only normal, seasonal, working capital demands. The heavy seasonal buildup in inventory and accounts receivable requires financing, but the financing is temporary and self-liquidating. As the peak season passes, inventory is sold down and receivables are collected. The inflow of cash in January and February provides the means to repay working capital loans. Stated another way, the time

Table 8.5

THE AVANTI COMPANY
Cash Budget
Pro Forma 19X3

	July	August	September	October	November
Cash Inflows:					
Total Inflows	$26,540	$27,650	$23,450	$22,580	$31,180
Cash Outflows:					
Payment for Purchases	11,400	11,400	16,530	20,292	26,334
Wages and Salaries	2,933	2,933	2,933	2,933	2,933
Rent and Leases	300	300	300	300	300
Utilities	433	433	433	433	433
Insurance	1,058	1,058	1,058	1,058	1,058
Advertising	425	425	425	425	425
Vehicle Maintenance	1,792	1,792	1,792	1,792	1,792
Accounting & Legal	200	200	200	200	200
Payroll Taxes	437	437	437	437	437
Owner's Withdrawals	-0-	-0-	2,000	-0-	-0-
Income Taxes	-0-	-0-	4,000	-0-	-0-
Capital Expenditures	4,000	3,020	-0-	-0-	-0-
Total Outflows	$22,978	$21,998	$34,108	$27,870	$33,912
Net Cash Flow	3,562	5,652	-10,658	-5,290	-2,732
+ Beginning Cash Balance	5,000	8,562	14,214	3,556	-1,734
Total Cash	8,562	14,214	3,556	-1,734	-4,466
– Minimum Balance Required	5,000	5,000	5,000	5,000	5,000
Required Financing	$ -0-	$ -0-	$ 1,444	$ 6,734	$ 9,466
Excess Cash	$ 3,562	$ 9,214	$ -0-	$ -0-	$ -0-

This table contains the monthly projections of an annual cash budget. The forecast cash flows reflect the impact of planned operations on the firm's financial resources. This information is used by management to estimate required operating cash balances, to plan financing needs, and to identify periods of cash surplus.

December	January	February	March	April	May	June
$38,850	$46,210	$44,600	$20,050	$20,480	$22,680	$28,480
30,096	11,400	11,400	1,970	14,592	20,634	23,256
2,933	2,933	2,933	2,933	2,933	2,933	2,933
300	300	300	300	300	300	300
433	433	433	433	433	433	433
1,058	1,058	1,058	1,058	1,058	1,058	1,058
425	425	425	425	425	425	425
1,792	1,792	1,792	1,792	1,792	1,792	1,792
200	200	200	200	200	200	200
437	437	437	437	437	437	437
4,000	-0-	-0-	4,000	-0-	-0-	4,000
6,000	-0-	-0-	6,000	-0-	-0-	6,000
-0-	-0-	-0-	-0-	-0-	-0-	-0-
$47,674	$18,978	$18,978	$29,548	$22,170	$28,212	$40,834
-9,094	27,232	25,622	-9,498	-1,690	-5,532	-12,354
-4,466	-13,560	13,672	39,294	29,796	28,106	22,574
-13,560	13,672	39,294	29,796	28,106	22,574	10,220
5,000	5,000	5,000	5,000	5,000	5,000	5,000
$18,560	$ -0-	$ -0-	$ -0-	$ -0-	$ -0-	$ -0-
$ -0-	$ 8,672	$34,294	$24,796	$23,106	$17,574	$ 5,220

required to convert Avanti's seasonal buildup in inventory to sales, and receivables to cash is more than sufficient to replenish drained liquidity, repay used outside financing, and rebuild the cash account. Because Avanti's financing will be needed for a short time, short-term financing would be used.

Conversely, consider what would happen if the buildup in inventory and receivables had extended beyond normal seasonal requirements. Avanti would again face a serious liquidity drain and find itself in the same position as 19X2 — large profits but no cash. If this were the case, the cash budget would tell the story before the fact: The final total cash figure for the budget horizon would be negative. A negative figure indicates that financing requirements extend beyond temporary working capital needs. To satisfy longer-term demands, long-term rather than short-term financing should be used.

Dealing with the Risks in Cash Budgeting

Regardless of how adept you become at the art of forecasting, you must be realistic and realize that any forecast is not going to be perfectly accurate. Your firm operates in an uncertain world, and in an uncertain world forecasts are subject to error regardless of how well they are prepared. This does not mean that risk and uncertainty cannot be dealt with. It can, and the best method for doing so is to understand the types of risk and the nature of the uncertainty your firm faces. Some suggestions for developing this understanding are listed below.

- Instead of preparing a single cash budget for a given planning horizon, prepare a set of three cash budgets for that horizon. These budgets would be prepared using different assumptions for forecast sales, the receivables collection pattern, and any other variables deemed important. One budget would be prepared using the most likely forecast values for key variables such as sales and the collection pattern for receivables; another would be prepared using the most optimistic set of forecast variables; and the third using pessimistic forecast values.

  This approach provides two important benefits. First, you obtain a good feel for the range of possible outcomes in the key budget variables: net cash flow, required financing, and excess cash. By having a realistic estimate of the possible range (or variability) for these variables, you have an estimate of the size of the contingency balance that must be held, and the total amount of financing capability required to conduct planned operations. Second, these insights help you prepare for the worst possible case. This may well be the most important task that you, as small firm manager, can undertake.

- Careful analysis of deviations between actual and expected cash flows will help you identify the margin of error involved in your forecasts, and indicate the protective measures that must be taken to compensate for this error (recall from Chapter 6 the discussion of management control). For example, where there are large deviations between actual and expected cash flows (large fluctuations in the actual outcomes), larger contingency balances of cash can be held, the credit terms offered your customers can be altered, or larger precautionary stocks of inventory can be held.

An important part of this control process is the careful documentation of the assumptions used in making budget forecasts. This means that key assumptions should be made in writing and attached to the budget at the time the budget forecasts are prepared. By so doing, they will not be forgotten several months or a year later when actual outcomes are evaluated. Having the assumptions available allows you to judge the quality of the reasoning used in preparing the forecasts. These judgments are necessary to improve the art of forecasting and budgeting.

- Cash forecasts and plans, once prepared, are not etched in stone. When periodic budget reviews indicate conditions different from what was expected, you must make the necessary changes in your plan. This is the reason for planning. When you plan, you look at alternative possible futures and make advance preparation for dealing with them.

Some Parting Thoughts on the Cash Budget

The power of the cash budget as a planning tool increases as you gain experience with its use and as your ability to forecast improves. Both of these will occur with:

- Taking time to record the assumptions and reasoning used in your budget forecasts at the time the budget is prepared.

- Taking time to review and compare actual results with budgeted expectations, and to evaluate the assumptions and reasoning used in preparing the budget.

- Practice, practice, and more practice.

By following these steps, you are able to identify budget deviations that require attention, the reason for the deviations, and, most importantly, you will be able to evaluate the quality and accuracy of the assumptions and reasoning that went into the forecast. It is only through this latter step that you get better at forecasting. By knowing what you do right and what is faulty, you know what to repeat and what to correct. Without an analysis of forecast and actual data, it is impossible to determine if an outcome results from something you did well, something you did poorly, or something you did not do.

It is the assumptions that go into the budget forecast that are the important and the difficult part of cash budgeting. The actual mechanics of cash budgeting are not difficult. They require nothing more than simple arithmetic and some number crunching, which can be done by hand or automated with a computer model. Information on financial models software is provided on the card enclosed at the back of this book.

Where to Now?

While the cash budget is the most important tool of financial planning, it is not the only one used. In the next chapter, you will investigate the roles that pro forma financial statements, the pro forma contribution statement, and breakeven analysis also play in the financial planning process.

Chapter 9
Profit Planning with Pro Forma Statements

The previous chapter described how the cash budget is used to measure the impact of planned operations on cash flows. This chapter examines the role of profit planning in the financial planning effort.

Profit planning is the process surrounding a forecast and plan of a firm's future profit performance and financial position. The primary tool used in this effort is the pro forma financial statement.

Profit planning is a matter of concern both to managers and to outside parties that have an interest in a firm. For example, have you noticed how the profit or loss figure attracts the attention of your banker? While cash flow is an important short-term consideration, profits are a key long-term indicator of a firm's progress. In fact, over extended time periods, a firm's ability to generate profits and cash flows is closely correlated.

TOPIC	CONCEPTS DISCUSSED
The Pro Forma Income Statement	How the concept of pro forma applies to the accounting income statement.
	How to use the percent of sales method to estimate projected expenses.
	How to interpret and use the pro forma income statement.
The Pro Forma Contribution Format Income Statement	How the concept of pro forma applies to the contribution format income statement.
	When the contribution format should be used for profit planning.
	How to interpret and use the contribution contribution statement.

TOPIC	CONCEPTS DISCUSSED
Projected Breakeven and the Target Level of Profit	How breakeven analysis is used in profit planning.
	The concept of the target level of profit.
The Pro Forma Balance Sheet	How the pro forma concept applies to the balance sheet.
	How to interpret the pro forma balance sheet.
	How the pro forma balance sheet is used to estimate the financing required to support planned operations.

As a management tool, profit planning provides answers to such vital questions as:

- What effect will long-term plans have on a firm's financial position, and how will this be reflected on its financial statements?

- What level of profits will planned operations produce?

- Approximately what total investment in current and fixed assets is required to support planned operations, and to generate the the target level of profits?

- Approximately how much outside financing will be required to accommodate long-term plans?

- What is the minimum level of sales a firm will have to generate to break even, and to earn the target level of profit?

The Concept of the Pro Forma Income Statement

Pro forma, as used in the context of planning, means *projected* or "*as if.*" A *pro forma income statement,* then, is a projected statement prepared as if forecast conditions and planned activity had actually occurred. The statement is prepared in the same format as its historical counterpart, but reflects estimated values based on planning assumptions rather than actual events.

The pro forma statement depicts the effect of planned operations on sales, expenses, and profits for a given planning horizon. Technically, the time period covered by the pro forma income statement depends on the stability of a firm's operations, its management's needs, and the degree of certainty management has in its forecast. In practice, the pro forma income statement is prepared as a part of a firm's long-term plan and covers a time frame, divided into appropriate budget intervals, of up to five years.

For example, a strategic plan may be prepared for a five-year planning horizon. If operating plans are prepared for one year, the long-term plan would be divided into five one-year intervals. A pro forma income statement would be developed for each year, and for the total five-year period as well.

Preparation of a pro forma income statement begins with a forecast of expected sales. This forecast would include individual sales estimates for each planning interval, and an aggregate figure for the entire planning horizon. The fact that preparation of the pro forma income statement starts with a sales estimate should come as no surprise. Sales serves as the major revenue item on the income statement, and the activity measure on which expenses and profit are predicated.

Preparing a Pro Forma Income Statement — The Percent of Sales Method

Given the sales forecast, the expenses associated with projected revenue must be estimated to complete the statement. The most commonly used technique for this purpose is the percent of sales method. This method is based on the assumption that expenses vary with sales, and the relationship between the two can be expressed as a percentage. For example, if cost of sales has historically averaged 57% of sales, and forecast sales is $100,000, then the cost of sales estimate on the pro forma income statement would be $57,000. This is calculated as:

Estimated Cost of Sales = Forecast Sales x Cost of Sales Percentage
$$= \$100,000 \times .57$$
$$= \$57,000$$

The same procedure would be used to establish estimates for each of the remaining expense items on the statement. The projected net operating income and net profit figures would be calculated by subtracting the appropriate expense estimates from sales revenue.

The initial or starting percent of sales value for each expense item on the income statement is usually established from historical financial statement relationships. Expense items for a given statement period are calculated as percentages of sales for that statement date (this was discussed in chapters 1 and 4). The percentages can be calculated from last year's income statement, from a statement for a year considered typical, or as averages calculated from statements for several years.

Calculating the Percent of Sales Percentages

If historical percentages are not appropriate proxies for expected future conditions, initial percentage values should be adjusted for anticipated changes. At times, planned activities may be based on expected conditions that differ from those of the past. If so, initial percentage values must be adjusted for these expectations.

For example, economic or market conditions may differ because of a change in the direction of economic activity, or the introduction of a new marketing strategy designed to attract a different customer base. Also, planned changes in the way business is conducted such as the introduction of lower- or higher-priced product lines, implementation of new production techniques, or a change in the credit terms offered a firm's customers will alter historical expense to sales relationships.

An Example of the Percent of Sales Method

To illustrate the percent of sales technique, take a look at The Avanti Company. Avanti management has estimated an 8% growth rate in sales for the planning period 19X3 through 19X5. This translates to projected sales levels of $367,200, $396,576, and $428,302. Because the cost control problems which caused profit margins to deteriorate during 19X2 have been corrected, Avanti's management feels that the percent of sales figures from the 19X2 income statement are not appropriate for the pro forma statements. Upon investigation, it was determined that the percentage relationships from the 19X1 income statement were representative of what could be accomplished over the planning horizon. These percentages are shown in Table 9.1 below.

Table 9.1 Percent of Sales from 19X1 Income Statement

Expense Item	Percent of Sales
Cost of Sales	51.0 %
Wages & Salaries	11.0
Rent & Leases	2.0
Utilities	1.9
Insurance	4.0
Advertising	2.0
Vehicle Expense	7.0
Accounting & Legal	0.8
Payroll Taxes	1.7
Depreciation	0.6
Total Operating Expenses	31.0 %
Interest Expense	1.0
Income Taxes	7.0

This table contains percent-of-sales data used to prepare pro forma income statements for the indicated planning horizon. The percent-of-sales values were calculated as historical relationships between sales and various income statement items. If necessary, these percentages are adjusted to reflect any anticipated changes in conditions during the planned period.

Each percent of sales value was obtained by dividing the amount of the expense item by the sales figure, which both came from the income statement in Chapter 1. For example, Avanti's cost of sales percentage of 51% for 19X1 was calculated as:

Cost of Sales Percentage (19X1) = Cost of Sales ÷ Sales

Cost of Sales Percentage (19X1) = $148,000 ÷ $290,000

$$= 51\%$$

Each of the remaining percent of sales values for 19X1 were calculated in the same manner.

To obtain Avanti's pro forma income statement for 19X3 (see Table 9.2), the projected sales figure of $367,200 is entered as revenue for the period, and each percent of sales value is applied to the sales figure to obtain the various expense amounts. Profit projections are calculated by subtracting expense items from sales revenue. For example, the gross profit figure of $179,928 can be determined by subtracting cost of sales from sales revenue.

Gross Profit = Sales Revenue – Cost of Sales

Gross Profit = $367,200 – $187,272

$$= \$179,928$$

It should also be noted that gross profit could have been calculated by applying the historical percentage relationship between gross profit and sales (49%) to the sales figure.

Gross Profit = Gross Profit Percentage x Sales Estimate

Gross Profit = .49 x $367,200

$$= \$179,928$$

The pro forma income statement for 19X3 is shown on Table 9.2. As indicated by the statement, if planned sales materialize and its management is able to improve profit margins to the 19X1 level, Avanti will enjoy a healthy jump in net income to $36,720.

A Final Word on the Pro Forma Income Statement

While it is important to be familiar with the mechanics of preparing a pro forma income statement, it does not have to be done manually. Computer software makes the necessary calculations and generates statements automatically. This automation eliminates tedious number crunching, and allows the convenience of testing alternative planning assumptions with lightning speed.

Suppose, for example, that Avanti management is interested in determining the level of sales that would be required to produce a target level of profit of $50,000. Using available software, Avanti's management could quickly explore different combinations of estimated sales

Table 9.2

THE AVANTI COMPANY

Pro Forma Income Statements

For the Planning Period 19X3 to 19X5

	19X3	19X4	19X5
Net Sales	$367,200	$396,576	$428,302
Cost of Sales	187,272	202,254	218,434
Gross Profit	$179,928	$194,322	$209,868
Operating Expenses:			
Wages & Salaries	40,392	43,623	47,113
Rent & Leases	7,344	7,932	8,566
Utilities	6,977	7,535	8,138
Insurance	14,688	15,863	17,132
Advertising	7,344	7,932	8,566
Vehicle Expense	25,704	27,760	29,980
Accounting & Legal	2,938	3,173	3,426
Payroll Taxes	6,242	6,742	7,281
Depreciation	2,203	2,379	2,570
Total Operating Expenses	$113,832	$122,939	$132,772
Net Operating Income	$ 66,096	$ 71,383	$ 77,096
Less: Interest Expense	3,672	3,966	4,283
Net Taxable Income	$ 62,424	$ 67,417	$ 72,813
Less: Income Taxes	25,704	27,760	29,981
Net Income	$ 36,720	$ 39,657	$ 42,832

The pro forma income statements shown on this table reflect the impact of projected sales and planned operations on profit performance during the planning period. These statements were prepared by applying the appropriate percent-of-sales values to forecast sales.

and costs of operation that would produce the $50,000 profit. This type of what-if probing is at the heart of financial analysis, planning and decision making, and a well-designed computer model allows management to concentrate solely on these important tasks. Software information is provided on the card enclosed at the back of this book.

The Pro Forma
Contribution Statement

From your reading of Chapter 5 on cost-volume-profit analysis, you may recognize a possible weakness in the percent of sales method when used for very short-term projections. This technique implicitly assumes that all expense items and profit will vary directly or proportionately with sales. For example, a 10% increase in sales will result in a 10% increase in expenses and a 10% increase in profit. While this assumption is appropriate for the ballpark estimates used in long-term planning, it may produce short-term distortions. The reason for possible distortions is the existence of short-run fixed costs. Recall that by definition, fixed costs do not vary with sales in the short run.

As discussed in Chapter 5, variable costs normally change in proportion to sales. For example, it is reasonable to assume that cost items such as those for materials, labor cost, and payroll taxes increase as sales increase. Fixed costs, on the other hand, will change very little (if at all) over short budget intervals. In Avanti's case for instance, it is unlikely that such items as rent, insurance, and accounting and legal costs would change during the one-year budget period, regardless of the change in sales.

If a traditional pro forma income statement based on percent of sales method is used in short-term situations where fixed cost is a large proportion of total costs, the profit projection will be understated. The reason is simple: The percent of sales method will increase fixed cost items even though fixed costs do not change in the short run. Thus, projected costs will be higher and projected profit lower than it should be. When fixed costs are a significant part of your firm's cost structure, the contribution format income statement may be more useful for short-term profit planning than the traditional income statement format. For long-term planning, however, the traditional income statement is the appropriate tool. Over the long run, even fixed costs will vary with sales.

Avanti's Pro Forma
Contribution Statement

A 19X3 pro forma contribution format statement for Avanti is shown on Table 9.3. This statement reflects Avanti management's assumptions that operations will be conducted at the same level of efficiency experienced in 19X1. The historical variable cost percentages for this year were applied to the sales forecast of $367,200 to obtain the variable cost and contribution margin figures. For example, the projected contribution margin of $150,552 was determined by multiplying the historical 41% contribution margin ratio and estimated sales of $367,200.

Table 9.3

THE AVANTI COMPANY

Pro Forma Contribution Income Statement

For 19X3

		Percent of Sales
Net Sales	$367,200	100.0 %
Less Variable Costs:		
Cost of Sales	187,272	51.0 %
Sales Commissions	16,524	4.5 %
Vehicle Delivery Expense	12,852	3.5 %
Total Variable Costs	$216,648	59.0 %
Contribution Margin (Ratio)	150,552	41.0 %
Less Fixed Costs:		
Wages & Salaries	16,275	
Rent and Leases	3,600	
Utilities	5,399	
Insurance	12,700	
Advertising	6,120	
Vehicle Expense	5,253	
Accounting & Legal	2,400	
Payroll Taxes	5,100	
Depreciation	2,100	
Total Fixed Costs	$ 58,947	
Net Operating Income	$ 91,605	25.0 %

The pro forma contribution format income statement, which is often a more accurate short-term forecasting tool than the traditional pro forma income statement, indicates how costs and profits behave, given the projected level of sales and operations.

Contribution Margin = Historical Contribution Margin Ratio x Sales

Contribution Margin = .41 x $367,200
$$= \$150,552$$

Avanti further assumed that wages and salaries and payroll taxes would increase by 5% for the year, utilities expense by 6%, vehicle expense by 3%, and advertising expense by 20% (the result of a planned promotion campaign). No change in rent, insurance, and accounting and legal expenses was anticipated. The results of these assumptions are reflected in the various fixed cost items shown on the pro forma contribution format statement on Table 9.3.

It is interesting to note the sizable difference in the projected net operating income figure of $66,096 shown on the traditional statement, and the projected $91,605 shown on the contribution format statement. Much of this difference can be attributed to the different assumption underlying the estimate of fixed cost.

Breakeven and the Profit Target

The concept of breakeven as discussed in Chapter 5 is well suited to profit planning. The breakeven calculation can be used to estimate the sales level needed to break even, and to achieve a target (desired) amount of net operating profit. To understand how this tool is used to estimate a target profit level, recall two important points about the breakeven concept.

1. The breakeven level of sales is calculated as fixed costs divided by the contribution margin ratio.

2. Once the breakeven level of sales is reached (i.e., fixed costs are covered), the contribution margin from each additional dollar of sales goes directly to operating profit.

Since net operating profit depends on the amount of contribution generated beyond the breakeven point, a slightly modified breakeven formula can be used to estimate the sales level required to produce the profit target. The modification involves nothing more than adding the target net operating income figure to fixed cost before dividing by the contribution margin ratio.

Suppose, for example, that Avanti management sets as a goal a net operating income target of $120,000. Management estimates that fixed costs will be $75,000 and that the firm will be able to achieve the contribution margin ratio of 41% earned in 19X1. Given these estimates, the level of sales required to generate the $120,000 in net operating income is $475,610.

Target Operating Profit = (Fixed Costs + Profit Target)
$$\div \text{ Contribution Margin Ratio}$$
$$= (\$75,000 + \$120,000) \div .41$$
$$= \$475,610$$

The Pro Forma Balance Sheet

The pro forma balance sheet is the fourth tool used in the profit planning process. This statement serves two important purposes:

1. It provides a financial profile of planned operations.

2. It is used to make a rough estimate of the financing that will be required to support long-term plans.

The Pro Forma Balance Sheet as a Financial Profile

A *financial profile* is simply a monetary picture of the effects that planned operations have on the financial position of a firm. These effects are reflected as estimated levels of assets, liabilities, and owner's equity on a pro forma balance sheet.

Analogous to the preparation of a pro forma income statement, a *pro forma balance sheet* can be prepared by using assumed relationships between balance sheet items and projected sales. Over long planning horizons (more than one year) most asset, liability, and equity items will vary proportionately with sales. Consequently, the percent of sales method is an effective technique for projecting most balance sheet items. Where necessary, percent of sales values can be adjusted for or replaced by management-determined values.

Establishing the Estimating Values

The percent of sales method and management-estimated values were used to project pro forma balance sheets for Avanti's three-year plan covering the period 19X3 through 19X5. The percent-of-sales and management-estimated values are shown on Table 9.4.

The Percent of Sales Estimates

The percent of sales values shown on Table 9.4 reflect 19X1 balance sheet to sales relationships. They were calculated using the specific 19X1 balance sheet items, and the 19X1 sales figure of $290,000. For example, the accounts receivable percent of sales value of 8.9% was obtained as follows:

Accounts Receivable Percentage = Accounts Receivable ÷ Sales

Accounts Receivable Percentage = $25,778 ÷ $290,000
$$= 8.9\%$$

Likewise, the accounts payable percent of sales value of 4.2% was obtained as follows:

Accounts Payable Percentage = Accounts Payable ÷ Sales

Accounts Payable Percentage = $12,200 ÷ $290,000
$$= 4.2\%$$

Each of the remaining percent of sales values shown on Table 9.4 was calculated in the same manner. The decision to use 19X1 relationships reflects management's opinion that operations will be returned to the level of efficiency experienced in that year.

Table 9.4 Percent of Sales/Estimated Dollar Data

Statement Item	Percent of Sales or Estimated Dollar Amount	
Cash	4.5%	
Accounts Receivable	8.9%	
Inventory	8.3%	
Accounts Payable	4.2%	
Accruals Payable	0.8%	
Land	$ 30,000	(No Change)
Building	$150,000	(No Change)
Vehicles	$ 55,000	up to 19X5
"	$ 75,000	in 19X5
Equipment	$ 33,000	up to 19X5
"	$ 40,000	in 19X5
Addition to Retained Earnings	$ 26,720	19X3
" " "	$ 19,658	19X4
" " "	$ 12,830	19X5
Notes Payable, Additional Long-Term Debt, and Additional Capital Stock	Plug Figure	

This table contains percent-of-sales and estimated dollar data used to prepare pro forma balance sheets for the indicated planning horizon. The percent-of-sales values were calculated using historical relationships between sales and select balance sheet items. If necessary, these values are adjusted to reflect any anticipated change in conditions during the planning period.

Fixed Asset Estimates

While Avanti's management considered using the percent of sales method to project the balance sheet value of fixed assets as well, it was ultimately decided that estimated dollar amounts would better reflect planned capital expenditures. The results of this decision are shown on Table 9.4. No expenditures for land or buildings are anticipated during the planning horizon, but purchases of additional vehicles and equipment are expected. Management feels that if sales grow at the projected 8% rate, a $20,000 outlay for a new vehicle in 19X3 and another in 19X5 would be required as would equipment purchases of $10,000 in 19X3 and $7,000 in 19X5. These expenditures would raise the pro forma balance sheet accounts to the levels indicated on the table.

Calculating the Addition to Retained Earnings

The addition to retained earnings values shown on Table 9.4 are determined by subtracting planned dividends (owner's withdrawals) from projected net income. They are needed to determine the amount of the retained earnings accounts on the three pro forma balance sheets on Table 9.5. The calculation of the balance sheet retained earnings account will be discussed in a subsequent section of this chapter, for now, trace through the calculation of the addition to retained earnings figures.

Avanti's management anticipates dividend payments of $10,000, $20,000, and $30,000 for 19X3, 19X4, and 19X5, respectively. As shown on the pro forma income statements, a projected net income for each of the three years is $36,720, $39,658, and $42,830 respectively. Subtracting the expected dividend from the projected net income figure provides the amount of addition to retained earnings. For example, the addition to retained earnings of $26,720 for 19X3 was calculated as follows:

Addition to Retained Earnings = Net Income – Dividends

Addition to Retained Earnings = $36,720 – $10,000
$$= \$26,720$$

The remaining values shown on the table are calculated in the same manner.

Preparing the Pro Forma Balance Sheet

Once the necessary estimates have been made, preparation of the pro forma balance sheet involves nothing more than plugging in the numbers. Avanti's statements for 19X3, 19X4, and 19X5 are shown on Table 9.5, and the calculations are explained below.

Calculating Assets and Liabilities

To obtain current asset, fixed asset, and the indicated current liability figures on the pro forma balance sheets, the available percent of sales values on Table 9.4 are applied to estimated sales. For example, the 19X3 current asset account, inventory, is determined by multiplying the projected sales figure of $367,200 by the inventory percent of sales value of 8.3%.

Projected Inventory = Projected Sales x Inventory Percentage

Projected Inventory = $367,200 x 8.3%
$$= \$30,478$$

The indicated current liability accounts were determined in the same manner. For example, pro forma payables for 19X3 were calculated as:

Projected Payables = Projected Sales x Accounts Payable Percentage

Projected Payables = $367,200 x 4.2%
$$= \$15,422$$

Fixed asset values in this case were determined by plugging the dollar amounts estimated by Avanti's management into the statement. If the

Table 9.5

THE AVANTI COMPANY
Pro Forma Balance Sheets
For the Planning Period 19X3 through 19X5

Assets	19X3	19X4	19X5
Current Assets:			
Cash	$ 16,524	$ 17,846	$ 19,274
Receivables	32,681	35,295	38,119
Inventory	30,478	32,916	35,549
Total	$ 79,683	$ 86,057	$ 92,942
Fixed Assets:			
Land	30,000	30,000	30,000
Buildings	150,000	150,000	150,000
Vehicles	55,000	55,000	75,000
Equipment	33,000	33,000	40,000
Less: Accumulated Depreciation	(23,100)	(26,000)	(30,000)
Total	$244,900	$242,000	$265,000
Total Assets	$324,583	$328,057	$357,942
Equities			
Spontaneous Liabilities:			
Accounts Payable	15,422	16,656	17,989
Accruals Payable	2,938	3,173	3,426
Total	$ 18,360	$ 19,829	$ 21,415
Existing Long-Term Debt	131,688	131,688	131,688
Owner's Equity:			
Existing Capital Stock	30,000	30,000	30,000
Retained Earnings	140,175	159,833	172,633
Total Owner's Equity	$170,175	$189,833	$202,663
Total Equities	$320,223	$341,350	$355,766
PLUG FIGURE	$ 4,360	$(13,293)	$ 2,176

Sales for each year of the planning horizon are $367,200, $396,576, and $428,302, respectively. These figures reflect an estimated growth rate of 8% per year from 19X2 sales of $340,000.

percent of sales method had been used to estimate fixed assets, the procedure would be the same as that used for other balance sheet items. The fixed asset percentage would be applied to the projected sales figure.

Calculating Retained Earnings

The retained earnings figure for each pro forma year is obtained by adding the projected addition to retained earnings value to the retained earnings figure shown on the balance sheet from the previous year. For example, the retained earnings value of $140,175 for pro forma 19X3 was obtained by adding the 19X3 addition to retained earnings of $26,720 to the $113,455 of retained earnings shown on the 19X2 balance sheet.

Projected Retained Earnings = Previous Retained Earnings
+ Addition to Retained Earnings

Projected Retained Earnings = $113,455 + 26,720
= $140,175

The retained earnings value of $159,833 for pro forma 19X4 was obtained by adding the 19X4 addition to retained earnings of $19,658 to the 19X3 retained earnings value of $140,175. In like manner, the 19X5 retained earnings value of $172,663 is obtained by adding the addition to retained earnings of $12,830 to $159,833.

Calculating the Plug Figure

The *plug figure*, shown on the pro forma balance sheet, is an adjustment value that balances any difference between total assets and the sum of total liabilities and owner's equity. Recall from Chapter 1 that the balance sheet must balance; total sources of funds (liabilities and owner's equity) must equal total uses (current and fixed assets). If sales are expected to increase over the planning horizon, then the total asset value on the pro forma balance sheet will increase as well. The increase in the amount of assets will cause the value total assets to exceed the value of total liabilities and equity. The plug figure serves to bring the two amounts into balance. It also plays an important role in the long-term financial planning process.

Since the plug figure serves to bring total liabilities and equity into balance with total assets, it is, in balance sheet terms, a required source of funds. As such it represents either notes payable, long-term debt, or owner's capital, or some combination of the three. In financial terms, the plug figure is the estimated amount of external financing required to support planned operations. External refers to financing raised beyond the firm's normal sources such as the addition to retained earnings (a rough proxy for cash flow from operations), and spontaneous current liabilities (accounts payable and accruals). It is financing that comes from negotiated short-term or long-term debt such as bank loans, and owner's paid-in capital.

Understanding the rationale behind this figure is the key to understanding how the pro forma balance sheet is used to estimate long-term financing needs.

The basis for using the pro forma balance sheet plug figure as a financing estimate lies in some elementary financial logic. This logic can be expressed as follows:

The Importance of the Plug Figure

- To operate the business and generate sales, your firm requires current and fixed assets.

- The existing asset base supports the current volume of sales and operations, but an increase in the volume of sales and operations requires additional assets. For example, increased sales will require additional inventory and will create larger accounts receivable balances; or, increased operations may require more labor, equipment, or buildings.

- To purchase additional assets, your firm must have additional funds.

- Some of the needed funds will be provided internally, such as the addition to retained earnings, and some will come from routine or spontaneous sources, such as accounts payable and accruals.

- If internally generated funds and spontaneous financing are not sufficient to meet total financing needs, the remainder must come from external sources (negotiated short- and long-term debt, and owner's paid-in capital).

This logic is easily traced through balance sheet relationships. The increases in current and fixed assets caused by planned operations are reflected in percent of sales or management-estimated values. Available financing from spontaneous sources appears as increases in accounts payable and accruals, and the estimate of internally generated funds is reflected in the addition to retained earnings figure. The difference between financing needs (increased assets) and routine financing sources (spontaneous financing and internally generated funds) is the plug figure. This is the amount, if any, that must be raised from external sources.

A positive plug figure indicates an increase in assets (financing needs) that exceeds the sum of spontaneous financing and the addition to retained earnings (financing sources). The amount of the plug figure in this case represents the additional external financing needed to meet planned operations. Note that Avanti's pro forma balance sheets for 19X3 and 19X5 indicate positive plug figures, $4,360 and $2,176 respectively. These values represent the amount of expected external financing that must be raised in these years.

A negative plug figure indicates that the sum of spontaneous financing and the addition to retained earnings exceeds the increase in assets. This means that surplus funds should be available during that planning period. Note that this is the case for Avanti in 19X4, $(13,293). In that year, the sum of spontaneous financing and internally generated funds is expected to exceed financing needs by $13,293.

If the plug figure was zero, no additional external financing is required. The amount produced by spontaneous financing and the addition to retained earnings is expected to equal the increase in assets.

Some Final Thoughts on the Pro Forma Balance Sheet

The pro forma balance sheet, along with the plug figure, highlights the impact that your policies and actions have on your firm's financial resources. For example, with only a slight reduction in Avanti's planned dividend payments in 19X3 and 19X5, the firm would enjoy a surplus cash position rather than a financing problem. At this stage in the planning process, Avanti's management may wish to reconsider their dividend policy and pay heed to previously stated advice: Resist the temptation to take excessive dividends in good years so that financial resources are available to survive the lean years.

While the pro forma balance sheet is an excellent tool for long-term planning, it is not (as you may already suspect) well suited to short-term planning horizons. Long-term planning is by its very nature more iffy and less certain than short-term planning. The rough approximations of year-end aggregate values produced by the pro forma balance sheet are acceptable estimates for extended time frames. They give Avanti management a reasonable estimate on which to plan the firm's long-term financial future.

In the short-run, forecasts are more certain and financial planning should reflect the detail necessary to effectively manage the firm's liquidity position. The pro forma balance sheet does not provide this needed detail. The proper tool for this purpose is the cash budget.

Where to Now?

The final chapter in this section is intended as a practical, step-by-step, how-to guide to financial planning. It consists of a series of questions designed to lead you through the entire process.

Chapter 10
Planning Worksheets

Often, the major obstacle to financial planning is knowing how to start and how to proceed through the planning process. The planning worksheets included in this chapter will help you overcome these hurdles. They will show you where and how to start your financial planning effort, and then lead you step by step through the process.

Planning your firm's financial future begins with an assessment of the environment in which it will operate. This means identifying the major economic, political, legal, and social factors that affect your firm's markets, sales and profits. Answering the questions on Worksheet 1 should provide the type of information that must be gathered to do so.

Worksheet 1: Evaluating Your Firm's Environment

The impact of the general economic, social, and political factors that are related to your firm's business activity is channeled through the particular market(s) in which it operates. It is important, therefore, that you understand and monitor the major determinants of activity in those market(s). Rarely will your firm do well if conditions in its market(s) are unfavorable. Worksheet 2 is designed to help you identify major market factors.

Worksheet 2: Evaluating Your Market

Financial planning for your firm begins with an informed forecast of a reasonable range for sales over a specified planning horizon (one year, three years, five years, etc.) and for the budget intervals or sub-periods within this horizon. This forecast should be a careful blend of:

Worksheet 3: Forecasting Sales

- Your knowledge and understanding of historical relationships between sales for your firm and economic, social, and political events.

- Realistic estimates of reasonable ranges for the key economic, social, and political factors.

- A projection of future sales from historical trends.

- Adjustments to projected sales for anticipated changes in the firm's external and internal environment.

(For review, see Chapter 6.)

Worksheet 4: Short-Term Cash Planning

Planning your firm's financial profile begins with an estimate of the working capital or temporary financing that will be required to support operating plans for the most immediate budget interval in your planning horizon. This estimate is made with the cash budget. As your experience with cash budgeting grows, this tool will become the most effective weapon in your financial planning arsenal. The questions on Worksheet 4 are designed to guide you through the cash budgeting process. It may be useful at this point to review the material on the subject in the planning section of the book. (For review, see chapters 7, 8, and 9.)

Worksheet 5: Planning Long-Term Financing Needs

To complete the financial planning process, you must supplement the cash budget with a plan for your firm's long-term financial profile, and Worksheet 5 will help you to estimate required financing. This estimate is made using pro forma statements. Having an estimate of the firm's financial profile allows you to make advance preparation for the amount and types of financing (debt and/or equity) that must be acquired.

Structuring a reasonable mix of debt and equity financing is necessary to keep financial risk within acceptable limits, and to identify the amount of unused debt capacity (borrowing capability) that should be preserved for unforeseen opportunities or contingencies. By not borrowing up to the limit of the firm's debt capacity, you maintain the flexibility to deal with future uncertainties and opportunities. (For review, see Chapter 8.)

Worksheet 6: Preparing the Financial Plan — The Target Debt Ratio

The long-term financial plan serves two important purposes: it provides the information needed to make advance preparation for the financing that will be required to support planned operations; and, it is used to establish an appropriate debt level for the firm. Your firm's debt level, which is measured by its debt ratio, should reflect a reasonable tradeoff between the advantages of using creditor financing and the risk that this type of financing creates for your firm. (For review, see Chapter 4.)

Ideally, the debt ratio, calculated from the balance sheet as total liabilities divided by total liabilities and equity, should reflect:

- An adequate equity capital cushion to protect your firm during periods of economic adversity;
- Some unused debt capacity (borrowing ability) to take advantage of unforeseen opportunities or for contingencies; and
- A level of risk that management can tolerate.

Worksheet 6 should help you make decisions on financing mix and debt level for your firm.

Worksheet 1: Evaluating Your Firm's Environment

Consensus Outlook for the Economy

What is the majority opinion of professional economists' forecasts for:

- Changes in gross national product and the rate of economic growth?

- Changes in the level of disposable income?

- Changes in credit conditions and interest rates?

- Changes in the rate of inflation?

- Changes in unemployment levels?

- Other key aggregate economic variables?

To which key economic variables is your firm's business activity closely related? For example, how are your markets and sales affected by such general economic factors as:

- Retail sales?

- Auto sales?

- Interest rates?

- New housing starts?

- The level of disposable income

- Industrial production?

- Durable goods orders?

- Unemployment rates?

- Other related variables?

What is the consensus outlook for each of the related variables, and how will this outlook affect your firm's markets and its sales? That is, will expected change in related variables cause an increase or decrease in sales for your firm?

Consensus Outlook for the Socio/Political Environment

What is the prediction of a majority of professional forecasters for such socio/political factors as:

- Tax laws?

■ Small business legislation?

■ Relevant state and local legislation?

■ Technological developments?

■ Demographic patterns?

■ The mood, attitudes, and values of our society?

■ Other related variables?

To which socio/political factors is activity in your firm's markets and its sales related?

What impact will predicted changes in related socio/political variables have on the level of activity in your firm's markets and its sales?

Worksheet 2: Evaluating Your Market

Trend of Activity in Your Market(s)

What is the outlook for the critical factors that drive activity in your market area? For example, what can be expected for:

■ The rate of growth in your markets?

■ The composition of your target customer group(s). Is this base stable or changing?

■ The tastes and preferences for your target customer group(s). Are these stable or changing?

■ New additions to your customer base?

■ The plans and activities of major competitors. How would these affect your firm's sales?

■ The entry or departure of a competitor?

■ The entry or departure of large noncompetitive firms or organizations in your market area. What impact will any such changes have on the level of business and economic activity in your market area?

■ The employment or payroll level of major firms or organizations in your market area. What economic impact will any such changes have?

■ The development of competitive or substitute new products or services. How would these changes affect sales for your firm?

■ The level of building and construction in your market area. What economic impact will this have?

■ Federal, state, or local government contracts or grants awarded, or to be awarded, to firms or organizations in your market area. What economic impact would such awards have?

■ The plans and activities of local development or planning authorities. What impact would they have on the local economy and on sales for your firm?

Worksheet 3: Forecasting Sales

Trend of Activity in Your Market(s)

- What is the existing general economic trend, and the trend of activity in your firm's market(s)?

- What is the existing trend of sales for your firm?

- What is the relationship between general economic trends, trends in your firm's markets, and sales for your firm?

- What sales figure(s) are projected for the planning horizon from an extrapolation of your firm's historical sales trend?

- Based on your understanding of historical relationships and your estimate of future conditions and planned activities, by what amount should projected sales be adjusted to obtain the most likely sales forecast?

- Assuming that the best set of forecast conditions were to occur over the planning horizon, what adjustments to the projected sales figures are necessary to obtain the optimistic sales forecast?

- Assuming the worst-case scenario for the planning horizon, what adjustments to the projected sales figures are necessary to obtain the pessimistic sales forecast?

- What budget intervals or subperiods have you established for the planning horizon?

- What are your most likely, optimistic, and pessimistic sales forecasts for the entire planning horizon and for each budget interval or subperiod in the horizon?

- What is the sales forecast for each of the periods within the most immediate budget interval? For example, if your planning is divided into one year budget intervals, and the intervals are divided into one-month periods, what are the forecast sales values for each of the next 12 months?

Worksheet 4: Short-Term Cash Planning

Making the Necessary Cash Budget Estimates

- Into how many periods (weeks, months, quarters) will the budget interval be divided?

- What are forecast sales for each period in the budget interval?

- What percentage of forecast sales is expected to be for cash?

- What are the accounts receivable collection pattern percentages to be applied to expected credit sales?

- What percentage of sales values will be used to estimate inventory purchases for each period in the budget interval?

- What is the expected lag in payments on the accounts payable created by inventory purchases?

- What are the expected cash costs of operations (payroll, rent, advertising, etc.) for each period in the budget interval?

- What are the expected cash outlays for loan repayment, fixed asset expenditures, taxes, and owner's withdrawals (dividends) for each period in the budget interval?

■ What is the minimum cash balance (contingency balance) that should be maintained to protect against forecasting error and unexpected adverse developments?

■ Using your most likely, optimistic, and pessimistic forecasts, what are the ranges of the cash budget estimates for each period in the upcoming budget interval?

■ What assumptions were made in preparing the cash budget? What are the critical assumptions underlying the economic and market forecasts? On what assumptions were the sales forecast and the cash flow estimates based? (These assumptions should be put in writing so they can be evaluated as part of the comparison of actual and forecast cash flows.)

Preparing the Short-Term Financial Plan

■ Using the largest financing required figure produced by your cash budget estimates for the budget interval, what are your firm's total working capital or temporary financing needs?

■ What specific working capital needs (inventory, accounts receivable, payroll, etc.) must be financed and in what amounts?

■ What are the excess cash figures produced by your cash budget estimates for each interval in the budget period?

■ Using the excess cash figure estimates, what loan repayment schedule can be established for the required working capital or temporary financing?

■ If the requested working capital loans were obtained and the worst-case scenario were to materialize, how and when would the loans be repaid?

Worksheet 5: Planning Long-Term Financing Needs

Estimating Required Financing

- What are the forecast sales values for each period in the planning horizon? For example, if you are preparing a long-term plan with a five-year horizon, what are the five annual forecast sales values?
  The forecast sales values should consist of projected historical trend values adjusted for any expected changes in the firm's internal or external environment.

- What are the percent of sales values for the expense and tax items to be used in the pro forma income statement calculations.
  These percentages should consist of historical relationships (for either a typical year or for an averaged set of relationships) between the expense items and sales. They should be adjusted for any anticipated changes in conditions.

- Based on the sales forecast and the expense and tax percent of sales values, what are the pro forma income statements for each year in the planning horizon?

- What projected net income figures are shown on the pro forma income statements for each year in the planning horizon?

- What are the percent of sales values for the current assets, accounts payable, and accruals to be used in the preparation of the current asset and current liability section of the pro forma balance sheet?
  These percentages should consist of historical relationships (for either a typical year or for an averaged set of relationships) between the various current asset and current liability items and sales. They should be adjusted for anticipated changes in the firm's policies or those of its trade creditor. For example, a change in inventory policy, or the credit terms offered to a firm's customers or by its suppliers.

■ What are the expected fixed asset levels that will appear on the pro forma balance sheet for each year in the planning horizon?
These values can be estimated using historical percent of sales values (for either a typical year or for an averaged set of relationships), or actual dollars for planned expenditures.

■ What is the expected addition to retained earnings amount for each year in the planning horizon?
These values are calculated by subtracting planned owner's withdrawals (dividends) from the pro forma net income figures.

■ What are the plug figure amounts for each year in the planning horizon?
These values are obtained by subtracting the spontaneous sources of funds (accounts payable, accruals, and the addition to retained earnings) from total assets (current assets plus fixed assets).

Worksheet 6: Preparing the Financial Plan—The Target Debt Ratio

■ What is your firm's average debt ratio for the last three years?

■ Using the banker's rule-of-thumb maximum debt ratio of 50% as a rough guideline, is your firm's average debt ratio within acceptable limits?

■ Based on the worst-case scenario cash budget for the next budget interval, will your firm generate the cash flows necessary to meet its existing debt obligations? Will surplus funds be available after debt obligations have been paid?

■ Given the banker's rule of thumb, the information produced by the worst-case cash budget, and your attitude toward risk, is your firm's existing average debt ratio within acceptable limits?

If the answer to this question is no, then plans should be scaled back unless financing needs can be met with additional owner's capital.

■ Given the banker's rule of thumb, the information produced by the worst-case cash budget, and your attitude toward risk, does your firm have excess debt capacity (borrowing ability)? That is, is the existing debt ratio lower than the acceptable maximum?

■ Using the pro forma balance sheets prepared for your planning horizon and treating any positive plug figures as debt financed, what is the projected debt ratio for the planning horizon?

■ Is this debt ratio within acceptable limits?

If the answer to this question is yes, your long-term plans are financially feasible without additional owner's investment.

- If the projected debt ratio exceeds acceptable limits, by how much can planned dividends (owner's withdrawals) be reduced to improve the projected debt ratio?
  Recall that as dividends are reduced, the amount of funds from operations available to meet financing needs is increased.

- Can the projected debt ratio reach acceptable limits after reducing planned dividends?

- If the projected debt ratio is still above acceptable limits after dividend adjustments, how much additional owner's capital are you or others willing to invest to support planned operations?

- If the additional owner's investment needed to bring the projected debt ratio within acceptable limits is not possible or desirable, do you have enough confidence in your plans to risk using an amount of debt financing that produces an excessive debt ratio?

- Can you convince a prospective lender that there is sufficient justification for your plans to loan an amount that produces an excessive debt ratio?

If the answer to the final questions is no, plans must be scaled back to a level that can be adequately financed. To find this level, you must redo the steps in the long-term planning process using different assumptions for sales growth, dividends, owner's investment, and target debt ratio until an acceptable combination of these variables is found.

Where to Now?

This chapter concludes the section on financial planning. Up to this point, you have examined the two primary sources of information for financial management: financial analysis and financial planning. Armed with this background, you are now ready to learn how this information is applied in the most critical area of financial management of the small firm: working capital management.

Introduction to Working Capital Management

The dominant theme throughout this book has been the importance of cash flow to the success and longevity of the small firm. As the next three chapters will reveal, nothing is more important to the cash flow process than the rate at which it circulates as working capital. Management and control of cash flow is a vital part of the firm's operations. What you will learn about working capital management in Part Three is outlined below.

The Third Ingredient of Sound Financial Management

TOPIC	CONCEPTS DISCUSSED
Account Receivable Management	The impact of accounts receivable on the cash cycle.
	The nature of credit terms and the cost of extending credit.
	The information and techniques necessary to effectively manage and control accounts receivable balances.
Inventory Management	The impact of inventory on the cash cycle.
	The cost of carrying inventory.
	The techniques and information necessary to effectively manage and control inventory balances.
Cash Management	The nature, role, and cost of holding money assets.
	Techniques for managing liquidity balances.
Accounts Payable Management	The nature, role, and cost of using trade credit.
	The information and techniques necessary to effectively manage accounts payable balances.

Part Three

The Meaning of Working Capital

Like the concept of cash flow, working capital is something everyone seems to understand, but it can be difficult to adequately describe. Often, small business managers think of working capital only in terms of the cash or financing needed to operate the business. While this is true in part, it is neither a complete nor a useful working definition of the concept. Thinking of working capital as a given quantity of cash ignores the fact that only a portion of the firm's cash or liquid balances actually sits idle at any given moment. Most dollars of working capital are constantly on the move. They first circulate from purchases into a temporary home as inventory. When the product is sold the cash takes the form of accounts receivable. If and when the customer pays the bill, working capital is finally released back into the cash account.

Given the elusive nature of this beast, what then is a good working definition of working capital? It is useful for you to think of *working capital* as the amount of financing required to sustain optimal balances in your firm's working assets. *Working assets* are those assets that will turn over or release cash within a relatively short period of time; they include inventory, accounts receivable, and the firm's stock of liquid assets. The concept of working capital is built on three important elements:

- Financing working assets.
- The amount of cash tied up in working assets.
- The speed with these assets are converted to cash.

In essence, working capital management is really cash flow management. It involves managing the cash flows associated with each of its major components.

Managing the Components of Working Capital

The final three chapters of this book detail the principles that underlie the management of working capital and each of its components. As you study these principles, keep this point in mind: When unnecessary working capital balances are avoided, the movement of dollars through the various working capital components is accelerated, and a firm's cash flows and profitability are improved. The following overview of the subject of working capital management highlights this point.

Accounts Receivable Management

The current asset accounts receivable represents credit sales that have trapped a firm's valuable cash. The longer that credit customers delay or are allowed to delay payment, the longer the average collection period, the slower the cash turnover rate, and the greater the cost of carrying accounts receivable. The goal then of receivables management is to maintain a credit policy that balances the benefits from extending credit against the cost and risk of doing so.

Good credit management and control can be a positive force for a firm. Effectively applied, it will increase sales volume and minimize cash needlessly tied up in unnecessary receivables balances. As you will learn, the prime ingredient of good credit management is good information.

Inventory Management

While a firm's inventory represents stocks of raw materials and/or finished goods, it is also a holding stage for cash. Cash is trapped in inventory from the time of delivery to the final acceptance of the product by the customer. As inventory balances increase, the amount of cash tied up in inventory increases and the rate at which cash circulates through working capital is reduced.

The obviously unattainable goal of inventory management is to have zero inventory balances, and no cash tied up in this asset. Realistically, however, the stock of inventory must be sufficient to smooth out any imbalance between purchasing, production, and sales; to ensure that all reasonable demands on inventory can be met as expeditiously as possible; and to provide a hedge against uncertainty. The goal then of inventory management is to maintain ideal balances — neither too much nor too little. To do so requires good forecasts, good information, and the application of rational techniques for controlling inventory levels.

Cash Management

It is not possible to manage and control a firm's cash flows without controlling its cash balances. Cash and other money assets are important components of working capital. Without sufficient liquidity, normal operations are impaired and there is no protection against unforeseen contingencies. Yet the amount of the firm's scarce financial resources held in the form of money assets should be carefully controlled. Carrying excessive liquidity is an unnecessary waste of financial resources, and insufficient liquidity places the firm at risk. The goal then of cash management is to hold only those amounts that are necessary to meet identified needs.

Accounts Payable Management

The current liability accounts payable represents obligations that arise from credit purchases of inventory. Commonly referred to as trade credit, accounts payable is often the most important source of financing working capital needs for the small firm. The focus then of accounts payable management is the information and techniques needed to maximize the benefits gained from this form of credit, while at the same time maintaining sound supplier relations.

Chapter 11
Accounts Receivable Management

Actively controlling the funds invested in accounts receivable is a key component of working capital management, and the focus of credit policy. Credit policy involves decisions on what credit terms should be offered customers, which customers should receive credit, and how the receivables should be collected, managed and controlled. These activities determine both the amount of receivables that are generated for a given volume of sales, and the length of time they are outstanding. Learning about the rudiments of credit policy and how to manage and control receivables are the topics of this chapter.

What you will learn about accounts receivable management is outlined below.

TOPIC	CONCEPTS DISCUSSED
Accounts Receivable and Cash Flow	Why accounts receivable represents an investment of your firm's scarce funds.
	How accounts receivable affects your firm's cash cycle, and why the investment in this asset requires financing.
	How to calculate the cost of carrying receivables.
Accounts Receivable Management	Guidelines for extending credit.
	The information needed to monitor and control receivables.
	Techniques used to monitor and control receivables.
	Guidelines for an effective collection policy.

If your firm is typical of most small businesses, a large percentage of its limited financial resources are invested or tied up in the receivables created by credit sales. Credit sales are similar to a dangerous two-edged sword: The sword cuts favorably as well as unfavorably. On the one hand, extending credit enhances sales by attracting customers that may otherwise be lost if credit is not available. Conversely, careless or nonexistent control over accounts receivable results in scarce cash tied up in slow-paying accounts, unnecessary losses from bad debts, and the need for additional financing.

Because the two unfavorable outcomes can spell financial disaster for your firm, careful control over the investment in accounts receivable is crucial to having a sound working capital position. You must make every effort to maximize the benefits of extending credit and carrying receivables, while minimizing the cost of doing so. To achieve effective management of your firm's accounts receivable, it is necessary to:

- Monitor credit sales to detect unintended changes in the amount of funds invested in receivables, or the rate at which outstanding accounts are collected.

- Stay apprised of the length of time individual accounts have been outstanding.

- Identify potential problem accounts before the fact.

- Detect changes in the behavior or payment pattern of key accounts.

- Establish and enforce a sound collection policy, and effective procedures for dealing with delinquent accounts.

Accounts Receivable and Required Financing

Receivables arising from credit sales are listed by the accountant as a current asset on a firm's balance sheet. They are considered an asset because each receivable represents ownership of a valuable claim on the customer's net worth in the event of default. Because receivables are assumed to be highly liquid, near-cash assets, they are treated as current items. This latter characterization, while appropriate to sound accounting, is not a useful way for you to view receivables.

From the standpoint of the small business manager, accounts receivable should be considered a "so near, yet so far" near-cash asset. Credit sales may be an important revenue item for the accountant preparing a firm's income statement, but to a small firm strapped for cash, a credit sale is not really a sale until the account has been collected. This is a subtle but important point. Prior to collection, the only thing tangible a credit sale produces for a firm is a financial burden that strains its cash resources. Up to the point of collection, an unpaid account represents an insidious pool that traps and holds a firm's scarce cash.

When a credit sale rather than a cash sale is made, the firm is denied the liquidity necessary to replace the resources used in creating that sale. A credit sale does not produce the funds to replace inventory, pay creditors, meet payroll, or do anything else that requires the use of cash. Yet, while the credit sale is outstanding, a firm's normal responsibilities for meeting its financial obligations continue. It is not until the receivable is actually collected that this asset releases cash and a firm is able to recoup its investment. In essence, accounts receivable literally traps a firm's scarce cash and, as is the case with any other asset investment, must be financed.

The idea of financing accounts receivable may, at first glance, seem to be a mistake. Certainly, no checks are written when the credit sale is made, and no bills for the sale are received at a later date. But in a very real sense, receivables represent a drain on funds until the last, critical step in a firm's normal cash or working capital cycle is completed — the point at which receivables are collected.

Recall from the discussion in Chapter 4 that the normal working capital or cash cycle is the length of time elapsed from the date inventory is purchased or produced, through the time the inventory is sold for credit, to the date the receivable is actually collected. The time lapse associated with the cash cycle often creates a firm's most pressing need for recurring financing; and, the more liberal a firm's credit terms or the more lax its collection efforts, the longer the cycle and the greater the need for financing.

To clarify this point, re-examine the concepts associated with the cash cycle, average expenditures per day, required working capital financing, and Avanti's cash cycle that were discussed in Chapter 4.

Accounts Receivable and the Cash Cycle

Avanti's Cash Cycle and Working Capital Needs

Recall that the number of days in the cash or working capital cycle was calculated as inventory turnover in days, plus the average collection period (ACP) for accounts receivable, minus the average payment period for accounts payable (APP).

Cash Cycle = (Inventory Turnover in Days + ACP) – APP

The average expenditures per day ratio is calculated as cash operating expenses (cost of sales plus operating expenses minus depreciation) divided by 360.

Average Expenditures Per Day = Cash Operating Expenses ÷ 360

A rough estimate of the financing required to support the cash or working capital cycle can be obtained by multiplying the cash cycle in days by the average expenditure per day.

Required Financing = Cash Cycle in Days x Average Expenditures per Day

In Chapter 4, it was determined that Avanti had a cash cycle of 37 days in 19X1 and 97 days in 19X2. Avanti's 19X1 income statement shows cost of sales of $148,000, total operating expenses of $90,428, and depreciation expense of $1,800. Using this data to calculate average expenditures per day and required financing, you can see that Avanti needed approximately $24,309 in 19X1 to finance its working capital needs.

$$\text{Average Expenditures Per Day} = (148,000 + 90,428 - 1,800) \div 360$$
$$= 236,628 \div 360$$
$$= \$657$$

$$\text{Required Financing (19X1)} = 37 \text{ days x } \$657$$
$$= \$24,309$$

In 19X2, Avanti's cash cycle increased by 60 days and the financing needed to support working capital grew to $63,729. This is an increase of $39,420 over 19X1.

$$\text{Required Financing (19X2)} = 97 \text{ days x } \$657$$
$$= \$63,729$$

Much of this $39,420 ($63,729 – $24,309) increase in Avanti's required working capital financing can be attributed to the burden created by the dramatic increase in accounts receivable. From 19X1 to 19X2, the ACP increased by 26 days — from 32 days to 58 days. This meant that the increase in receivables accounted for an additional $17,082 in required working capital financing.

$$\text{Financing Related to Receivables} = \text{Average Expenditures per Day}$$
$$\text{x Change in ACP}$$
$$\text{Financing Related to Receivables} = \$657 \text{ x } 60 \text{ days}$$
$$= \$17,082$$

It is no small wonder that Avanti's use of debt financing increased during this period.

The Cost of Extending Credit

Since credit sales delay the flow of cash into the business, there is a definite cost associated with granting credit. Again, this cost is not obvious because there is no immediate payment involved. This cost exists, however, and it is a real part of the cost of doing business.

To illustrate how the cost of carrying receivables arises, assume that your firm sells its product for $15, has a cost of sales of $10, and can borrow from Friendly Bank at an annual interest rate of 13%. This interest rate represents both an out-of-pocket cost if your firm borrows from the bank, and an opportunity cost if it can avoid borrowing. An *opportunity cost* can be thought of as a cost that is avoided or saved by not borrowing.

If your firm sells its product for cash, its gross profit margin is 33.3%. This is calculated as sales minus cost of sales, which is gross profit, divided by sales (recall from Chapter 4 the concept of the common-size income statement).

Gross Profit Margin = (Sales – Cost of Sales) ÷ Sales
Gross Profit Margin = ($15 – $10) ÷ $15
            = 33.3%

Conversely, if the sale is made for credit, your firm incurs the additional cost of the financing needed to carry the credit sale for the length of the credit period. In this case, the financing cost is $0.13 (13 cents) on every dollar borrowed for a year. This is a real cost of doing business and, when incurred, increases your firm's cost of operations and reduces its profit margin.

In this example, if you extend 30-day terms to your customers and borrow from the Friendly Bank for 30 days to carry the credit sale, your "true" gross profit margin drops from 33.3% to 32.6%. The revenue of $15 is reduced by the $10 cost of sales and about 11 cents in financing cost ($10 x 13% x 30 ÷ 365).

Gross Profit Margin = (Sales – Cost of Sales – Financing Cost) ÷ Sales
Gross Profit Margin = ($15 – $10 – $0.11) ÷ $15
            = $4.89 ÷ $15
            = 32.6%

If the credit sale remains unpaid for longer than 30 days, the length of time for which financing is needed also increases. The increased financing costs reduce the real gross profit margin even further. For example, if the receivable remains outstanding for 60 days (or your firm extends 60-day terms), interest costs rise to $0.21 for each dollar borrowed ($10 x 13% x 60 ÷ 365), and the profit margin declines to 31.9%.

Gross Profit Margin = ($15 – $10-- $0.21) ÷ $15
            = $4.79 ÷ $15
            = 31.9%

The message from this example is clear: It costs money to carry credit sales. If your credit terms are too liberal or if receivables are carried longer than indicated by your credit terms, the cost of doing business is increased unnecessarily and profit margins are eroded. Effective management of accounts receivable minimizes such problems.

Delinquent Accounts and Cash Flow

The volume of receivables your firm carries at any given time is determined by two factors: the volume of credit sales, and the collection pattern associated with those sales. Obviously, sales create accounts receivable, and higher sales rates increase the rate at which receivables are created. What may not be obvious is the fact that the longevity of credit sales also determines the level of receivables that must be carried. The longer the time period required to collect receivables, the greater the amount of receivables outstanding, and the greater the amount of scarce cash tied up in those receivables.

This message is also clear: While the volume of sales in any given period may be beyond your control, the length of time that a given level of receivables is outstanding is not. Outstanding receivables are a function of how effectively you monitor your accounts and administer your collection policy.

You have seen how delays in customer payments strain a firm's cash position and raise the cost of doing business. There is another, equally important side to accounts receivable management. If the length of time receivables are outstanding can be reduced, cash that would otherwise be tied up is freed for other uses, and the need for that amount of financing and its associated costs are avoided. Again, you can use Avanti's experience to illustrate this point.

Another Receivables Management Lesson for Avanti

Avanti's average collection period of 32 days in 19X1 was virtually ideal. Thirty-two days was close to both the firm's stated credit terms of Net 30 days, and to the average collection period for the industry (the experience of other firms in the same line of business). As seen in Chapter 4, things took a definite turn for the worse in 19X2. Avanti's receivables swelled to $54,600 from the 19X2 level of $25,778. Some of this increase was due to the increase in sales from 19X1 to 19X2; but most resulted from the increase in the average collection period to 58 days.

Since receivables were now on Avanti's books for an additional 26 days, cash inflows were delayed for that period. To offset the cash shortage, Avanti had to obtain additional working capital financing from the bank at an interest rate of 14%. Much of this costly financing could have been avoided with careful control over accounts receivable.

If the average collection period for 19X1 of 32 days had been maintained in 19X2, the average level of accounts receivable would have been $30,124 instead of the $54,600 that the firm actually carried. This means that 26 days of cash flow or a total of $24,476 ($54,600 – $30,124) would have been freed to meet operating needs, and costly bank financing in this amount would have been avoided. At an interest rate of 14%, Avanti would have saved $3,426 in interest charges ($24,476 x .14) that year.

The lesson that Avanti learned, and the message of this chapter, is the critical need for effective management of those aspects of accounts receivable that are under the direct control of the small firm manager.

At best, the cost for not doing so is high; at worst, the cost of poor receivables management is a firm's survival. Now, explore guidelines that will assist you in establishing a sound credit policy, techniques that will help you effectively manage your accounts receivable, and recommendations for conducting your collection efforts.

Extending Credit

The first credit policy decision that you must make as manager is whether credit should be extended and, if so, the terms to be offered. These decisions involve a delicate trade-off between the desire for sales, and the risks associated with committing scarce funds to an uncertain return. A no-credit policy, or a policy which stresses stringent credit terms, highly selective credit customers, and aggressive collections will work to eliminate or minimize bad-debt loss and the funds tied up in receivables. However, these policies may work to restrict sales and profits. At the other extreme, an overly lenient credit policy and/or sloppy receivables management may inflate receivables, collection and administrative expenses, and bad-debt loss without a compensating increase in profits.

For better or worse, the decision on the credit terms to be offered is usually made for a typical small firm by competitive pressure and industry custom. If competitors offer credit or prospective customers expect credit terms to be offered, a small firm is virtually coerced into doing as the competition does or risk losing sales. Being forced to offer credit does not, however, mean that the cost and risks associated with extending credit cannot be controlled. You can employ preventive measures that minimize overall credit costs.

Know the Real Cost of Granting Credit

In order for your firm to maintain acceptable profit margins, extending credit and carrying receivables must be cost-justified. Benefits, in the form of increased sales, must exceed the overall cost of granting credit. In addition to the cost of financing receivables as discussed above, credit costs include a variety of related hidden expenses that management must identify and evaluate. These include the out-of-pocket expense of analyzing customer credit capability, recordkeeping, monitoring receivables, collecting problem accounts, bad debt loss, and the cost of your time spent on administering credit-related activities. The impact of all these costs on your firm's profit margin must be factored into each individual decision to extend credit. If profit margins cannot support the cost and risk associated with a particular credit sale, do not make the credit sale. It is better to miss a sale than to make a credit sale that will lose money.

Receive Compensation for Waiting

In addition to the cost of extending credit, your firm incurs additional financing costs when receivables are carried beyond the normal credit period. Customers who delay payment disrupt the firm's normal cash flow cycle and increase its cost of extending credit. These customers should pay for this privilege. Do not be afraid to institute a reasonable credit charge, such as $1^{1}/2\%$ per month, on balances that extend beyond the net period. This is nothing more than sound business practice. If you cannot cover all credit costs, you cannot stay in business.

Know Your Credit Customer

This first commandment of credit management is as straightforward as the old adage that "an ounce of prevention is worth a pound of cure." It is essential that information on the credit applicant's character, financial position, and capacity to pay is gathered and evaluated before credit is extended. Judicious selection of creditworthy customers, and the careful determination of reasonable customer credit limits will prevent the vast majority of difficult collection problems and bad debt losses.

The author is reminded of a succinct summary on the importance of discriminating credit selection made by an owner of a small chain of paint stores. He stated:

> *"Competition in this business is fierce and I simply cannot afford to extend credit to everyone who walks in off the street wearing white coveralls and a painting hat claiming to be a painting contractor. If a credit application does not indicate the customer is worthy of receiving credit, I don't extend it."*

The information gathering process starts with a prospective customer's completed credit application. Regardless of the format or level of sophistication of this document, it should provide you with certain vital information. The application should contain questions that allow you to determine the customer's:

- References, which should include the customer's bank and other credit suppliers;

- Business and credit history;

- Payment practices and reputation for honesty; and

- Financial condition.

It is your responsibility to evaluate the information provided on the credit application as well as what can be gleaned from other sources such as local or industry credit bureaus, credit rating agencies such as Dun & Bradstreet, or competitors. While the investigation and analysis takes time, it is an investment that pays large dividends.

If the credit analysis indicates that a prospective customer is marginal but still a desirable risk, you can minimize its loss exposure by limiting the customer's initial credit line. Later, the credit limit can be increased as payment practices warrant.

It is good business practice to make clear to each customer, before credit is granted, the exact nature and details of your firm's credit policy, and what is expected of customers in return for receiving credit. Each customer should understand two critical facts of credit life. First, receiving credit is a privilege that your small firm is not in a financial position to have abused. Your firm's suppliers and creditors expect to be paid on time, and to do so your firm must receive timely payment from its customers. Second, granting credit creates a two-way promise: your firm's promise to provide goods or services according to established terms, and the customer's promise to meet those terms. The customer's failure to do so is a broken promise, and the deliberate theft of your firm's critical cash flow.

Announce Your Credit Policy

Monitoring accounts receivable involves generating the information necessary to determine whether credit policy is being administered as intended, and whether the investment in receivables is consistent with the current level of sales. As we learned in Chapter 4, unless management has made a deliberate change in credit policy or in its collection effort, the level of accounts receivable should vary directly with the volume of sales. If sales increase, receivables expand and scarce funds are absorbed; if sales decline, receivables decline and funds are released. It is the unintended increase in accounts receivable, however, that is your concern and the focal point of any monitoring effort. Investigate the tools that are used for this purpose. They are recordkeeping, the average collection period ratio, and aging schedules.

Monitoring Receivables

It has been suggested throughout this book that a major determinant of good management is good information. Good information means good data, and this implies the existence of good records. While it takes time to record the necessary details surrounding your receivables, it is time well spent. Without such records, it is impossible to maintain satisfactory control over receivables, and the absence of adequate controls jeopardizes your firm's ability to survive.

Recordkeeping

In Chapter 4, we identified the average collection period (ACP) ratio as a measure of the average rate at which receivables are collected and, as such, an indicator of the relationship between sales and the level of receivables. While this ratio provides insight into the overall behavior of receivables, its usefulness is limited to this purpose. Effective control over receivables requires both aggregate information, and detailed information on the crucial fluctuations that take place during the year.

The Average Collection Period Ratio

The information most essential to the effective management and control of accounts receivables is the length of time accounts have been

Aging Receivables

outstanding. While there are a variety of ways this information can be prepared for analysis, each approach involves some form of an age distribution or age schedule. This type of report is usually prepared monthly for both individual accounts and aggregate receivables, and the focus is the length of time receivables have been outstanding.

The simple, yet informative, set of monthly aging schedules used by Avanti are shown on tables 11.1 and 11.2. Both the individual and aggregate schedules have been prepared for the month ending January, 19X3. When evaluating these schedules, Avanti's management looks for:

- An indication of the overall effectiveness of credit policy.

- Signs of deterioration in the rate at which receivables are being collected.

- Accounts that are past due, and the length of time they have been delinquent.

- Signs of potential problem accounts.

- Signs of change in large or key accounts.

- Accounts that show abnormal increases in size, or peculiarities in the pattern of payments.

Examine Avanti's schedules more closely and learn what they discovered about the results of their newly adopted receivables management policy. Recall from chapters 2 and 4 that control over receivables had been virtually nonexistent in 19X2. The result was a disproportionate growth in the level of receivables, and a costly increase in the average collection period. Correcting these problems was the goal of Avanti management's rigorous control efforts.

Who's Overdue

First, look at the schedule of individual accounts shown on Table 11.1. This schedule identifies each of Avanti's active customers, the existing balance from each purchase, the number of days the account is past due, and the percent of total receivables that each account balance represents. The values for the "Balance Due" and "Due Date" were obtained from Avanti's internal records, while those for the "Days Past Due" and "% Total" were calculated.

The number of days past due is the difference between the due date and the date of the aging report (January 31, in this case). For example, the difference between January 15, 19X3 and January 31, 19X3 is 16 days past due. In Avanti's aging report, positive numbers in the Days Past Due column, such as 16 days for the Gary Slayton account, indicate the length of time the account has been outstanding beyond its due date.

Table 11.1
THE AVANTI COMPANY
By-Customer Aging Schedule
For the Period Ending January, 19X3

Customer Name	Balance Due	Due Date	Days Past Due	% of Total
Debi Brewer	$ 500	02/15/X3	(15)	1.1%
Charles Dennis	600	12/10/X2	21	1.3%
Charles Dennis	1,100	12/15/X3	16	2.3%
Kenny Gallagher	300	02/20/X3	(20)	0.6%
Andy Hamsley	900	12/30/X3	1	1.9%
Greg Almond	1,500	12/20/X2	11	3.2%
Lisa Marie	500	02/30/X3	(30)	1.1%
Morris Repairs	1,800	02/10/X2	(10)	3.8%
Rainbow Bicycle	1,700	02/15/X3	(15)	3.6%
Rally Bicycle	3,000	02/10/X3	(10)	6.3%
Rally Bicycle	6,000	01/25/X3	6	12.7%
Swan Bicycle	10,000	01/25/X3	6	21.1%
Swan Bicycle	7,000	02/30/X3	(30)	14.8%
Gary Slayton	1,000	01/15/X3	16	2.1%
Trip Bicycle	7,000	10/30/X2	91	14.8%
Trip Bicycle	2,000	11/30/X2	61	4.2%
Twelve-Speed Drive	2,500	12/30/X2	1	5.3%
Total	$47,400			100%

This table contains an example of a monthly aging schedule that details the status of individual customer accounts. This by-customer report provides the information needed to monitor and control credit.

To suit their own preferences, Avanti's management has decided to embellish the aging report by showing the number of days remaining until the scheduled due date as a negative number. For example, from February 15, 19X3 to January 31, 19X3 is a negative 15 days, and is shown in the Days Past Due column as (15). This is the case for the Debi Brewer account. Avanti management has found that by displaying the days remaining until the due date as negative values, it is easier to identify the accounts that should be paid, and the time at which they should be paid. This information is valuable for tracking customer payment behavior, spotting potential trouble accounts, and for cash flow planning.

The % Total values are calculated as the percentage that each outstanding balance represents of total receivables on that date. In Avanti's case, outstanding receivables on January 31, 19X3 total $47,400. The $500 balance for the Debi Brewer is 1.1% of total receivables ($500 ÷ $47,400), and the balance for the Gary Slayton account is 2.1% of the total ($1,000 ÷ $47,400). With an understanding of how the numbers are derived, interpreting the customer aging schedule can be easy.

Avanti's management uses the customer aging schedule to highlight:

- Accounts that are past due.

- The status of key customer accounts.

- Unusual activity in accounts.

- Account balances that exceed established credit limits.

Notice that the customer analysis report shown on Table 11.1 indicates that Swan Bicycle is Avanti's most important customer. Swan accounts for 35.9% (21.1% + 14.8%) of total receivables. Since the largest portion of Swan's balance is only six days past due and the remainder is current, the account requires no managerial action.

Rally Bicycle is also a large desirable customer. The account represents 19% (6.3% + 12.7%) of total receivables, and is mostly current. The same cannot be said for Avanti's other large customer, Trip Bicycle. Trip's balance represents 19% (14.8% + 4.2%) of total receivables, and most of the account is over 90 days past due. These numbers convey a clear signal that action on this problem account is long past due.

A quick scan of the other values in the Past Due and % Total columns suggests that Avanti's other customers are small, mostly current accounts. None of these balances represent more than 5.3% of total receivables; the majority of the past due values are negative numbers (current accounts); and, Avanti's management has determined that none of the outstanding balances in this group exceed their established credit limits.

With the exception of the Trip account, Avanti's credit policy controls seem to be working. Further evidence of this fact is provided by the aggregate aging schedule shown on Table 11.2.

An aggregate aging schedule, such as that shown below, is designed to furnish information on the rate at which receivables are being collected. Notice that this report lists the total of all outstanding balances falling into established past due categories, and the percentage of total receivables that each represents. Since Avanti has net 30-day terms, its management has chosen to divide the aging schedule into the commonly used 30-day age categories.

Aggregate Aging Information

Table 11.2 Example of Avanti's Aggregate Aging Schedule

Dollar & Percentage		Period Outstanding				
	Current Accounts	1 – 30 Days	31 – 60 Days	61 – 90 Days	Past 90 Days	Total
Dollar Amount	$14,800	23,600	0	2,000	7,000	$47,400
Percentage	31.1 %	49.8 %	0	4.2 %	14.9 %	100 %

The aggregate aging report shown on this table provides management with information on the overall rate at which receivables are being collected. The key piece of information shown on this report is the percentage of total receivables contained in each past-due category.

The Current Accounts column contains the total of outstanding balances that are not past due. Listed below the dollar total is the percentage of total receivables that this amount represents. As indicated by the remaining headings, each column represents more distant 30-day age categories.

The dollar amount in each age category is obtained by summing the appropriate balance due values from Table 11.1, the Aging Schedule — By Customer. For example, the $14,800 amount in the Current Accounts column is the sum of all outstanding balances with negative days past due values, and the $23,600 amount in the next column is the sum of the outstanding balances that are between 1 and 30 days past due. The percentages in each column are obtained by dividing the dollar value in that column by the total outstanding receivables figure. For instance, the 31.2% in the Current Accounts column was calculated as $14,800 ÷ $47,400.

Before you interpret the information produced by Avanti's aging report, it would be useful to ask yourself this question: If I could dictate the ideal situation, how would the aging schedule for your firm look? You would undoubtedly want to avoid past due accounts and have the total of all outstanding balances in the current accounts category. If past dues do exist, you would want the delinquency period minimized and balances appearing in the most recent past due category. In short, the larger the dollar amounts, the number of customers, or the percentages in distant age categories, the further from the ideal, and the more alarming the situation.

From Table 11.2, you can see that Avanti management's efforts have credit policy headed in the right direction. Almost one-third of the outstanding receivables are current, and about 81% (31.1% + 49.8%) are less than 30 days past due. While management should work to reduce the percentage of receivables in the 1- to 30-day past-due category, the only major problem indicated by the report is the relatively large dollar amount over 61 days past due. As you know from the analysis of Table 11.1, this is the Trip account.

Collection Policy

It has been suggested that credit policy involves three main activities: 1) the decision on granting credit and the terms to be offered; 2) monitoring receivables to control the funds tied up in this asset; and 3) formulating and carrying out an effective collection policy. This latter activity is as crucial to sound credit management as the first two. Regardless of how carefully credit applicants are screened, a firm is likely to have delinquent accounts and experience bad debt loss. With an effective collection effort, however, the length of delinquent periods and the chance of delinquencies becoming losses can be minimized.

The Fundamentals of Good Collection Policy

Designing and maintaining an effective credit policy is not a simple task. The policy must strike a delicate balance between generating the pressure needed to obtain payment from delinquent accounts and avoiding jeopardizing future business by offending customers. Unfortunately, there are no rules or formulas that will guarantee a successful policy. In most cases, you have to move toward an acceptable approach to collections, gradually using judgment and learning by trial and error. There are, however, some guidelines that, when coupled with good business judgment, provide the nucleus of an effective collection policy. These guidelines include:

- The foundation of a collection policy should be clear, effective communication between a firm and its customers. This begins with the customer's application for credit, and continues through any subsequent contact with a customer. The emphasis of this communication should be a customer's responsibility as a recipient of credit, and a firm's tenuous position as a creditor.

- When customer records indicate that an account is approximately 10 to 15 days past the net period (for example, 40 to 45 days old when credit terms are net 30 days) the first contact should be made. This can be done by either telephone or mail, but in either case the message should be a gentle reminder that there has been an "oversight" on the customer's part. The date of the contact, and the nature of the response (hopefully, a promise to "put the check in the mail") should be noted in the customer's file. Also, the account should be flagged as delinquent and no further credit granted without satisfactory arrangements made to eliminate the existing balance.

- If the past due account reaches the next age category (for example, 60 days when credit terms are net 30 days), the customer should again be contacted. This contact should serve two purposes: to send the message that the customer has broken promises and abused the credit privilege; and, to determine the reason for the customer's failure to pay.

If the reason for nonpayment is financial inability and there seems to be little hope for improvement at some reasonable time in the future, the firm has little choice but to take immediate legal action. If the customer is unable to pay but has an encouraging financial future, a mutually acceptable repayment plan should be worked out. This plan should be accompanied by a legally enforceable promissory note.

If it is determined that the delinquent customer is financially capable but simply abusing the credit privilege, a message should be something as harsh as "although the firm values your business, you have not met your responsibilities and leave me no recourse but to take legal action." It is advisable to follow up this contact with a registered letter indicating that within 10 days the promised legal action will be taken. Again, the date and results of these contacts should be noted in the account's file. These notes and a registered letter serve as acceptable evidence of a "reasonable attempt to collect" for both the courts if legal action is taken, and the IRS if the account is written off as a bad debt.

- If the account reaches the next age category (for example, 90 days when credit terms are net 30 days) and the customer has failed to make payment or to abide by the established agreement, the promised vigorous action should be initiated. As a general rule, if the account is small it should be submitted to a collection agency. In the case of small accounts, it is usually not worth the manager's time and the legal expense involved to have the firm attempt collection itself. In the case of larger accounts, the firm should pursue legal action. Where dollar limits allow, small claims court should be used. Most often, cases in the small claims court can be successfully adjudicated without the need for legal representation.

It is worth noting that while generalizing human behavior is difficult, there is one common trait of which informed creditors are well aware: A debtor who shuns communication and fails to respond to telephone or mail contact is either unwilling or unable to pay. In these cases, do not wait until the account is 60 or 90 days past due before you take vigorous action.

Also, changes in the buying behavior and payment pattern of customers are often danger signals. For example, if a cash customer suddenly switches to credit, question why. If one order comes in larger than ever, find out if the customer is getting ready to stock up and run. If a regular customer pays less than usual on the account, find out if that means the customer is having financial difficulty. If partial payments are received on bills due in full, or payments are made with slow-to-clear out-of-town checks, determine if these are storm warnings.

A Final Thought

Given the importance of receivables management to the financial health of your firm, it would be useful to summarize the key points made in this chapter. These points can serve as fundamental rules by which you approach the administration of credit policy.

- **Adopt a Cash Flow Perspective**. Your accountant treats a credit sale as revenue at the time the sale is made. While the recognition of a credit sale as revenue is appropriate accounting practice, your firm's financial health is determined by cash flow, not the accounting concept of revenue. Conduct your activities as if the product is not sold until the account is actually collected.

- **Adopt a Banker's Perspective**. A banker views your receivables as an investment in an asset that must be financed. You must think of receivables the same way. Extending credit may enhance sales, but it also increases your need for funds.

- **Adopt a Financial Perspective**. While receivables represent potential cash flow, the cash does not flow until collection occurs. Up to that point, receivables represent invested dollars that cannot be used for other purposes. The cost of these dollars, the cost of administering the credit, and the cost of your firm's bad debt losses must be factored into your firm's normal profit margin. If the profit margin on a credit sale cannot support these costs, do not make the credit sale.

■ **Your Firm Must Be Compensated for Waiting**. Closely related to the concept of the cost of extending credit is the cost of carrying receivables beyond the normal credit period. Customers who delay payment disrupt your normal cash flow cycle, and add to your financing burden. They should pay for the privilege. Do not be afraid to institute a reasonable credit charge on balances that extend beyond the net period. This is nothing more than sound business practice. If you cannot cover your costs of doing business, you cannot stay in business.

■ **Be Alert to Changes in Economic Activity**. When the pace of overall economic activity slows, your customers will delay payments and you will suffer the cost and strains associated with lagging collections. To minimize this burden, investigate methods that can increase cash flow or reduce the cost of carrying receivables. For example, you may consider using either interim billing periods or billing when the invoice is received, rather than waiting until the end of the month to mail statements. Or, in a service firm or job order shop, adopt protective policies such as requiring a down payment before a large job is started as well as periodic progress payments. These and similar policies produce the survival tactics that maximize the chances of staying afloat when times get tough.

■ **Keep Good Records**. Good information means good data, and this implies good records. While it takes time to record and evaluate the details surrounding your receivables, it is time well spent. Control is impossible without good information. Note that the burden of recordkeeping and information production can be reduced substantially through the use of a well-designed, computerized receivables model. For information on available models software, see the card enclosed at the end of this book.

■ **Monitor Accounts Receivable Records**. Equally as important as keeping records is using the information. This requires an investment of time, but again it is time well spent. Careless or nonexistent control over receivables has sounded the death knell for all too many small firms. During the high interest rate period of the early 1980s, the bankruptcy rate for small firms reached the level of the Depression years of the 1930s. Far too many of the firms that failed during this period did so with large amounts of uncollected receivables on the books.

Equally as important as receivables management to the financial health of a typical small firm is control over inventory. Inventory management is discussed in the following chapter.

Where to Now?

Chapter 12
Inventory Management

Inventory, like accounts receivable, is a critical component of working capital and deserves your special attention. In a typical small firm, this asset represents a sizeable investment of funds and, for a merchandising concern (retail and wholesale), the lifeblood of the business. As used here, inventory refers to those items that are either currently ready for resale, or will be prepared for that purpose. For the merchandising firm this means the stock of salable goods available to satisfy anticipated customer demand. In the manufacturing firm, inventory refers to the raw materials and work-in-process that will be converted to salable goods, and the supply of finished goods needed to support expected sales volume.

In spite of its importance, poor physical and financial control of inventory is a common and often costly problem among small firms. At the very least, poor inventory control leads to substandard financial performance; and, at worst, results in financial ruin. From what you have learned about management's need for good information, it should come as no surprise that the primary reason for poor inventory control is the absence of good inventory records. All too often, the small business manager trusts important inventory information to memory, or limits information gathering to what can be obtained from physical inspection and/or the annual inventory count. These hit-or-miss approaches do not produce the quality of information necessary to effectively manage and control this critical asset. Good information results from a systematic effort to collect, organize, record, analyze, and evaluate inventory-transactions data. This information, along with the active management of inventory, will:

- Provide reliable information for planning and decision making.

- Reduce the occurrence of lost sales and/or production interruptions caused by inventory shortages or complete stockouts.

- Minimize the possibility of overstocking inventory which increases the cost of operations, drains scarce cash from the business, and increases the potential for large losses in value.

- Minimize the risk of inventory obsolescence.

■ Minimize the possibility of losses that result from unauthorized withdrawals from inventory.

What you will learn about inventory management and control is outlined below.

TOPIC	CONCEPTS DISCUSSED
Inventory Management	The purpose of inventory management.
	The benefits of an effective inventory management and control system.
Inventory and Cash Flow	How inventory affects your firm's cash position.
	How to calculate the target level of inventory using the turnover ratio.
Requirements for an Inventory Management and Control System	What constitutes a good record-keeping system.
	How to monitor and evaluate the information produced by your recordkeeping system.
	The ABC Method of inventory control.
	The role of the sales forecast in inventory management.
	The principles of inventory control.

Inventory Management and Control

The need to have stock on hand to meet either customer demand or production requirements, or both, creates a mandatory investment of your firm's scarce funds. For your small firm, it is essential that this investment is managed effectively. An over-commitment or an under-commitment of funds to inventory can be damaging to your firm's financial health. Investing in inventory can be compared to the purchase of business insurance. If too little insurance is obtained, you save the cost of premiums but risk losses that are suffered when unexpected events occur. On the other hand, excess insurance results in unnecessary costs that drain cash from the firm and provides little or no additional benefits in return. The investment of funds in inventory, like insurance, must be carefully managed and controlled.

Good inventory management and control results in appropriate inventory balances for a given set of forecast conditions and expected sales. Such balances maximize the cost/benefit trade-off associated with financing and carrying inventory. The benefits from holding appropriate balances come in the form of the cash flows and earnings generated by avoiding stockouts (lost sales and production delays). The costs that are avoided by holding optimum inventory balances are unnecessary carrying costs. Inventory carrying costs, which have been estimated to represent from 15 percent to 25 percent of the value of inventory, include:

- Interest paid on bank loans used to finance the investment in inventory.

- Lost earnings on cash tied up in excess inventory.

- Increased holding costs associated with storing and insuring excess inventory.

- Declining profits caused by the slowing of inventory and asset turnover; that is, inadequate sales for the level of inventory held.

- Reduced inventory value due to obsolescence of unsold and aging inventory.

- Reduced or lost profit margins on the forced sale of aging or obsolete inventory.

To get an idea of how costly it can be when appropriate inventory balances are not held, look at what happened at Avanti in 19X2.

Inventory and Cash Flows

In 19X2, Avanti enjoyed a welcomed increase in dollar sales. Unfortunately, and to the chagrin of management, other important indicators of performance, such as cash flow and profits, were extremely disappointing. One source of this disappointment, lax credit and collection controls, was discussed in Chapter 11, Accounts Receivable Management. Further analysis of Avanti's financial statements revealed an additional problem area: an inordinate and costly buildup of inventory.

Although sales increased during the period 19X1 and 19X2, both the level of inventory and the cash invested in this asset increased much faster. This was made clear when Avanti's management calculated the percentage changes in sales and inventory for the period. Sales increased 17% from 19X1 to 19X2, but inventory jumped by a whopping 132% during that year. While it is true that higher sales levels require more inventory, the percentage increase in each should be roughly proportional. For instance, a 10% increase in sales should require approximately 10% more inventory to accommodate the increase. In Avanti's case, the disproportionate buildup of inventory reduced the inventory turnover rate below that of former, more efficient levels. This over-investment was clearly unwarranted and, no doubt, the result of poor inventory management and control.

Because of this administrative lapse, Avanti suffered unnecessary financing and carrying costs, lost profits, and a major drain on the firm's cash position. Had Avanti exercised closer control over inventory, a favorable turnover rate would have been maintained, the investment in inventory would have been substantially less, and the firm's cash position substantially better.

Inventory Buildup and the Cash Cycle

In 19X1, Avanti was able to maintain an inventory turnover rate of 6.1 times per year. This means that cash was tied up in inventory for about 59 days (360 ÷ 6.1). Materials were purchased roughly every 59 days, and about 59 days elapsed before finished products were converted into sales. Had Avanti been been able to maintain this 6.1 inventory turnover rate in 19X2, the inventory investment that year would have been $31,885 as opposed to the actual amount of $56,125 (see the 19X2 balance sheet). This means that Avanti would have had to borrow $24,240 less than they actually did to finance the inventory investment. Let's see how the more desirable inventory figure of $31,885 was determined.

Calculating the Target Level of Inventory

Calculation of a desired or target level of inventory requires nothing more than minor manipulation of the familiar inventory turnover ratio. Instead of using the ratio to calculate the rate of inventory turnover, start with a given or desired turnover rate and work in reverse order to find the level of inventory consistent with that rate. Recall that the inventory turnover ratio is calculated as:

Inventory Turnover = Cost of Sales ÷ Inventory

From this relationship, you can obtain the desired inventory level as follows:

Desired Inventory = Cost of Goods Sold ÷ Inventory Turnover

Using the cost of goods sold figure of $194,500 from Avanti's 19X2 income statement and the 19X1 inventory turnover ratio of 6.1 as the desired rate, the target or desired inventory level is calculated as:

Desired Inventory = $194,500 ÷ 6.1
= $31,885

Since Avanti's actual inventory level in 19X2 was $56,125, there was an over-investment in inventory of $24,220 ($56,125 – $31,885). Stated differently, if 19X2 inventory levels had been managed at least as efficiently as in 19X1, Avanti would have been able to free up $24,200 of cash for alternative uses. As Avanti has learned, the penalty for poor inventory management and control fits the crime: It is severe.

It is worth noting that, while the desired inventory calculation was used to illustrate the cash flow effects of poor inventory management, it can be a useful planning tool. By setting a target turnover rate, management can obtain a quick estimate of what inventory levels should be, given a forecast set of conditions.

An effective inventory management and control system depends on the following requirements:

Requirements for Sound Inventory Management

- A perpetual inventory recordkeeping system.

- A systematic process of monitoring and evaluating inventory records and inventory stocks.

- The use of sales forecasts to project inventory needs.

- A system for controlling inventory levels.

The best possible source of information for inventory control is a well-designed and up-to-date record of your firm's inventory transactions. The orderly recording of transactions and updating stock levels at the time transactions occur is known as a *perpetual inventory system*. Such a system produces timely information on the movement of items into and out of inventory; the rate at which inventory items are being sold or used; and the status of existing balances. To maintain a perpetual inventory system requires information on:

Recordkeeping

- Beginning balances in units and in dollar value for each major item or item grouping in inventory.

- Recorded purchases data including date, description, quantity, cost, dollar value, and vendor information for each major item or item grouping.

- Recorded usage or sales data, or both, including date, quantity, dollar value, product produced, and customer.

There are a variety of manual or computerized formats on which this essential data may be recorded. Assuming that key information requirements are met, the particular format used is a matter of personal preference. So that you can get an idea of a typical approach to inventory recordkeeping, examine the manual system used by Avanti prior to the firm's conversion to a computerized inventory management model.

The recordkeeping system consists of inventory control sheets which display summary inventory values for raw materials and for finished goods, and file cards which contain purchase, usage, and sales data for individual items or item groupings. The control sheets are prepared

Avanti's Manual System

for monthly periods but are updated weekly to reflect transactions in items of major significance. Updatings for less important item groupings take place at the end of the month.

The recording process begins with an update of the monthly control sheets. The initial entry on the finished goods control sheet is for the number of units and dollar value of the balance at the start of the month for each item or item grouping. The beginning balance figures are the same as the ending balances from the previous monthly control sheet. Weekly updating entries include the number and dollar value of the units added to inventory during the week (purchased or produced), the units and dollar value deducted during the week (sales), and the units and dollar value of inventory on hand at the end of the week. An example of a finished goods inventory control sheet is shown on Table 12.1.

The entry procedure is virtually identical for the raw materials inventory control sheets. The ending balances from the previous month are transferred to the new month as beginning balances, and weekly and monthly updatings are made for the units and dollar values of what is purchased (units in) and used in production (units out). An example of a raw materials inventory control sheet is shown on Table 12.2.

The daily recordings for individual items or item groupings are made on separate file cards. These cards are prepared for a one month period. The information contained on the individual file card includes the beginning balance, the unit and dollar value of purchases, the unit and dollar value of what is used in production or sold, and ending balances. The monthly totals include units, dollar values, average unit cost (total dollar cost ÷ number of units used or sold), and the usage rate. This latter figure is an average of the number of units used to that date. The usage rate, which is discussed later in this chapter, is an important figure for projecting inventory needs. An example of a Finished Goods File Card is shown on Table 12.3.

A Final Word on Recordkeeping

There is no question that recordkeeping and the periodic evaluation of these records takes time. It should be emphasized again that this is time well spent. The benefits, in terms of improved cash flows, lower financing expense, and the reduced risk of inventory obsolescence will more than outweigh the costs. In many small firms, these benefits can mean the difference between success and failure.

One last point on inventory recordkeeping should be stressed. The degree of sophistication required of a firm's recordkeeping system should be determined by the character and importance of its inventory. If the stock of inventory is small and/or consists of easily identifiable items, any reliable, cost-effective method of tracking and controlling inventory is appropriate. In these cases, an orderly, handwritten system

Table 12.1

THE AVANTI COMPANY

Finished Goods Monthly Control Sheet — Competition Frame

For the Month Ending January, 19X3

Week	Beginning Balance Units	Beginning Balance Dollars	Production Units	Production Dollars	Sales Units	Sales Dollars	Ending Balance Units	Ending Balance Dollars	Sales Rate
One	10	$5,000	5	$2,550	7	$5,600	8	$4,080	7
Two	.	.	.	.	.	.	.	.	.
Three	.	.	..	.	.	.	.	.	.
Four	.	.	.	.	.	.	.	.	.
Totals	10	$5,000	?	?	?	?	?	?	?

The finished goods control sheet contains summary values for the amount of beginning inventory, the number of units produced and sold, and the amount of ending inventory during a given month. A control sheet is used in conjunction with inventory file cards to monitor and control inventory levels.

Table 12.2

THE AVANTI COMPANY

Raw Materials Monthly Control Sheet — Front Forks

For the Month Ending January, 19X3

Week	Beginning Balance Units	Beginning Balance Dollars	Purchases Units	Purchases Dollars	Used Units	Used Dollars	Ending Balance Units	Ending Balance Dollars	Usage Rate
One	700	$1,050	800	$11,200	200	$2,900	1300	$18,850	200
Two	.	.	.	.	.	.	.	.	
Three	.	.	.	.	.	.	.	.	
Four	.	.	.	.	.	.	.	.	
Totals	700	$1,050	?	?	?	?	?	?	?

The raw materials control sheet daily summary values for the amount of beginning inventory, the number of units used in the production process, and the amount of ending inventory. A control sheet is used in conjunction with inventory file cards to monitor and control inventory levels.

such as that formerly used by Avanti will do the job. If, on the other hand, inventory is large and costly and the business is complex, something as sophisticated as a computerized, on-line, real-time system may be needed. These systems are commonplace today in many business such as auto parts stores, wholesalers, or large grocery stores. For most small firms, however, less complex inventory management models are available that will reduce the recordkeeping burden and, at the same time, automatically produce information on inventory behavior. See the card enclosed at the back of this book for information on financial models software.

Monitoring Inventory Records and Stocks

As with all management control efforts, the inventory monitoring process should be designed to identify any facet of your firm's inventory function that requires attention. Your firm's recordkeeping system plays an important role in this process. First, good records provide you with information on what inventory should be. This information allows you to stay abreast of what has been sold or used in the production process; the rate at which items are being used or sold; what should be currently available from inventory stocks; the age of what is available; and what is not available that should be available. This latter information is necessary to minimize the occurrence of undetected inventory loss or theft. Information on the rate at which items are being used or sold (fast- and slow-moving items) is necessary for projecting inventory needs, determining quantities to be ordered, and identifying candidates for elimination.

The information that is shown on inventory records should be supplemented with periodic physical inspections. Actual counts of inventory on hand are used to verify the accuracy of the records, and to identify discrepancies between what should be available and what is available.

The time spent monitoring and evaluating inventory will produce benefits in the flow of improved cash flows and earnings but, equally important, will also provide you with a better understanding of the business. Monitoring and controlling inventory forces you to identify and understand the factors that affect the firm's operations and inventory levels. This knowledge results in improved planning and decision making.

Allocating Management's Time

To make monitoring and control efforts cost-effective, your limited time must be well-directed. For example, if your inventory consists of a large number of items with different dollar values, it would be virtually impossible for you to monitor each item with the same intensity. In fact, a blanket approach to controlling such an inventory would be counterproductive, even if sufficient time were available to do so. It would be poor management practice, for instance, to exert the same

Table 12.3

THE AVANTI COMPANY
Finished Goods File Card — Competition Frame
For the Month Ending January, 1990

Date	Beginning Balance Units	Dollars	Production Units	Dollars	Sales Units	Dollars	Ending Balance Units	Dollars	Sales Rate
01	10	$5,000	-	$ 0	2	$1,600	8	$4,000	2
02	.	.	.	.	.	.	.	.	.
03	.	.	.	.	.	.	.	.	.
04	.	.	.	.	.	.	.	.	.
05	.	.	.	.	.	.	.	.	.
06	.	.	.	.	.	.	.	.	.
07	.	.	.	.	.	.	.	.	.
Totals	10	$5,000	5	$2,550	7	$5,600	8	$4,080	7
Average	?	?	?	?	?	?	?	?	?
08	8	$4,080	.	.	.	.	.	.	.
09	.	.	.	.	.	.	.	.	.
10	.	.	.	.	.	.	.	.	.
11	.	.	.	.	.	.	.	.	.
12	.	.	.	.	.	.	.	.	.
13	.	.	.	.	.	.	.	.	.
14	.	.	.	.	.	.	.	.	.
Totals	?	?	?	?	?	?	?	?	?
Average	?	?	?	?	?	?	?	?	?
15	.	.	.	.	.	.	.	.	.
16	.	.	.	.	.	.	.	.	.
.	.	.	.	.	.	.	.	.	.
.	.	.	.	.	.	.	.	.	.
.	.	.	.	.	.	.	.	.	.
31	.	.	.	.	.	.	.	.	.
Totals	?	?	?	?	?	?	?	?	?
Average	?	?	?	?	?	?	?	?	?

The file card displayed on this table is used to record the daily movement of an individual product through the inventory account as well as beginning and ending balances of the item. Totals from the file card are periodically transferred to inventory control sheets to complete the inventory recording process.

time and effort monitoring a stock of one-cent paper clips as that spent on an inventory of uncut diamonds. Effective inventory control is achieved when time is allocated in proportion to the value of the inventory items involved. One simple approach to efficiently allocating the time spent on inventory control is known as ABC analysis.

ABC Analysis

ABC analysis involves nothing more than arraying inventory items or groups of items in order of dollar value, and then allocating the time spent on control accordingly. Classifying inventory in this manner allows you to identify the high dollar-value items (the important few) that require strict control, and the low dollar-value items (the trivial many) that require correspondingly less control.

It has been found that in many businesses approximately 10% of the inventory items account for about 50% of dollar sales or production volume; roughly 40% of inventory accounts for about 40% of sales or production; and the remaining 50% of inventory accounts for the last 10% of dollar volume. According to the ABC classification scheme, the inventory items that account for the 50% of dollar volume would be designated group "A". The middle group of items that account for the 40% of volume would be designated group "B", and the remaining 10% would be group "C" items.

These classifications or groupings serve as guidelines for allocating the time spent on inventory control. The A group would command the most attention; somewhat less time would be spent controlling items in the B group; and comparatively little effort would be expended on the C group. For example, it may be decided that A group items are of such importance that their status should be subject to continuous review. This may mean weekly or possibly daily evaluation. The B group may be reviewed once or twice a month, while C group items may be reviewed no more frequently than monthly or quarterly.

It is important to keep in mind that the 10%-40%-50% classification categories and the review periods used in the above example were only illustrations. These parameters may or may not fit the circumstances or needs of a specific business. Some firms may require more or less than three letter classifications, and longer or shorter review periods. It is up to you to decide what is appropriate for your firm's particular set of circumstances.

The Mechanics of ABC Analysis

The steps in ABC analysis are outlined below, and an example from The Avanti Company data is given on tables 12.4 and 12.5 in the next section. Working through the simple calculations of the Avanti example will clarify the concepts involved. To perform ABC analysis for your firm, you would:

- Determine the dollar value for each inventory item or item grouping. This involves multiplying the unit cost of the item by the number of units purchased or, if so desired, the units sold. These figures for The Avanti Company are shown in the Dollar Value column of Table 12.4.

- Rank the items on the basis of dollar value by listing the dollar value amounts in descending order. The rankings and the necessary percentage calculations for the Avanti example are shown in Table 12.5.

- Calculate the percentage of total dollar value that each inventory item represents. This involves dividing the dollar value for each item by total dollar sales. For The Avanti Company, these percentages are shown in the Dollar Value Percentage column of Table 12.5.

- Calculate the cumulatives for the dollar value percentages. These values are obtained by adding a given percentage figure to the sum of the previous percentage figures. The cumulative dollar value percentages for Avanti are shown in column 5 of Table 12.5.

- Use the total and cumulative percentage values to group inventory according to the desired classification scheme and assign the appropriate ABC designations.

Working Through the Calculations for Avanti

Notice on Table 12.4 that column 1 lists inventory items by their stock number (any descriptive indicator could be used), and columns 2 and 3 show the number of units purchased (sales could be used) and the cost of each. The dollar value calculations appear in column 4. Each amount in that column is obtained by multiplying the value in column 2 by that of column 3.

The rankings and various percentage calculations for the data from Table 12.4 are shown on Table 12.5. How these values are calculated and what they mean is discussed below.

Columns 1, 2, and 3 of Table 12.5 represent the dollar value rankings, in descending order, of each item in Avanti's inventory. These rankings reflect the relative contribution of each item to total sales. For instance, since item number 090 makes the largest contribution to total sales, $50,000, it ranks first in the distribution. Item number 100, on the other hand, generates the least amount of sales, $1,200, and ranks last. The dollar value amounts of column 3 are converted to percentages of total sales and shown in column 4. These percentages are calculated as dollar value divided by total sales. For example, item number 020 has a dollar value of $8,000. Dividing this amount by total sales of $100,000 produces the 8.0% figure shown in column 4.

Table 12.4
Inventory Dollar Value Extensions for The Avanti Company

Item Number	Units Purchased	Unit Cost	Dollar Value
060	200	$ 8.00	$ 1,600
010	1,000	15.00	15,000
080	400	7.00	2,800
050	500	10.00	5,000
030	400	6.00	2,400
090	10,000	5.00	50,000
040	1,000	2.00	2,000
070	20,000	6.00	12,000
100	600	2.00	1,200
020	10,000	0.80	8,000
Total			$100,000

The dollar-value extensions shown on this table are used to prepare the inventory classifications required for ABC analysis. These values are calculated as units purchased times unit cost.

Table 12.5
Inventory Ordering and Classifications for The Avanti Company

Rank	Item Number	Dollar Value	Dollar Value Percentage	Cumulative Dollar Value Percentage	Group
1	090	$ 50,000	50.0 %	50.0 %	A
2	010	15,000	15.0	65.0	B
3	070	12,000	12.0	77.0	B
4	020	8,000	8.0	85.0	B
5	050	5,000	5.0	90.0	B
6	080	2,800	2.8	92.8	C
7	030	2,400	2.4	95.2	C
8	040	2,000	2.0	97.2	C
9	060	1,600	1.6	98.8	C
10	100	1,200	1.2	100.0	C
Totals		$100,000	100.0 %		

The data shown on this table reflects the ranking or ordering of inventory items by percentage of total inventory value. This ranking allows management to establish the required cutoff points for ABC assignments. These assignments assist Avanti management in allocating the time spent on control of specific inventory items.

The cumulative dollar value percentages of column 5 are obtained by making a running total of the values in column 4. The running total is calculated by adding each percentage value of column 4 to the sum of the previous percentage values. For example, item 090 represents 50% of sales, and item 010 an additional 15% of sales. Together, these two items account for 65% of total sales. Since item 070 produces another 12% of sales, the running total of the percentages for the first three items is 77%.

After the data is accumulated, it is Avanti management's job to establish the appropriate cutoff points for the ABC assignments. At Avanti, the ABC letter designations were decided from an evaluation of the dollar value percentage (column 4) and cumulative dollar value percentage (column 5) figures, and Avanti management's knowledge of its inventory. The A group, which will receive constant attention, includes only item 090. This one item constitutes 50% of the firm's dollar volume. The B group, which includes the next 40% of the items, consists of items 010, 070, 020, and 050. Management feels that the behavior of these items must be examined no less than once per week. The remaining 50% of the items in the C group represent only 10% of total sales and will be monitored only once per month.

Before you leave this section, it is important to emphasize that:

- ABC analysis provides guidelines, not sacred laws. The number of cutoff points and associated percentages used to establish inventory categories and allocate the time spent on control, depends on your specific circumstances, needs, and priorities. For example, your inventory may require four categories (A, B, C, D), a 40%-30%-20%-10% classification scheme, and more frequent review periods.

- ABC cutoff points and percentages, once established, are not permanently etched in stone. Everything changes, including your firm's product and sales mix. Periodic review is necessary to determine if changing conditions necessitate changes in your approach to inventory control.

- Your analysis of inventory data will not provide a clear picture of product and sales mix unless it covers a representative time period. This means a period of time sufficiently long to include seasonal influences or other market conditions that are peculiar to your firm. How long is sufficiently long? Only you can answer this question from a study of your sales and inventory records. As a general rule, however, data for no less than six months to one year is needed to make the necessary judgments.

A Final Word on Monitoring Inventory Records

One important goal of inventory control is to minimize obsolescence. Obsolete inventory means everything that is antiquated, has lost its usefulness, or has been superseded by something better. The systematic monitoring of inventory records makes an important contribution to this goal.

Periodically, all inventory items should be reviewed with the thought of preventing excess accumulation of items that have a slim chance for sale or usage. This review is conducted by identifying what has not been sold or used since the last review period. If an evaluation indicates these items have little or no future value, they should be candidates for immediate elimination.

Forecasting Sales

In Chapter 6, sales was identified as the activity which determines the pace and level of virtually all of a firm's activities. Of these various activities, none is more closely linked to sales than inventory movements. Expected sales or the production, or both, required to meet this demand should govern the size and rate of inventory purchases as well as the level of stock that is carried. A good sales forecast is the logical starting point for effective inventory management and control.

The more accurately sales are forecast for a given planning period, the better the estimate of an optimal level of inventory for that period. As the level of inventory approaches this ideal, the funds invested in inventory are minimized, and cash flows and profits are maximized. If sales estimates are vague or highly uncertain, an excessive inventory safety stock must be carried to protect against the possibility of lost sales due to stockouts and/or costly interruptions to production schedules. Excessive safety stocks drain a firm's scarce cash, reduce inventory turnover, and reduce profits. As learned from Avanti's experience, improved sales forecasts lead to improved inventory management, which means improved financial performance.

Controlling Inventory Levels

Once the sales forecast has been made and inventory requirements for that volume of sales estimated, it is necessary to establish when purchase orders should be placed and what quantity should be ordered. While these responsibilities can never be reduced to an exact science, there are fundamental inventory management principles that can give you some guidance for making these difficult decisions.

The basis for many inventory management systems is a concept known as *maximum and minimum Control.* As the name suggests, this approach requires that lower (minimum) and upper (maximum) stock levels be established for each item or item grouping in inventory. Also required is a reorder point which indicates when a purchase order should be placed, and an order quantity which indicates the size of the order.

An inventory reorder point has three basic components. These are:

What Is a Reorder Point?

- ■ An estimate of the rate at which inventory is either sold, or used in the production process. This estimate is known as the usage rate.

- ■ An estimate of the amount of inventory safety stock needed to protect against uncertainty.

- ■ An estimate of the length of lead time required to receive a shipment once the purchase order has been placed.

In short, the reorder point is the lowest level to which the stock of an inventory item should be allowed to fall before a purchase order is placed. This point reflects the minimum level of inventory that must be on hand to avoid stock shortages during the period of time required to receive shipment (lead time). You should first investigate the concept of the reorder point under ideal conditions.

Deciding the Reorder Point Under Ideal Conditions

If the rate of sales and/or production (usage rate) is relatively constant throughout the year, and the length of lead time required to fill orders placed with a supplier is absolutely certain, estimating the reorder point for inventory is straightforward: The reorder point is determined by multiplying the usage rate per day (or any appropriate time period) by the number of days (or any appropriate time period) of lead time.

For example, assume that the average rate of sales (usage rate) for your firm's product is 2 units per day, and it takes 10 days from the time the need for inventory is recognized to the time a purchase order is received from your supplier (lead time). The reorder point would occur when inventory reached a level of 20 units (2 units x 10 days).

Reorder Point = Usage Rate x Lead Time

Reorder Point = 2 x 10
         = 20 units

When inventory reached a level of 20 units, there would be just enough inventory on hand to meet demand until inventory is replenished. With a lead time of 10 days and usage rate of 2 units per day, the shipment would be received from the supplier on the day the last two units of inventory are sold.

If the length of the lead time is not absolutely certain, then the reorder point must be increased to reflect possible delays. Suppose that it takes between 10 and 14 days to fill an order. To be conservative and guard against unforeseen delays, the maximum lead time (14 days) would be used to calculate the reorder point. In this case, a purchase order would be placed when the inventory level is at 28 units (14 days x 2 units per day). In effect, the firm is willing to maintain a safety stock (contingency balance) to protect against uncertainty.

A *safety stock* is simply an amount of inventory held in excess of the expected reorder point. Its purpose is to protect against the uncertainties surrounding the reorder point and lead time estimates. In the above example, the ideal reorder point is 20 units. The actual reorder point is 8 units above that level.

Reorder Points and Seasonal Activity

Unfortunately, most firms do not enjoy stable sales and/or production (usage rates) throughout the year. Activity in a typical small business is subject to seasonal patterns or other periodic influences. Since demand for inventory in any firm will vary from season to season, a single reorder point is not suitable for effective inventory control. For example, a small manufacturing firm specializing in custom-made bicycle frames does 70% of its business in the six-month period from March through August. If this firm's manager used a single reorder point based on the average annual sales rate, the reorder point would always miss the mark. During the slow season, when the inventory usage rate declines, the reorder point would be too high, and scarce cash would be tied up in excessive inventory. During the busy months, the reorder point would be too low, and stockouts would disrupt production schedules and cause lost sales.

For firms experiencing periodic swings in activity, a reorder point must be calculated for each distinct season or period of activity. The frame- maker, for example, would have two reorder points, one for the slack season from September to February, and another for the peak season from March to August. Each reorder point would be calculated using:

- An estimate of the lead time for that season.
- An estimate of the usage rate (sales demand or production requirements) for that season.
- The desired safety stock for that season.

The reorder point would be determined as the desired safety stock, plus the usage rate times the lead time.

To illustrate, assume that the bicycle framemaker manages to make and sell only one frame per day (usage rate) during the slow season from August to February, the lead time is seven days, and the framemaker's desired safety stock is two units. In this case the reorder point would be nine units of materials.

Reorder Point = (Usage Rate x Lead Time) + Safety Stock

Reorder Point = (1 x 7) + 2

$\qquad$ = 9 units

If sales during the peak season average four units per day, the reorder point with the same lead time and safety stock would be 30 units. This is calculated as follows:

Reorder Point = (Usage Rate x Lead Time) + Safety Stock

Reorder Point = (4 x 7) + 2
= 30 units

Estimating the Usage Rate and Lead Time

As is true with all planning and decision making, the quality of the choices made depends on the quality of the estimates made. With regard to inventory control, obtaining a reasonable reorder point estimate requires reasonable usage rate and lead time estimates. This observation begs the question, "Where do you obtain good estimates for these variables?" Unfortunately, there is no magical formula or book of facts that will provide an easy answer. Usage rate and lead time estimates are judgments that must be developed from your knowledge and understanding of the firm's sales and inventory behavior patterns. This knowledge is gained from maintaining and monitoring detailed inventory records which will provide critical information such as order size and dates, dates on which purchase orders are received, and amounts sold or used during specific time periods. There simply is no substitute for this approach.

Deciding Order Quantities

The reorder point is an estimate of when a purchase order should be placed. To complete the process, you must have an estimate of how much should be ordered. This latter estimate is known as the order size or quantity. While there are sophisticated mathematical techniques available for estimating inventory order quantity, a simple concept known as the *desired covering period* provides guidelines for making reasonable working estimates for many small firms.

The desired covering period is the length of time, such as the number of days-of-sales or days-of-inventory usage, that a given stock of inventory will last at some given inventory usage rate. In other words, given the average demand per day for inventory, the desired covering period is the number of days of sales or usage that a given stock of inventory will cover before it is exhausted. Using this definition for the desired covering period, the order size is calculated as the usage rate times the length of the desired covering period.

To illustrate the use of the order size concept, return to the hypothetical bicycle framemaker. Suppose the framemaker decides that each order placed during the slow season should be sufficient to cover 30 days of production and sales. The desired covering period, then, would be 30 days. If the average usage rate is 1 unit per day, the order quantity for each order placed would be 30 units.

Order Size = Usage Rate x Desired Covering Period

Order Size = 1 x 30

= 30 units ordered

If the desired covering period of 30 days is used during the peak season when the inventory usage rate is 4 units per day, the order quantity for each order placed would be 120 units.

Order Size = Usage Rate x Desired Covering Period

Order Size = 4 x 30

= 120

Estimating the Desired Covering Period and Order Quantity

As is true of the usage rate and lead time estimates, the estimate of the desired covering period is determined by the pattern of sales and inventory usage peculiar to each firm during a specific time frame. Again, you gain the understanding required to make this estimate from inventory records, and the learning experiences created by the monitoring and control effort. This effort forces you to identify and evaluate the factors that affect inventory, and this in turn results in improved inventory estimates.

Some Final Thoughts on Inventory Management

Given the financial and strategic importance of inventory to most firms, it would be useful to summarize the key points made in this chapter.

- **Don't Underestimate the Importance of Inventory**. The management of inventory deserves special attention. This asset often comprises the bulk of your firm's working capital investment, yet it is by far the least liquid working asset. As such, errors in judgment about inventory are not easily or quickly remedied. For a typical small firm, inventory mismanagement or the absence of effective management procedures can be an expensive, often fatal oversight.

- **Take a Financial Perspective.** Inventory includes the physical goods that make up such things as raw materials, purchased parts, supplies, and the finished goods that are available for delivery to customers. It is also considerably more than this. Inventory is really cash disguised as various forms of metals, fabrics, liquids, or other materials. This means that inventory management is a question of how much, in terms of both units and dollars. The goal is to strike a reasonable balance between an appropriate number of units, and what the firm can afford to invest.

- **Know The "Four Horsemen."** There are many factors that influence inventory management decisions, but the four key points emphasized in this chapter are:

Inventory Costs: These include the opportunity cost of the funds invested in inventory, the costs of acquiring inventory, and the costs of carrying inventory such as storage, taxes, insurance, and obsolescence.

Sales or Usage Rate: The inventory control process starts with an estimate of the sales or usage rate for a given planning horizon. This estimate should be based on a combination of historical demand and a sales forecast. It is important to realize, however, that the usage rate must be modified for changing conditions and forecasting error. Rarely will an expected usage rate exactly coincide with actual usage, but a well-founded estimate is far superior to no estimate, an uneducated guess, or trusting to luck.

Value of Inventory: Inventory dollar values should be stratified into groups, with high-valued items controlled more rigidly than low-valued items.

Impact of Inventory Decisions: Inventory is a major component of the firm's network of physical, financial and human resources as well as the many activities that influence these resources. You must understand what factors affect inventory, as well as how inventory decisions affect the other aspects of the firm's network.

■ **Be Information Insatiable.** The more you know about your product, customers, and how the effects of these factors take place, the more effective your inventory management will be. Scientific principles can be useful aids to solving some aspects of the inventory management problem, or as checks against judgmental decisions, but they are not a substitute for sound judgment and experienced intuition. These qualities are developed from knowledge and understanding of the business and its products, and this know-how comes from good information. The information system must consist of data on those factors within your firm that affect inventory decisions, and data on the external forces that cause demand for your firm's products or services to fluctuate.

The two remaining elements of working capital are the current asset cash, and the current liability accounts payable. Neither is typically as large nor potentially as destructive as accounts receivable and inventory, although both are important to sound working capital management.

Where to Now?

Chapter 13
Cash & Accounts Payable Management

The two preceding chapters stressed the importance of controlling the investment required to grant credit and to hold a firm's physical inventory. This chapter examines the principles, techniques, and policies that will maximize the benefits derived from a firm's liquidity position, and from the credit extended by its trade suppliers. A firm's liquidity position is a "money asset" similar in principle to other asset investments, and accounts payable is the mirror image of accounts receivable. What you will learn about these two important components of working capital is outlined below.

TOPIC	CONCEPTS DISCUSSED
Cash Management	Cash and the concept of liquid assets.
	Why liquid assets are necessary to the efficient operation of your firm.
	The goal of liquidity management.
	Techniques for managing your firm's liquid assets.
Accounts Payable Management	The meaning of trade credit and its role in the cash cycle.
	The implicit cost of using trade credit as a form of working capital financing.
	The components of a good accounts payable recordkeeping system.
	Guidelines for establishing the effective management of accounts payable.

As a small business manager, there is a natural tendency for you to think of your firm's stock of liquid assets only in terms of cash on hand: coin, currency, and checking account deposits. Liquidity, however, is a far broader concept. It encompasses all of the resources that are available to meet your firm's need for liquidity. These include:

Cash Management: The Concept of Liquid Assets

- Cash on hand and checking account deposits.

- Near-cash items that can be easily converted to cash, such as savings certificates, money market investments, money market account deposits, or a variety of short-term debt investments.

- Readily available sources of credit.

While diverse, these money assets have a common characteristic: They provide a suitable outlet for holding the firm's operating and contingency balances. These important functions of liquidity are discussed in the next section of this chapter.

You may also think of a liquid balance as a residual, nonworking asset — the nonproductive by-product of normal operations. Nothing could be further from the truth. Money assets are critical to the efficient operation of your firm. Without sufficient liquidity, your firm is exposed to the risks of being illiquid. Conversely, excessive liquidity is as debilitating to a healthy financial position as sluggish inventory or excessive receivables. The question then is not whether your firm should carry liquid balances, but rather, what is the appropriate balance to hold given the expected set of conditions facing it.

The Role and Importance of Liquidity Balances

Money assets are a critical component of working capital and play an important role in the efficient operation of your firm. The stock of resources held as liquidity balances serve as a necessary form of financial insurance. By maintaining adequate liquidity, you buy the protection necessary to ensure that normal activities can be pursued without exposing your firm to undue risk. To gain a clear picture of how this is accomplished, it is necessary to understand the important functions that money assets perform.

Meet Operating Requirements

Liquid balances are necessary to ensure your firm's ability to conduct normal operations, meet obligations in a timely manner, and implement and carry out planned activities. If your small firm existed in an ideal world, all cash flows would be perfectly synchronized; cash receipts would exactly match needed cash outflows. In the real world, however, this is not the case. Cash inflows are seldom, if ever, perfectly timed to meet upcoming cash obligations, and liquidity balances are needed to absorb or smooth the normal ebbs and flows of funds through the business.

For example, assume your firm buys from a supplier whose terms call for payment on the 10th of the month, but your cash inflows are received fairly evenly throughout the month. As a result, sufficient cash has not accumulated by the 10th to pay the account in full, so liquid operating balances must be maintained to offset the temporary deficiency.

It is also clear that the size of your firm's liquidity balance should be related to the level of its operations. Increased operating activity requires larger liquidity balances, and slowdowns require less. For example, during periods of peak seasonal activity, your firm experiences a higher level of operating transactions such as larger inventory purchases and payments, higher payroll costs, and additional overhead expense. This increased pace of operations requires more supporting liquidity.

Provide a Cushion Against Uncertainty

An additional purpose of money assets is to provide a defense or protective reserve against unexpected drains on liquidity. For example, planned operating balances would usually be insufficient to protect against unanticipated emergencies such as an interruption to production caused by late shipments, a decline in sales resulting from an adverse change in your firm's competitive position, or the degree of error in the forecast underlying the cash budget. To protect against unexpected events, a portion of your firm's liquidity position must be earmarked as a contingency balance. This balance serves as a floor or minimum figure below which the level of money assets should not fall.

Maintain Lower-Cost Financing

By maintaining a sound liquidity position, you not only avoid high-cost crisis financing, but you are able to favorably influence your firm's credit rating. A good credit rating is a symbol of stability and sound management. These virtues translate into lower borrowing costs, and an advantage for your firm in all credit negotiations.

Enhance Bank Relationships

Banks need deposits to make loans and investments, so customers with reasonably stable average account balances are highly desirable. The small firm that fits this profile is often the recipient of both tangible and intangible benefits from its bank. For example, some banks may charge for each service rendered, while others are willing to be compensated in the form of account balances that are, on average, reasonably stable. These services include such "perks" as providing credit information on potential customers, advice on business opportunities, and information on economic and business conditions.

Good customers are also the beneficiaries of intangibles that may be vital to a firm's financial health. During periods of tight credit conditions, banks are forced to curtail lending activities. Yet a typical bank will find a way to meet the credit needs of its good customers. Given the difficulty most small firms encounter in locating financing, such an intangible may be a virtually priceless asset.

The Goal of Liquidity Management

The objective of liquidity management is to maintain an appropriate liquidity balance for the expected set of conditions facing your firm.

This means having sufficient liquidity to conduct operations, while at the same time avoiding excessive balances. An appropriate liquidity balance maximizes the trade-off between the cost of carrying money assets, and the benefits these assets provide.

By having liquid assets, your firm would enjoy the tangible benefits listed above, and at the same time, eliminate the risks associated with illiquidity. These risks include the uncertainty surrounding the firm's ability to meet its maturing obligations, and the crippling actions creditors may take when the firm fails to do so. Yet, committing some portion of the firm's financial resources to liquid balances represents an often sizable opportunity cost. The cost is the earnings lost because these financial resources are not invested in working assets. This is a deceptive, insidious cost since no bill comes due and no check is written to pay it. Nevertheless, the cost is real and it can be significant.

The Opportunity Cost of Being Liquid

Investment in liquid assets provides only minimal returns at best. For example, interest earned on checking account deposits and yields on savings certificates or money market accounts would normally be substantially less than the rate of return a firm earns on its working assets. When financial resources are held in the form of money assets, they are withheld from investment in working assets. In doing so, a firm gives up or loses the difference between the return on each. This lost differential is the opportunity cost of holding liquid balances.

This does not mean that the investment in money assets can be avoided. It means that the investment should be managed so that liquidity balances are efficiently utilized, and are appropriate for the set of conditions a firm is expected to encounter.

Techniques for Managing Money Assets

Sound management of a firm's money assets involves three primary objectives. These are:

- Maintaining liquid balances that are appropriate for expected economic and competitive conditions.

- Keeping surplus funds fully invested.

- Using available money assets as efficiently as possible.

The techniques listed below are designed to accomplish these goals.

Maintaining a Reliable Cash Budgeting System

As discussed in Chapter 8, by studying historical patterns of cash inflows and outflows and by learning from the experience of doing, it is possible for you to achieve a high degree of cash forecasting skill. The more precise the cash flow estimates for a given planning horizon, the more accurate will be the estimate of appropriate liquidity balances for that period. Improved cash budgeting leads to improved liquidity management in a variety of ways.

- By clearly defining future operating needs, alternative methods for meeting cash outflows can be explored. For example, it may be possible to make arrangements with suppliers to set due dates that coincide with your firm's expected periods of peak cash inflows. Or, your firm can use the cash budget to examine the effects of possible changes in its own credit terms or payment practices in order to iron out differences in the pattern of cash inflows and outflows. Also, if periods of peak cash inflows are known, it may be possible to negotiate debt repayment schedules that coincide with these periods.

- By identifying periods when surplus cash will be available, you have the time to investigate attractive alternatives for investing temporarily idle funds.

- By studying historical cash flow patterns, the deviations between forecast and actual cash flows, and the events that caused the deviations, you gain the experience and judgment required to estimate appropriate contingency balances. It is not sufficient to understand that some portion of your firm's money assets must be earmarked as self-insurance against the unknown. The real question is what amount is appropriate. An effective cash budgeting system provides the information for making this judgment.

Using Alternative Methods of Maintaining Protective Liquidity

A sound liquidity position favorably influences your firm's credit rating, and a good credit rating provides the opportunity to use alternative methods of meeting contingency needs. One possible alternative to your firm carrying its own contingency balances is to have your bank carry these balances in the form of loan commitments or unused borrowing capacity. To the financially experienced, loan commitments and borrowing capacity represent the most important money assets a firm owns.

For example, if your firm has the credit capability to establish a bank line of credit, it enjoys the luxury of having the bank carry the balances to meet its working capital and contingency needs. A line of credit assures you of available funds up to the amount of the credit limit. In addition, these funds are only drawn as needed, and interest is only paid on what is actually used.

Unused borrowing capacity represents an equally attractive form of contingency balance. By reserving a portion of the total borrowing capacity that its credit capability allows, your firm has readily available credit to meet emergency needs. This eliminates the necessity of allocating a portion of normal liquidity balances for this purpose.

Keeping Temporarily Idle Funds Fully Invested

When periods of temporary cash surplus are identified, plans should be made to ensure that these idle funds are kept productive. This is accomplished by investing in any of several suitable outlets. It is important to keep in mind that these funds will be needed to meet upcoming operating expenses, so the investment media must be carefully chosen. The criteria governing such investments should be:

- **Safety of Principal**. Since these funds will be needed in the near future, speculative investments are not suitable. What is needed is an investment vehicle free (or virtually free) from the risk of default.

- **Appropriate Maturity**. Since the funds will be needed at some definite future date, the chosen investment should mature (repayment of principal) at that time.

- **Immediate Liquidity**. In addition to selecting an investment with an appropriate maturity, it is necessary to protect against the possibility of unexpected need. This can be accomplished by selecting an investment that is easily converted into cash at a moment's notice.

- **Maximum Return**. While yield is not the primary consideration for this type of investment, the highest yielding alternative should be selected once the other criteria have been satisfied.

There are a variety of investments for temporarily idle funds that meet these criteria. Some take the form of short-term, highly liquid marketable securities such as United States Treasury Bills, commercial paper, or negotiable certificates of deposit. Others, which are attractive for firms with lower amounts of surplus funds, take the form of sophisticated accounts such as negotiated orders of withdrawal (NOW) accounts, money market accounts, or asset management accounts that are offered by a variety of financial institutions.

A Final Thought on Cash Management

The cash and other money assets that flow through a business are the result of a complex interrelated set of decisions and transactions. Seldom can a single decision on the management of such flows be isolated from other decisions. Effective cash management can only be achieved if conducted as an integral part of the overall system of cash flow management. For example, it is of little consolation to know that a cost-effective cash management system is in place or optimal liquidity balances are held, yet funds are needlessly tied up in excessive inventory or accounts receivable.

Accounts Payable Management

Accounts payable is the accounting term used to indicate the obligation that is created when inventory is purchased on credit. In financial parlance, this widely used form of delayed payment financing is referred to as trade credit. For many small firms, especially those in the wholesale and retail fields, trade credit is the most important source of inventory financing. Often, these firms are without the continuous supply of cash or bank financing needed to maintain desired inventory levels, and trade credit fills this need.

The importance of trade credit dictates that accounts payable be carefully managed and controlled. You should take the steps necessary to minimize the cost of this type of financing, and at the same time, eliminate the possibility of jeopardizing supplier relations.

Your firm's outstanding accounts payable at any given time is determined by the volume of purchases, the credit terms offered by suppliers, and your payment practices. The most critical of these factors is the terms under which goods are purchased. Credit terms stipulate the conditions of sale, the date or dates on which the obligation should be paid, and the amount of the payment to be made. Credit terms typically consist of three distinct parts:

Understanding Trade Credit Terms

- The net period

- The size of the cash discount, if offered

- The cash discount period

The *net period* is the length of time between the billing date and the date the invoice should be paid in full. This time span varies from industry to industry, but a net period of 30 to 90 days is typical. Of particular importance to the interpretation of credit terms is the date at which the net period is assumed to start. For example, the net period may be expressed as 30 days with billing to start from the date of the invoice (DOI); from the end of the month (EOM); from the middle of the month (MOM); or from the date the goods are received (ROG). In highly seasonal industries, seasonal dating is common practice. Under this arrangement, goods are shipped to the buyer in advance of the selling season, but payment is not due until the end of that season.

The Net Period

Often, credit terms will include the opportunity to obtain a cash discount in exchange for early payment. A *cash discount* allows a specified percentage deduction from the face amount of the invoice for payment made within the cash discount period. For example, if purchases are made under terms of 2/10, net 30 (EOM), the full amount of the invoice is due 30 days from the end of the month of purchase. If payment is made by the 10th day following the end of the month of purchase, 2% of the invoice price can be deducted from the payment. Likewise, if terms of 5/15, net 90 (ROG) are granted, only 95% of the invoice price is due if payment is made within 15 days following the receipt of the goods. If the discount is not taken, the full amount of the invoice must be paid in 90 days following receipt of the goods. The purpose of the cash discount is to speed collections for the seller, but as

Cash Discounts

you will learn, the discount plays an important part in the cost of using the seller's offer of trade credit.

The Cost of Trade Credit

Your first reaction to the idea that there is a cost associated with trade credit might be, "Wrong. I don't pay interest when using trade credit, so there is no cost. Trade credit is free financing." In some cases that is true, but in others it is not. The use of trade credit can be a costly form of financing.

If no cash discount is offered by a supplier (for example, terms are net 30 days or net 60 days), the above statement is true. There is no cost associated with the use of trade credit. The statement is also true if a cash discount is offered, and the discount is taken by paying on the cash discount date.

If, however, a cash discount is offered and the discount is not taken (payment is not made by the earlier discount date), there is a cost associated with the use of trade credit. In fact, missing cash discounts is usually a very costly method of financing inventory purchases. This cost does not take the form of explicit interest charges as in the case of bank financing. Rather, it is a hidden opportunity cost. Again, this opportunity cost is not obvious because no check is written for payment, yet the impact on a firm's cash position of missing a cash discount is real.

The Opportunity Cost of Trade Credit

By foregoing a cash discount, a manager elects not to pay on the earlier discount date but delay payment until the more distant net date. To gain these additional days of financing (the difference between the discount date and the net date), a firm must give up the amount of the discount. This loss is a real cost to a firm. It is the cost of paying the full invoice price rather than the lower discount price.

For example, assume your firm's supplier offers terms of 2/10, net 30. With these terms, you can earn a 2% discount if payment is made by the 10th day. If you choose to take the longer credit period and pay at the end of 30 days, you pay the full amount of the invoice. Delaying payment until the 30th day provides an extra 20 days of financing (day 10 to day 30), but this additional time is not free. In this case, the cost of the additional 20 days of financing is the missed 2% discount.

You might feel that 2% is not much of an opportunity cost to suffer for missing the discount. This would be true if 2% was the opportunity cost for the entire year, but it is not. In this case, the cost is 2% for 20 days. If you purchase from this supplier on a continuous basis, 2% for every 20-day period in a year amounts to an annual effective cost of 37.23% for foregoing discounts. This is a hefty opportunity cost to suffer for the extra 20 days of financing gained.

Calculating the annual effective cost of missing a cash discount is actually quite simple. What is needed are two fractions: the first is the percentage discount divided by one minus the percentage discount; the second is 365 divided by the difference in days between the net period and the discount period. These two fractions are multiplied to obtain the annual effective cost (AEC) of missing a cash discount.

Making the Calculation

AEC = (% discount ÷ 1 – % discount)
    x (365 ÷ net period – discount period)

In the above example, the annual effective cost of missing the cash discount when credit terms are 2/10, net 30 was 37.23%. This was calculated as follows:

AEC = (.02 ÷ 1 –.02) x (365 ÷ 30 – 10)
    = (.02 ÷ .98) x (365 ÷ 20)
    = .0204 x 18.25
    = 37.23%

Calculating the annual effective cost of missing the cash discount with credit terms of 3/15, net 45 is 37.63%.

AEC = (.03 ÷ 1 – .03) x (365 ÷ 45 – 15)
    = (.03 ÷ .97) x (365 ÷ 30)
    = 37.63%

The point made by these examples is clear:

> The cost of missing a cash discount depends on the specific credit terms offered, but as a general rule, missing cash discounts can be a costly method of financing. If the cash is available, take the discount; if it is not, consider borrowing the funds to take advantage of the discount. If your firm has the necessary credit capability, and the interest cost of borrowing is less than the annual effective cost (AEC) of missing the discount, there is a definite financial advantage to borrowing the funds and taking the discount. It is important to note that any advantage to the borrowing alternative assumes the loan will be repaid on the net date. This is the date the supplier would have to be paid if the discount is not taken.

Now that you are familiar with the concept of the cost of trade credit, you need to know how the use of this subtle form of financing benefits your firm. To do so, recall the concept of the cash cycle and the financing needed to support this cycle. As discussed in previous chapters, the cash cycle is the number of days from the date inventory is purchased to the date the credit sale is collected. The length of this cycle is approximated by subtracting the average payment period

Accounts Payable and Financing the Cash Cycle

(APP) from the sum of the inventory turnover in days and the average collection period (ACP).

Cash Cycle = (Inventory Turnover in Days + ACP) – APP

This time period is critical to the financial management of your firm because it must be financed. Recall again that the financing required to support the cash cycle can be estimated by multiplying the number of days in the cash cycle by the average expenditures per day.

Required Financing = Cash Cycle x Average Expenditures per Day

The longer the cash cycle, the greater the amount of financing required to support normal operations. While cash is tied up in inventory and credit sales, it is not available for such necessities as meeting payroll, paying suppliers, or making loan payments. These and other working capital needs must be financed for the duration of the cycle. This financing burden is eased, however, if a firm is the fortunate recipient of trade credit. To find out how this is accomplished, study Avanti's cash cycle and working capital needs.

Avanti's Cash Cycle and Working Capital Needs

In 19X1 Avanti's cash cycle was 37 days, and in 19X2 it jumped to 97 days. These values were calculated as follows:

Cash Cycle = (Inventory Turnover in Days + ACP) – APP
Cash Cycle (19X1) = (59 + 32) – 54
$$= 37 \text{ days}$$
Cash Cycle (19X2) = (103 + 58) – 64
$$= 97 \text{ days}$$

The working capital financing required to support each cash cycle was approximately $24,309 in 19X1 and $63,050. These values were calculated as follows:

Required Financing = Cash Cycle x Average Expenditures per Day
Required Financing (19X1) = 37 days x $657
$$= \$24,309$$
Required Financing (19X2) = 97 days x $650
$$= \$63,050$$

In each year, the amount of required financing reflects the 54 days and 64 days of trade credit received by Avanti. To highlight the importance of trade credit as a method of financing, calculate the required financing figure using the assumption that trade credit had not been available. The difference between actual financing needs and what they would have been without trade credit is the contribution of this type of financing.

If Avanti were not able to qualify for trade credit, purchases would be made for cash and there would be no accounts payable. This would lengthen the 19X1 cash cycle to 91 days, and the 19X2 cycle to 161 days.

Cash Cycle = (Inventory Turnover in Days + ACP) – APP

Cash Cycle (19X1) = (59 + 32) – 0
= 91 days

Cash Cycle (19X2) = (103 + 58) – 0
= 161 days

Accounts Payable and Working Capital Financing

The consequence of the extended cash cycles is an increase in financing needs to $59,787 in 19X1 and to $104,650 in 19X2. These values were calculated as follows.

Required Financing = Cash Cycle x Average Expenditures per Day

Required Financing (19X1) = 91 days x $657
= $59,787

Required Financing (19X2) = 161 days x $650
= $104,650

To determine the amount of financing provided by accounts payable, we need only subtract the financing needs with accounts payable (actual) from the financing needs without accounts payable (hypothetical).

Financing from Payables = Financing Without Accounts Payable
– Financing With Accounts Payable

Financing from Payables (19X1) = $59,787 – $24,309
= $35,478

Financing from Payables (19X2) = $104,650 – $63,050
= $41,600

The difference of $35,478 in 19X1 and $41,600 in 19X2 represent the valuable contribution of trade credit to working capital financing for Avanti. While trade credit does not involve the direct loan of funds, it does allow the firm to use goods provided by the supplier for the length of the payment period. Since payment for these goods is delayed, cash is retained in the business. This is cash that would otherwise be immediately paid to suppliers for inventory purchases if trade credit was not extended.

It may also be useful to think of the contribution of trade credit in this way. In 19X2, Avanti's cash cycle was 97 days. If the firm had not qualified for trade credit from its suppliers, the cash cycle would have been 161 days. Because Avanti's suppliers were willing to wait an average of 64 days before requiring payment for purchases, the firm had to finance only 97 days of operations rather than the 161 that would have been necessary without the use of trade credit. At an average expenditure rate of $650 per day, Avanti's estimated financing needs were reduced by $41,600. This difference is bank financing and associated interest cost that Avanti was able to avoid.

Stretching Accounts Payable

If Avanti had been able to increase the payment period to trade creditors beyond the 64-day average of 19X2, financing needs and the annual effective cost of missing discounts would have been reduced even further. For example, if payment to suppliers had been delayed an average of 75 days, the cash cycle would decline to 86 days (161 – 75) instead of the actual 97 days. A corresponding drop in the required financing from $63,050 to $55,900 (86 x $650) would also have occurred.

Stretching payments beyond the net date also reduces the annual effective cost of missing a cash discount. Recall that the cost of missing a discount with terms of 2/10, net 30 was 37.23%. If payments are delayed until day 60, the annual effective cost of missing the discount declines to 14.91%. This percentage is calculated using the AEC relationship, and a 60-day rather than 30-day payment period.

$$AEC = (\% \text{ discount} \div 1 - \% \text{ discount})$$
$$x \ (365 \div \text{net period} - \text{discount period})$$
$$AEC = (.02 \div 1 - .02) \ x \ (365 \div 60 - 10)$$
$$= (.02 \div .98) \ x \ (365 \div 50)$$
$$= 14.91\%$$

As this example illustrates, there is a strong incentive for stretching payments beyond the net date. Yielding to this temptation, however, is poor business practice, and it is risky. As many small business managers have learned, there can be a substantial implicit cost associated with stretching payables. Abusing the trade credit privilege can lead a supplier to:

- Put a firm on a "cash only" status, or refuse to fill purchase orders until outstanding obligations are paid.

- Jeopardize a firm's credit rating by making its poor payment practices known to the firm's bank or its other creditors.

- Eliminate a firm from future considerations, such as placing it on the bottom of the priority list for filling orders when goods are in short supply.

As a general rule, the long-run benefits of prompt payment practices outweigh the limited, short-run gains from stretching payables. For a small firm attempting to maximize its long-run value, there is no substitute for good business practice. A firm's trade creditors are a valuable source of financing, and as such are a major contributor to its long-run value.

As is true with all aspects of financial management, the key ingredient to effective accounts payable management is good information. Trade credit is an invaluable resource, and as the small business manager, you must have good information to use wisely. This information takes the form of timely data on the status of outstanding obligations. Such information comes from the dual effort of maintaining appropriately designed records, and your involvement in the monitoring and evaluation of the data provided by those records.

Recording and Monitoring Payables

The accounts payable recordkeeping system is a simple extension of the firm's inventory records. Appropriate information on the nature of the purchase, the vendor, and the terms surrounding the purchase should be recorded at the time inventory is acquired. While the specific format for recording payables information may vary, a minimum of the following essential data items should be logged and monitored.

- The discount date, if any, on each invoice, and the number of days remaining to the discount date.

- The dollar and effective annual percentage cost of missing the offered discount.

- The net payment date on each outstanding account, and the number of days remaining to the net date.

- Past due accounts, and the number of days that they are past due.

In order to gain insight into the design and use of an accounts payable recordkeeping system, let's look at the manual system used by Avanti before the firm converted to a computerized accounts payable model.

The focus of the Avanti system is timely information on the status and cost of outstanding obligations. To obtain this information, the data outlined above is recorded on a separate vendor card for each invoice. A sample vendor card is shown on Table 13.1.

Avanti's Accounts Payable Records

The vendor card is an important part of the inventory control process. By recording information on the vendor, nature of the purchase, and purchase terms, you have the data necessary to monitor and control the purchasing of inventory.

Most of the information contained on the vendor card is taken directly from the invoice. The only calculated amounts are the discount amount and the effective cost. The discount amount is determined by multiplying the purchase amount by the discount percentage. For example, the $30 discount amount shown on Table 13.1 is calculated as:

Discount Amount = Purchase Amount x Discount Percentage

Discount Amount = $1000 x 3%
$$= \$30$$

Table 13.1 Accounts Payable Vendor Card Information

NAME: Peleton Parts
ADDRESS: 1 Veledrome Drive, Cycletown, Georgia 30001
TELEPHONE: (912) 247-1085
INVOICE NUMBER: 107   DATE: 02/01/X3   TERMS: 3/15, net 45

Purchase Amount	Discount Date	Discount Amount	Effective Cost	Net Date
$1,000	02/15	$30	37.6%	03/30

The effective cost of 37.6% is calculated using the annual effective cost relationship.

AEC = (% discount ÷ 1 – % disc.) x (365 ÷ net period – discount period)
AEC = (.03 ÷ .97) x (365 ÷ 30)
      = 37.6%

In order to keep track of the critical payment date on each purchase, the vendor card is filed in a simple "tickler" arrangement. In this case, the tickler file is nothing more than a drawer with 31 slots arranged in sequence from the 1st to the 31st day. When a shipment is received, the vendor card is prepared and placed in the appropriate due date slot. Since Avanti attempts to take advantage of cash discounts, the appropriate due date is the cash discount date. At the beginning of each day of the month, the vendor cards in the tickler slot corresponding to that date are reviewed for payment. If an invoice is paid on that date, it is stored in the paid file. If Avanti cannot take the discount, the vendor card is moved to the slot in the tickler file that corresponds to the net date.

Guidelines for Managing Accounts Payable

The following guidelines, coupled with maintaining and monitoring accounts payable records, will help you maximize the benefits gained from the use of trade credit.

- **Take Cash Discounts**. Good financial practice suggests that cash discounts should be taken as long as your firm has the necessary liquidity, and the transaction is cost justified. In most cases, the cost of missing the discount can be substantial. If payment cannot be made by the discount date, but the firm has the credit capability to borrow the funds to do so, it is usually cheaper to borrow and take advantage of the discount than to suffer the cost of missing it. To determine whether such a transaction is cost justified, compare the annual effective cost of missing the discount with the interest rate charged on a loan for the same period. If the bank borrowing rate is lower than the annual effective cost of missing the discount, it is cheaper to borrow the cash, take the discount, and repay the loan on the net date.

- **Be Greedy**. If your supplier offers a cash discount for early payment, you may be able to negotiate an even larger discount for a COD purchase. If so, the COD purchase should be made if doing so is cost justified. To make this decision, it is necessary to compare the additional cost savings from paying COD rather than on the discount date with the firm's average return on investment. If the savings exceed the firm's average ROI, it is cheaper to buy for cash and secure the larger discount.

For example, assume your firm's average ROI is 20%, its supplier's normal terms are 2/10, net 30, and the firm is able to negotiate terms of 5/COD, net 30. The annual effective cost of missing the regular cash discount is 37.23%, while that of the COD transaction is 64.03%. These calculations are made using the AEC relationship:

$$AEC \text{ (normal)} = (.02 \div .98) \times (365 \div 20)$$
$$= 37.23\%$$

$$AEC \text{ (COD)} = (.05 \div .95) \times (365 \div 30)$$
$$= 64.03\%$$

The difference between the two AEC values is 26.8% (64.03% − 37.23%). Since this difference is greater than the firm's ROI of 20%, your firm is better off by purchasing COD.

- **Be On Time, But Not Too Early**. While it is important that you follow good payment practices and pay on time, you do not want to lose the use of your money by paying too early. If your cash discount or net period dates are 10 days and 30 days, respectively, you would pay on either the 10th day or the 30th day. There is no advantage to paying before the 10th day when taking the discount, and before the 30th day if the discount is missed. Remember, there is an opportunity cost associated with the use of money. If you have needlessly paid early, it is not available for use in the business. Not having the cash to use is an opportunity cost you suffer.

- **Shop For The Longest Credit Terms**. If it is not possible to take a cash discount, find the longest terms available from suppliers. The further the payment can be extended into the future, the lower the effective cost of missing the discount, and the greater the financing effect of trade credit. For example, if your firm had a relatively short operating cycle and could obtain terms with an extended credit period, it is conceivable that trade credit could provide the bulk of your working capital needs.

- **Don't Hide From Your Suppliers**. When temporary financial problems occur and payments cannot be made on time, the natural tendency is to avoid contact with your supplier or employ transparent stall tactics such as failing to sign the check, or responding with the ruse "the check is in the mail." Hiding and stalling are without question the worst courses of action to take. Business people understand that business firms encounter occasional problems. What is not understood is managers who try to hide from them. As a general rule, you are better able to preserve the relationship with your supplier if you make contact. Explain the problem, make it clear that you have a definite plan for resolving it, and indicate how and when you plan to make payment. This approach sends a clear message: The firm is in the hands of competent management. Hiding from your creditor leaves the impression that the firm is in the hands of management that is either oblivious to, or hides from its problems. Neither impression instills confidence.

- **Employ Sound Financial Practices**. Good payment practices are first a function of available liquidity. Adequate liquidity is often an extremely scarce asset for a typical small firm. To get the most mileage out of available financial resources, they must be carefully managed and controlled. Remember, cash management is a system within your firm's other financial systems; it affects and is affected by all your decisions.

Where to Now?

The next step is up to you. You have been exposed to a wealth of information on financial management practices. Whether you continue to study, apply, and develop facility with the principles espoused in these pages depends on you. Years of working with small firms have convinced this author that such an effort will translate into bottom line benefits for your firm. Regardless of the size of your firm, sound management is important to your success, but in the case of the small firm, it is a prerequisite.

As you contemplate incorporating this newly acquired financial knowledge into your management process, the question of "Where do I begin" may surface. The most effective place to start applying financial management techniques is at the beginning. Start by applying the principles and tools of financial analysis. By doing so, you will gain invaluable insight into your firm's past and current financial position, its past and current financial performance, the inner workings of the business, and the quality of the decisions that have been made. Given this awareness, a picture of the financial planning and management activities that should be implemented will begin to take shape.

Conclusion

This book has stressed the importance of financial analysis, planning, and management to the success of the small firm, and demonstrated how you can approach these tasks in practice. It seems fitting, therefore, that its conclusion consist of a summary of key points.

1. **The goal of financial management is to ensure that decisions essential to your firm's existence are not frustrated by the lack of available financial resources.** This means that careful planning and management are required to ensure that financial resources are deployed to their maximum advantage.

2. **Your firm's continued financial success depends on its ability to generate cash flow.** The small business manager should focus his or her planning and decision making efforts on maximizing this lifeblood of the business.

3. **Net income is not cash.** To understand the inner workings of your firm's financial system, you must understand the critical factors that determine cash flow.

4. **Your firm's financial statements can provide valuable information on its financial position and performance.** To obtain this information, you must first understand the construction and limitations of traditional statements, and then apply the appropriate tools of financial analysis.

5. **Your firm's financial statements do not provide all of the information necessary for sound financial analysis, planning, and decision making.** You must make certain that the specialized reports needed for these purposes are routinely prepared and evaluated.

6. **To make sound financial decisions you must have a clear understanding of your firm's cost structure, and how this cost structure behaves with changes in the volume of operations.**

7. **The gross profit margin figure calculated from your firm's income statement is a useful financial indicator, but the important figure for financial analysis, planning, and decision making is the contribution margin.**

8. **The prerequisites for sound financial decisions are realistic forecasts and sound plans.** Good forecasting and planning occur when you maintain an information system that provides a clear picture of the trend and direction of the critical factors that affect your firm and its markets.

9. **Good forecasting, planning, and decision making is the art of informed judgment.** Sound business judgment is developed through the continuing process of documenting the assumptions upon which plans and decisions are built, and subsequently evaluating them to determine what went right, what went wrong, and why.

10. **Cash, receivables, and inventory are insidious pools that trap your firm's scarce financial resources.** These working assets and the financing used to support them must be carefully managed and controlled.

These 10 points will hopefully be constant reminders of the financial principles that should be incorporated into the administrative process of your firm. By following these points and remembering the related topics discussed throughout this book, you will be a more informed, better organized manager, and you will only increase your firm's degree of success.

Index

If you are in business, or if you are thinking of starting a business, our resources on the following pages may provide exactly what you've been looking for:

- **Expert advice on business issues**

- **Clear explanations of laws and taxes**

- **Worksheets to help you think through decisions**

- **Step-by-step guidance to plan out actions**

Please look through the list, then mail, fax, or call in your order toll-free

800-228-2275

Acquiring Outside Capital

The Loan Package
Book

Preparatory package for a business loan proposal. Worksheets help analyze cash needs and articulate business focus. Includes sample forms for balance sheets, income statements, projections, and budget reports. Screening sheets rank potential lenders to shorten the time involved in getting the loan.

Venture Capital Proposal Package
Book

Structures a proposal to secure venture capital. Checklists gather material for required sections: market analyses, income projections, financial statements, management team, strategic marketing plan, etc. Gives tips on understanding, finding, and screening potential investors.

Financial Templates
Software for IBM-PC & Macintosh

Software speeds business calculations including those in PSI's workbooks, *The Loan Package, Venture Capital Proposal Package, Negotiating the Purchase or Sale of a Business, The Successful Business Plan: Secrets & Strategies*. Includes 40 financial templates including various projections, statements, ratios, histories, amortizations, and cash flows. *Requires Lotus 1-2-3, Microsoft Excel 2.0 or higher, Supercalc 5, PSI's Spreadsheet (described in the Financial Management section of this resource list), or Lotus compatible spreadsheet and 512 RAM plus hard disk or two floppy drives.*

Managing Employees

A Company Policy and Personnel Workbook
Book

Saves costly consultant or staff hours in creating company personnel policies. Provides model policies on topics such as employee safety, leave of absence, flextime, smoking, substance abuse, sexual harassment, performance improvement, grievance procedure. For each subject, practical and legal ramifications are explained, then a choice of alternate policies presented.

Software for IBM-PC & compatibles and Macintosh

The policies are on disk so the company's name, specific information, and any desired changes or rewrites can be incorporated using your own word processor to tailor the model policies to suit your company's specific needs before printing out a complete manual for distribution to employees. *Requires a word processor and hard disk and floppy drive.*

Staffing A Small Business: Hiring, Compensating and Evaluating
Book

For the company that does not have a personnel specialist. Clarifies the processes of determining personnel needs; establishing job descriptions that satisfy legal requirements; and advertising for, selecting, and keeping good people. Over 40 worksheets help forecast staffing needs, define each job, recruit employees, and train staff.

Managing People: A Practical Guide
Book

Focuses on developing the art of working with people to maximize the productivity and satisfaction of both manager and employees. Discussions, exercises, and self-tests boost skills in communicating, delegating, motivating people, developing teams, goal-setting, adapting to change, and coping with stress.

Mail Order

Mail Order Legal Manual
Book

For companies that use the mail to market their products or services, as well as for mail order businesses, this book clarifies complex regulations so penalties can be avoided. Gives state-by-state legal requirements, plus information on Federal Trade Commission guidelines and rules covering delivery dates, advertising, sales taxes, unfair trade practices, and consumer protection.

To order these tools, use the convenient order form at the back of this book or call us toll-free at: 800-228-2275

Marketing & Public Relations

Marketing Your Products and Services Successfully
Book

Helps small businesses understand marketing concepts, then plan and follow through with the actions that will result in increased sales. Covers all aspects from identifying the target market, through market research, establishing pricing, creating a marketing plan, evaluating media alternatives, to launching a campaign. Discusses customer maintenance techniques and international marketing.

Customer Profile and Retrieval (CPR)
Software for IBM-PC & compatibles

Stores details of past activities plus future reminders on customers, clients, contacts, vendors, and employees, then gives instant access to that information when needed. "Tickler" fields keep reminders of dates for recontacts. "Type" fields categorize names for sorting as the user defines. "Other data" fields store information such as purchase and credit history, telephone call records, or interests.

Massive storage capabilities. Holds up to 255 lines of comments for each name, plus unlimited time and date stamped notes. Features perpetual calendar, and automatic telephone dialing. Built-in word processing and merge gives the ability to pull in the information already keyed into the fields into form or individual letters. Prints mail labels, rotary file cards, and phone directories. *Requires a hard disk, 640K RAM and 80 column display. (Autodial feature requires modem.)*

Publicity and Public Relations Guide for Businesses
Book

Overview of how to promote a business by using advertising, publicity, and public relations. Especially for business owners and managers who choose to have promotional activities carried out by in-house staff rather than outside specialists. Includes worksheets for a public relations plan, news releases, editorial article, and a communications schedule.

Cost-Effective Market Analysis
Book

Workbook explains how a small business can conduct its own market research. Shows how to set objectives, determine which techniques to use, create a schedule, and then monitor expenses. Encompasses primary research (trade shows, telephone interviews, mail surveys), plus secondary research (using available information in print).

EXECARDS®
Communication Tools

EXECARDS, the original business-to-business message cards, help build and maintain personal business relationships with customers and prospects. Distinctive in size and quality, EXECARDS get through even when other mail is tossed. An effective alternative to telephone tag. Time-saving EXECARDS come in a variety of handsome styles and messages. Excellent for thanking clients, following up between orders, prospecting, and announcing new products, services, or special offers. *Please call for complete catalog.*

How To Develop & Market Creative Business Ideas
Paperback Book

Step-by-step manual guides the inventor through all stages of new product development. Discusses patenting your invention, trademarks, copyrights, and how to construct your prototype. Gives information on financing, distribution, test marketing, and finding licensees. Plus, lists many useful sources for prototype resources, trade shows, funding, and more.

International Business

Export Now
Book

Prepares a business to enter the export market. Clearly explains the basics, then articulates specific requirements for export licensing, preparation of documents, payment methods, packaging, and shipping. Includes advice on evaluating foreign representatives, planning international marketing strategies, and discovering official U.S. policy for various countries and regions. Lists sources.

Related Resources from PSI Successful Business Library

Business Communications

**Proposal Development: How
to Respond and Win the Bid**
Book

Orchestrates a successful proposal from preliminary planning to clinching the deal. Shows by explanation and example how to: determine what to include; create text, illustrations, tables, exhibits, and appendices; how to format (using either traditional methods or desktop publishing); meet the special requirements of government proposals; set up and follow a schedule.

**Write Your Own Business
Contracts**
Book

Explains the "do's" and "don'ts" of contract writing so any person in business can do the preparatory work in drafting contracts before hiring an attorney for final review. Gives a working knowledge of the various types of business agreements, plus tips on how to prepare for the unexpected.

**Complete Book of Business
Forms**
New Book available Fall 1991.

Over 200 reproducible forms for all types of business needs: personnel, employment, finance, production flow, operations, sales, marketing, order entry, and general administration. Time-saving, uniform, coordinated way to record and locate important business information.

EXECARDS®
Communication Tools

EXECARDS, business-to-business message cards, are an effective vehicle for maintaining personal contacts in this era of rushed, highly-technical communications. A card takes only seconds and a few cents to send, but can memorably tell customers, clients, prospects, or co-workers that their relationship is valued. Many styles and messages to choose from for thanking, acknowledging, inviting, reminding, prospecting, following up, etc. *Please call for complete catalog.*

PlanningTools™
Paper pads, 3-hole punched

Handsome PlanningTools help organize thoughts and record notes, actions, plans, and deadlines, so important information and responsibilities do not get lost or forgotten. Specific PlanningTools organize different needs, such as Calendar Notes, Progress/Activity Record, Project Plan/Record, Week's Priority Planner, Make-A-Month Calendar, and Milestone Chart. *Please call for catalog.*

**Customer Profile
& Retrieval (CPR)**
Software for IBM-PC & compatibles

Easy computer database management program streamlines the process of communicating with clients, customers, vendors, contacts, and employees. While talking to your contact on the phone (or at any time), all notes of past activities and conversations can be viewed instantly, and new notes can be added at that time. *Please see description under "Marketing & Public Relations" section on previous page.*

Business Relocation

**Company Relocation
Handbook: Making the
Right Move**
New Book available Fall, 1991

Comprehensive guide to moving a business. Begins with defining objectives for moving and evaluating whether relocating will actually solve more problems than it creates. Worksheets compare prospective locations, using rating scales for physical plant, equipment, personnel, and geographic considerations. Sets up a schedule for dealing with logistics.

Retirement Planning

**Retirement & Estate
Planning Handbook**
Book

Do-it-yourself workbook for setting up a retirement plan that can easily be maintained and followed. Covers establishing net worth, retirement goals, budgets, and a plan for asset acquisition, preservation, and growth. Discusses realistic expectations for Social Security, Medicare, and health care alternatives. Features special sections for business owners.

Career Recordkeeping

Career Builder
Book

This workbook collects all of an individual's career-related data in one place for quick access. From educational details, through work history, health records, reference lists, correspondence awards, passports, etc., to personal insurance policies, real estate, securities and bank accounts, this manual keeps it all organized. Gives tips on successful resumés.

To order these tools, use the convenient order form at the back of this book or call us toll-free at: 800-228-2275

Financial Management

Financial Management Techniques for Small Business
Book

Clearly reveals the essential ingredients of sound financial management in detail. By monitoring trends in your financial activities, you will be able to uncover potential problems before they become crises. You'll understand why you can be making a profit and still not have the cash to meet expenses, and you'll learn the steps to change your business' cash behavior to get more return for your effort.

Risk Analysis: How to Reduce Insurance Costs
Book

Straightforward advice on shopping for insurance, understanding types of coverage, comparing proposals and premium rates. Worksheets help identify and weigh the risks a particular business is likely to face, then determine if any of those might be safely self-insured or eliminated. Request for proposal form helps businesses avoid over-paying for protection.

Debt Collection: Strategies for the Small Business
Book

Practical tips on how to turn receivables into cash. Worksheets and checklists help businesses establish credit policies, track accounts, and flag when it is necessary to bring in a collection agency, attorney, or go to court. This book advises how to deal with disputes, negotiate settlements, win in small claims court, and collect on judgments. Gives examples of telephone collection techniques and collection letters.

Negotiating the Purchase or Sale of a Business
Book

Prepares a business buyer or seller for negotiations that will achieve win-win results. Shows how to determine the real worth of a business, including intangible assets such as "goodwill." Over 36 checklists and worksheets on topics such as tax impact on buyers and sellers, escrow checklist, cash flow projections, evaluating potential buyers, financing options, and many others.

Financial Accounting Guide for Small Business
Book

Makes understanding the economics of business simple. Explains the basic accounting principles that relate to any business. Step-by-step instructions for generating accounting statements and interpreting them, spotting errors, and recognizing warning signs. Discusses how banks and other creditors view financial statements.

Controlling Your Company's Freight Costs
Book

Shows how to increase company profits by trimming freight costs. Provides tips for comparing alternative methods and shippers, then negotiating contracts to receive the most favorable discounts. Tells how to package shipments for safe transport. Discusses freight insurance and dealing with claims for loss or damage. Appendices include directory of U.S. ports, shipper's guide, and sample bill of lading.

Accounting Software Analysis
Book

Presents successful step-by-step procedure for choosing the most appropriate software to handle the accounting for your business. Evaluation forms and worksheets create a custom software "shopping list" to match against features of various products, so facts, not sales hype, can determine the best fit for your company.

Financial Templates
Software for IBM-PC & Macintosh

Calculates and graphs many business "what-if" scenarios and financial reports. Forty financial templates such as income statements, cash flow, and balance sheet comparisons, break-even analyses, product contribution comparisons, market share, net present value, sales model, *pro formas*, loan payment projections, etc. *Requires 512K RAM hard disk or two floppy drives, plus Lotus 1-2-3 or compatible spreadsheet such as our program called "Spreadsheet" listed below.*

Spreadsheet
Software for IBM-PC & compatibles

Economically priced spreadsheet program. Compatible with Lotus 1-2-3® release 2.01 files. Creates and manipulates worksheets with up to 256 columns by 2,048 rows, and will automatically use Lotus 1A, 2.0, and 2.01 macros (even the most advanced). Comes with a detailed, yet understandable, reference manual. Requires 640K RAM and hard disk drive. This program doesn't have Lotus' fancy fonts, separate tutorial , or ability to use expanded memory, but it handles most of the calculations (even statistical) you'd ever require. A great business workhorse at an affordable price!

Related Resources from PSI Successful Business Library

Business Formation and Planning

Starting and Operating a Business in... series
Book available for each state in the United States, plus District of Columbia

One-stop resource to current federal and state laws and regulations that affect businesses. Clear "human language" explanations of complex issues, plus samples of government forms, and lists of where to obtain additional help or information. This book helps seasoned business owners keep up with changing legislation. It also guides new entrepreneurs step-by-step to start the business and do what's necessary to stay up and running. Includes many checklists and worksheets to organize ideas, create action plans, and project financial scenarios.

Starting and Operating a Business: U.S. Edition
Set of eleven binders

The complete encyclopedia of how to do business in the U.S. Describes laws and regulations for each state, plus Washington, D.C., as well as the federal government. Gives overview of what is involved in starting and operating a business. Includes lists of sources of help, plus post cards for requesting materials from government and other agencies. This set is valuable for businesses with locations or marketing activities in several states, plus franchisors, attorneys, accountants, and other consultants.

Surviving and Prospering in a Business Partnership
Book

From evaluation of potential partners, through the drafting of agreements, to day-to-day management of working relationships, this book helps avoid classic partnership catastrophes. Discusses how to set up the partnership to reduce the financial and emotional consequences of unanticipated disputes, dishonesty, divorce, disability, or death of a partner.

Corporation Formation Package and Minute Book
Book and software for IBM-PC, available for Texas, Florida, or California

Provides forms required for incorporating and maintaining closely-held corporations, including: articles of incorporation; bylaws; stock certificates, stock transfer record sheets, bill of sale agreement; minutes form; plus many others. Addresses questions on regulations, timing, fees, notices, election of directors, and other critical factors. Software has minutes, bylaws, and articles of incorporation already for you to edit and customize (using your own word processor).

Franchise Bible: A Comprehensive Guide
Book

Complete guide to franchising for prospective franchisees or for business owners considering franchising their business. Includes actual sample documents, such as a complete offering circular, plus worksheets for evaluating franchise companies, locations, and organizing information before seeing an attorney. This book is helpful for lawyers as well as their clients.

How To Develop & Market Creative Business Ideas
Paperback Book

Step-by-step manual guides the inventor through all stages of new product development. Discusses patenting your invention, trademarks, copyrights, and how to construct your prototype. Gives information on financing, distribution, test marketing, and finding licensees. Plus, lists many useful sources for prototype resources, trade shows, funding, and more.

The Successful Business Plan: Secrets & Strategies
Book

Start-to-finish guide to creating a successful business plan. Includes tips from venture capitalists, bankers, and successful leaders, such as Bill Walsh, Eugene Kleiner, and heads of companies of all types and sizes including The Price Club, Levi Strauss & Co., See's Candies, Aston Hotels. Features worksheets for ease in planning and budgeting with the Abrams Method of Flow-Through Financials. Gives a sample business plan, plus specialized help for retailers, service companies, manufacturers, and in-house corporate plans. Also tells how to find and impress funding sources.

The Small Business Expert
Software for IBM-PC & compatibles

Generates comprehensive custom checklist of the state and federal laws and regulations based on your type and size of business. Allows comparison of doing business in each of the 50 states. Built-in worksheets create outlines for personnel policies, marketing feasibility studies, and a business plan draft. *Requires 256K RAM and hard disk.*